Teaching Electronic Music

D1394243

Teaching Electronic Music: Cultural, Creative, and Analytical Perspectives offers innovative and practical techniques for teaching electronic music in a wide range of classroom settings. Across a dozen essays, an array of contributors—including practitioners in musicology, art history, ethnomusicology, music theory, performance, and composition—reflect on the challenges of teaching electronic music, highlighting pedagogical strategies while addressing questions such as:

- What can instructors do to expand and diversify musical knowledge?
- Can the study of electronic music foster critical reflection on technology?
- What are the implications of a digital culture that allows so many to be producers of music?
- How can instructors engage students in creative experimentation with sound?

Electronic music presents unique possibilities and challenges to instructors of music history courses, calling for careful attention to creative curricula, historiographies, repertoires, and practices. *Teaching Electronic Music* features practical models of instruction as well as paths for further inquiry, identifying untapped methodological directions with broad interest and wide applicability.

Blake Stevens is Associate Professor of Music History at the College of Charleston.

Modern Musicology and the College Classroom
Series Editor: *James A. Davis, SUNY Fredonia*

Modern Musicology and the College Classroom is a series of professional titles for current and future college instructors of musicology in its broadest definition—encompassing music history, ethnomusicology, music theory, and music courses for all majors. Volumes feature a basic introduction to a significant field of current scholarship, a discussion of how the topic impacts pedagogical methodology and materials, and pragmatic suggestions for incorporating these ideas directly into the classroom.

Listening Across Borders
Musicology in the Global Classroom
Edited by James A. Davis and Christopher Lynch

Teaching Electronic Music
Cultural, Creative, and Analytical Perspectives
Edited by Blake Stevens

Teaching Electronic Music
Cultural, Creative, and Analytical Perspectives

Edited by Blake Stevens

COLLEGE OF CHARLESTON

Routledge
Taylor & Francis Group

NEW YORK AND LONDON

First published 2022
by Routledge
605 Third Avenue, New York, NY 10158

and by Routledge
2 Park Square, Milton Park, Abingdon, Oxon, OX14 4RN

Routledge is an imprint of the Taylor & Francis Group, an informa business

© 2022 Taylor & Francis

Library of Congress Cataloging-in-Publication Data
Names: Stevens, Blake, editor.
Title: Teaching electronic music : cultural, creative, and analytical
    perspectives / [edited by] Blake Stevens.
Description: New York : Routledge, 2021. | Series: Modern
    musicology and the college classroom | Includes bibliographical
    references and index.
Identifiers: LCCN 2021004645 (print) | LCCN 2021004646
    (ebook) | ISBN 9780367415808 (hardback) | ISBN
    9780367415785 (paperback) | ISBN 9780367815349 (ebook)
Subjects: LCSH: Electronic music—History and criticism.
Classification: LCC ML1380 .T43 2021 (print) | LCC ML1380
    (ebook) | DDC 786.709—dc23
LC record available at https://lccn.loc.gov/2021004645
LC ebook record available at https://lccn.loc.gov/2021004646

ISBN: 978-0-367-41580-8 (hbk)
ISBN: 978-0-367-41578-5 (pbk)
ISBN: 978-0-367-81534-9 (ebk)

Typeset in Sabon
by Apex CoVantage, LLC

Contents

Figures

Acknowledgments

I would like to thank the contributors for their commitment to this project during a most challenging year, one that has brought a sharpened awareness of the spaces of teaching and scholarly exchange. The idea for this volume originated in discussions at the conference "Music as Cultural Education: Building New Bridges between Pre-College Schools and Universities," sponsored by the International Musicological Society (IMS) study group "Transmission of Knowledge as a Primary Aim in Music Education" and held at the University of Bologna in June 2018. I would like to thank the conference organizers, Giuseppina La Face Bianconi, Pierpaolo Polzonetti, and C. Matthew Balensuela, for arranging an ideally convivial and stimulating meeting. The involvement and enthusiasm of Marc Battier, Annie Yen-Ling Liu, and Robert McClure helped sustain the project in its early stages, and from the very beginning, Jim Davis offered expert guidance that kept it moving forward. I would also like to acknowledge financial support from Dean Edward B. Hart and the Dean's Excellence Fund for the College of Charleston School of the Arts, and from the Music Department at the College of Charleston and its chair, Dr. Michael O'Brien. Finally, my deepest thanks to my family and friends, far and near, for their continuous support.

Introduction

Narrative Histories, "Real" Music, and the Digital Vernacular

Blake Stevens

Electronic music presents unique creative possibilities and challenges to instructors of music history courses. Having initiated profound transformations in twentieth-century musical culture, musicians working with electronic and digital media continue to remap our conceptions of sound, spatial experience, identity, and agency as transformed through algorithmic and distributed processes. Traditional frameworks of musical production and knowledge have been destabilized through new forms of creative participation in digital culture. Modes of listening as well as analysis must, therefore, adapt to changing contexts and aesthetic aims. Probing into technologies of production may introduce forbidding levels of technical complexity and specialized languages—moving targets of study in a domain often characterized by radical experimentation— yet it will likely uncover opportunities for creative exploration in the classroom. The virtual archive of this media environment, itself a critical object of study for music in digital culture, is expanding into proportions that are difficult to map. Defining the field and its related terminology is itself a core, persistent challenge, given the diversity of its forms.

The adoption of "electronic music" in the title of this volume is meant to keep these issues mobile across various practices and to convey their interdisciplinary scope. A single volume cannot comprehensively treat so large a topic: the past decade alone has seen a staggering profusion of research guides, companions, handbooks, and monographs on electronic music, sound art, new media art, mobile music studies, digital culture, philosophy of education, and technology in education. This volume offers a sampling of current perspectives from practitioners in musicology, art history, ethnomusicology, music theory, performance, and composition. The contributors reflect on instructional strategies from their disciplinary backgrounds and pedagogical experience, speaking to issues such as curricular challenges, historiography, repertoires, analytical techniques, and the search for new or largely untapped methodological directions. The topics addressed are applicable to multiple settings, from specialized courses on electronic music and surveys of twentieth- and twenty-first– century music to courses for general student populations. The chapters balance a focus on specific practices and traditions with an interest in wide applicability.

One of the concerns shared by these contributions is exploring how the material affordances of working environments, media, instruments, and other tools inform musical production and analysis. Reflecting this premise is a set of recurring questions and themes: How can instructors expand and diversify students' knowledge of the field? How can the study of electronic music foster critical reflection on technology and digital culture more broadly? What are the implications of a musical culture whose technologies allow so many to be producers of music? How can music history instructors engage students in creative experimentation with sound? These questions—and the wide range of possible answers explored here—position music history courses as powerful sites of critical and creative engagement with the evolving intersection of electronic music, technology, and digital culture. This volume is directed toward this potential, offering both practical models of instruction and paths for further inquiry.

Narrative Ends

A well-traveled path into electronic music is the traditional survey course. The closing chapters of survey textbooks may inspire a particular fascination in readers interested in the subject, given that the entanglements of electronic music with technological innovation make it a potent marker of the fugitive "present moment." Amid the flux of genres, techniques, and instruments that seem primed for continuous evolution and thus obsolescence in their current forms, which are representative? And representative of what, precisely? Historical origins, norms, breakthroughs, institutional prestige and influence, market positioning, everyday experience, or other forces? Which aesthetic and critical discourses are necessary to understand these processes? Who are the most significant figures (and *types* of figures) currently active in the field? What exactly is this field or domain?

As the "present" draws near in Richard Taruskin and Christopher H. Gibbs's *The Oxford History of Western Music: College Edition* and J. Peter Burkholder's *A History of Western Music*, the compressions and omissions required to extend their narratives from prehistory and antiquity into the 2010s become more pronounced, especially as they involve electronic and digital media.[1] Selectivity is obviously required to navigate through the past several decades of an increasingly globalized and digitally mediated musical culture, whose aural practices, inaugurated by recording and electronic media, are increasingly supplanting the dominance of traditional musical literacy. These transformations involve musical production, material preservation, and dissemination as well as learning practices and standards of competency. Originating within narrative frameworks largely defined by live performance and literacy, technologies such as records, magnetic tape, synthesizers, digital sampling, Musical Instrument Digital Interface (MIDI) connectivity, and mp3s have created new sonic cultures that shift outside these frames. In this regard, Taruskin and Gibbs maintain a particularly sharp historiographical focus on literacy. Although the impact of these technologies has been decisive and widespread, the agents and forms of expression involved—musicians, composers, producers, inventors, institutions, genres, works, recordings— gradually recede in prominence as their narrative advances from the origins of innovative practices into the present. Postliterate ontologies withdraw from view, in part, because they would require analytical and descriptive methods distinct from those cultivated for literate art music. By contrast, Burkholder sketches the pluralistic range of these transformations from the 1970s into the early 2000s in considerable detail, giving particular attention to popular music and media; like Taruskin and Gibbs, however, he brings instrumental concert music and opera into the foreground in his close readings, along with analytical vocabulary and forms of mediation principally defined through literacy.

Students may wonder about their place within these maps of contemporary musical culture. Heirs of the "digital revolution" and, by and large, "digital natives," they are navigating through a process whose broad historical implications are profoundly disruptive yet whose local inflections are perhaps now commonplace. Some degree of tension or estrangement may nonetheless characterize their experience of this environment and their formal studies, particularly for students focusing on performance in Western art music. Having only roughly sketched the endpoints of these surveys so far, I next examine the rise of participatory digital culture as focalized through these accounts and in dialogue with the work of Christopher Small, Georgina Born, and Thor Magnussun. The resulting perspective suggests both the desirability and the necessity of pedagogies of sonic "making." These pedagogies reflect and embrace forms of participatory creativity that have become increasingly common in digital media, opening spaces for student experimentation, expression, and collaboration, as well as critical reflection on their enabling technologies.

Splices and Relays

Despite their differences in historiographical priorities and narrative voice, Taruskin-Gibbs and Burkholder position the origins and development of electronic music in broadly similar ways. Their accounts emphasize the period from the late 1940s to the 1970s and the emergence of pivotal practices within institutional frameworks: the founding of *musique concrète* and *elektronische Musik* in the Paris and Cologne studios at midcentury, followed by innovations at the Columbia-Princeton Electronic Music Center, Bell Telephone Laboratories (in Taruskin-Gibbs), The San

Francisco Tape Music Center (more directly discussed by Burkholder), and, finally, IRCAM. This last is the only such institution discussed at length after the 1960s. It is presented as the site of salient developments in acoustic research and electronic music from its opening in 1977 to the present. With varying degrees of detail, each text treats Karlheinz Stockhausen's *Gesang der Jünglinge* (1956) and Edgard Varèse's *Poème électronique* (1957–58) as key works in this early period. The latter is included in the accompanying Norton anthology of scores, along with Section I of Milton Babbitt's *Philomel* (1964), for live voice and fixed medium (tape), and Steve Reich's tape piece *Come Out* (1966).[2] In the absence of notated scores, *Poème électronique* and *Come Out* are represented in the anthology through sound recording and descriptive commentary.[3]

The internal histories of specific practices and traditions are typically set aside once their origins have been established. What is crucial, instead, is the launching of techniques and conceptions of sound production into other domains. The initial focus on studios and research universities privileges "institutional electroacoustic music," to invoke one of the three metagenres Joanna Demers has introduced to define the field of electronic music, along with "electronica" and "electronic sound art."[4] Composers associated with fixed-medium electroacoustic music are nearly absent after the 1970s, as are representative works in the medium. For instance, neither text remains within the institutional framework in which *musique concrète* emerged to follow subsequent developments at the Groupe de Recherches Musicales (GRM) after the early 1950s. This later history includes disputes over abstraction and mimesis that echo aesthetic controversies in the nineteenth and twentieth centuries that are presented earlier in each survey, the pivot to "acousmatic music" as a generic descriptor, the exploration of sound diffusion techniques with the Acousmonium, and experiments in electronic and digital sound processing.[5]

Instead, the surveys track the influence of electronic music on instrumental concert music and eventually opera. The key figures in this process are Iannis Xenakis, György Ligeti, and Krzysztof Penderecki in the 1950s–60s and Gérard Grisey and other composers associated with Spectralism beginning in the 1970s. The continuing influence of Spectralism on Kaija Saariaho via IRCAM serves as a connecting thread in each account, with Burkholder also linking Ligeti's piano étude *Vertige* (1990) to Jean-Claude Risset's work at the institute. Without a perspective of *musique concrète* or the GRM after the 1950s, however, Burkholder's references to "musique concrète" in Ryuichi Sakamoto's score for *The Last Emperor* (1987) and Osvaldo Golijov's opera *Ainadamar* ("Fountain of Tears," 2003–5) raise the question of whether the relevant context for these composers' understanding of such techniques was indeed the work of Schaeffer and Henry in the 1950s or more recent practices developing out of it that would be described as "acousmatic music" or, more generally, "electroacoustic music."[6]

Just as experimental practices radiate from electronic studios into concert music, they are also absorbed into and transformed by vernacular practices. In Taruskin-Gibbs, this process is exemplified by The Beatles, who drew upon *musique concrète* techniques in their turn to studio composition with *Revolver* (1966) and *Sgt. Pepper's Lonely Hearts Club Band* (1967). The final song on *Sgt. Pepper*, "A Day in the Life," also emulates aspects of experimental sound-mass composition.[7] The most substantial narrative payoff of *musique concrète* in Burkholder's text is a discussion of sampling practices in popular music, and more specifically, plunderphonics and mash-ups, including commentary on Danger Mouse's *The Grey Album* (2004).[8] These examples, traversing media affordances from the analog practices of the 1960s to digital platforms in the early 2000s, illustrate an evolution from stylistic emulation and collage to contemporary cultures of sampling and remixing. These are prominent forms of "relayed creativity," the term Georgina Born has introduced to describe the process by which music is "distributed across space, time and persons" to "become an object of recurrent decomposition, composition and re-composition by a series of creative agents."[9] Digital culture has intensified such forms of creative action, many of which began under analog affordances: Born observes that music is now able to be "scattered, flung via the internet in near-real time from any point of creation and departure to any number of points of destination."[10] Digital technologies are, therefore, shaping new models of authorship, collaborative networks, creativity, genre, and the musical "work."[11]

The *relay* is a dominant trope in the narratives of electronic music presented in Taruskin-Gibbs and Burkholder: it tracks the dispersal and transformation of creative techniques across historical periods and practices, and it also allows for strategic cuts or splices.[12] To the extent that electronic music is understood primarily in terms of its medium—the coherence of its field established through shared techniques and materials—its history is virtually synonymous with these multiple relays.[13] These are also subject to narrative selection: Burkholder only briefly alludes to the relays between Western European studios and those in East Asia and other regions, and neither text examines relays between experimental music and "sound art."

In noting these narrative choices, my purpose is not to raise objections or to suggest oversight or negligence, particularly given the obvious space constraints in single-volume histories. These choices reflect premises that are at once historiographical, institutional, and economic. Within the frame of literate art music, each text presents institutional electronic music as a dialectical and generative counterpart of instrumental concert music, opera, and vernacular music. It only rarely emerges as a focus of sustained interest, particularly once it has entered these other domains. The textbooks are written for students and courses in programs that have traditionally emphasized performance studies on acoustic instruments in

Western art music. Fixed-medium electroacoustic music after the 1960s, for instance, appears to be irrelevant for the professional training of this target audience. Its cultural relevance also appears marginal next to rock, hip-hop, techno, and mash-ups. What matters instead is the relay of experimental electronic techniques into both popular music (including forms of "electronica" such as techno and mash-ups) and live performance in art music. The latter includes "mixed music" combining performers and electronics, such as Babbitt's *Philomel* and Pierre Boulez's *Répons*, instrumental music, and opera.

Of the various relays that link electronic music to other practices, one has particular relevance for my purposes here: its dispersal from elite institutions into widespread participatory cultures of digital production and sharing via personal computing devices. Taruskin and Gibbs characterize this process as potentially destructive of the literate tradition. They observe that the "digital revolution foreshadowed above all liberation from the tradition of notated music," with personal computers and other technologies making it possible to "simplify and democratize music"; when considered in their cumulative effect, "these technological advances may well have dealt the literate musical tradition a slow-acting death blow."[14] In addition to the potential of democratizing musical production, these transformations led to a resurgence of folkloric oral practices in performance art of the 1970s and 1980s and have created the conditions for "a postliterate art music."[15]

Burkholder follows similar contours in his account, although commenting more on vernacular music over the past several decades. He seems more inclined toward the rhetoric of "liberation" than "death" when he describes how digital technology is "decentralizing" musical production by allowing "anyone to create, record, produce, and distribute music."[16] The literate tradition, he suggests, may now be returning to conditions of orality and aurality. The book's closing gesture, then, loops back to its opening:

> With new computer software and techniques of sampling and synthesis found in traditions from art music to hip hop, it is now possible for people with access to technology to make their own music, without training in performance. In some respects, we are surrounded by more music than we can ever consume. But perhaps we are also returning to something akin to the practice of music long ago, when every singer sang their own song.[17]

Configurations that have defined the past several centuries of art music unravel: both the musical "work" and the paradigm of the composer-score-performer lose their dominance, and creativities disperse beyond the elite institutional support of musicians and professionalized training.

The idea of producing one's "*own* music" and one's "*own* song" implies a kind of authenticity and independence, if not solipsism. By contrast, for

Born, traditional notions of originality and authenticity are disassembled by the social agencies of digital sampling and jazz improvisation. In place of ownership, music in these practices is characterized by mutation and dispersal: "The musical object eschews any absolute state as it is repeatedly relayed and transformed across time, space and persons."[18] Rather than viewing producers in isolation, this perspective focuses on the social mediations required for the circulation of materials and creative transformations within digital culture.

Considered together, these various socio-cultural maps may well prove defamiliarizing for students—perhaps productively so. If students seek out their own place in them, what will they make of this growing population of musicians "without training in performance"? For students currently engaged in this training and considering careers in teaching, how will these careers relate to cultures of informal learning and amateuring? What if "relayed creativity" and other forms of making become the principal focus of musicking—even within "art music"—and, therefore, displace the performance and reproduction of the works of professional composers? Do these students sense the ground moving beneath them? Do their instructors? Do we?

I invoke the concept of "musicking" to suggest a way of describing as well as responding to this disruption, which may well be (or become) a crisis. The term is also used by several contributors to this volume and of course points to Christopher Small's vision of the multiple social practices involved in musical activity. Although his vigorous advocacy for amateur participation was not oriented around electronic media, it resonates with and seems to anticipate participatory forms of digital musicking. Also congruent with these practices is the skepticism he repeatedly expressed concerning professionalization and conventional models of music education. So too is his celebration of creative process over finished work in his assertion that "the real power of art lies, not in listening to or looking at the finished work; it lies in the act of creation itself."[19]

Thor Magnussun has taken up these themes as they directly involve electronic music pedagogy. He has reappraised the training required of musicians working with digital media to propose the "virtuoso amateur" as a new model. His proposal rounds off a far-reaching exploration of electronic and digital instrumentality, notation, recording, and computational creativity. These diverse modes of inscription challenge the literate/nonliterate and notated/non-notated oppositions that often characterize accounts of electronic music. Magnussun suggests that as pedagogy responds to digital tools and environments, it will necessarily blend music and "music technology."[20] This fusing of competencies will better prepare music graduates for future careers and artistic pursuits. It will require collaboration and interdisciplinarity in place of the competitive ideal of the virtuoso. This last point is the crux of his argument for education: he argues that the "virtuoso performer can no longer be the purpose of music education" and that in its place, we should cultivate the "amateur."[21] Musicians aspiring to this new objective should seek to "become virtuoso amateurs of music, not necessarily through our physical motoric skills, but the understanding of the technology, how to apply it, navigate aesthetic taste, and the dedication to music as an interdisciplinary intermedia art form."[22] These virtuoso amateurs will develop fluency in new literacies, through coding and adapting to ever-evolving digital instruments and interfaces. Many sound artists already incorporate these skills into their work, yet their grounding in visual arts practices and institutions has often led to their exclusion from histories of music.[23]

Participatory digital culture offers a rich and complex terrain for the exploration of electronic music. In the remainder of this chapter, I consider potential applications and benefits of digital musicking for music history instruction, particularly in introductory courses for music majors and general student populations. To do this, I propose an instructional strategy oriented around Pierre Schaeffer's *In Search of a Concrete Music* that transforms this text from a historical source reading into a guide to sonic experimentation, creating an experiential and genealogical link between the foundations of *musique concrète* and sampling practices. The two journals collected in the book offer vivid insights into Schaeffer's creative process. At moments, they take on an autoethnographic quality as he examines the technological and cultural framework conditioning his work. Students encounter the questions, experiments, obstructions, dead ends, and provisional successes that led Schaeffer to develop *musique concrète* as fellow travelers, learning the possibilities of their own instruments as they begin to make music of personal and shared significance— amateurs in the art of "virtuoso amateuring." Schaeffer's text is uniquely useful for this purpose, as it leads into more sophisticated theoretical reflection in the essays that close the book and as it introduces germinal ideas for the subsequent development of electronic music beyond his own practice. I locate four of these key issues—instrumentality, agency, collaboration, and representation—that form a nucleus around which the chapters in this volume revolve. As my discussion proceeds, I point to the most salient of these connections.

"Real" Music and Processual Thinking

A starting point is the proposition that anyone can make music with a laptop. Skeptics may instead prefer to think of this as a testable hypothesis. Speaking in its favor is an expanding genre of pedagogical literature centered on sonic experimentation, including books by composers and educators such as Leigh Landy, Andrew R. Brown, and Andrew Hugill, as well as Robert McClure's contribution to this volume (chapter 1).[24] Hugill, for instance, combines projects in digital musicking with forays into historical and aesthetic issues, experientially combining production with listening and analysis. My own interest in this type of integrative pedagogy emerged through collaborating with a colleague in computer science in a first-year course that linked elements of music theory, history, and computer programming.[25]

In designing introductory experiences for students, accessible tools and methods, dependent on specific contexts, are critical. It makes sense to begin at ground level, empirically, with what is likely closest at hand, both materially and culturally: although by no means universally available, these tools will often include laptops, tablets, smartphones, the adoption of sound editing software and Digital Audio Workstations (DAWs), and the use of recorded sound, whether exclusively through sampling (borrowing) or by also recording sounds oneself. Many guides to digital musicking incorporate what Landy has characterized as a "sound-based" paradigm of music, which he discusses in advocating for "sonic creativity" within a holistic curricular philosophy in this volume (chapter 7).[26] There are many benefits to working with sound instead of with pitch, discrete tonal systems, and staff notation: it is accessible to novices, it cultivates and rewards skills that are often undervalued in formal musical training, and most appealingly, it allows for nearly inexhaustible stylistic eclecticism when conceived in terms of sampling. Although composing with recorded sound is historically rooted in *musique concrète* and is often theorized in terms of "acousmatic music" and "electroacoustic music," students are free to reference and emulate virtually any style, including pitch-based tonal systems, just as musicians from Pierre Henry to John Oswald and Danger Mouse have done. The process, in other words, is singularly open to relay.

Schaeffer's work has much to offer students in their early experiments with sound, including his monumental *Treatise on Musical Objects* (1966) and his narrated exploration of sound examples in the *Solfège de l'objet sonore* (1967), his most directly pedagogical enterprise. The journals collected in his *In Search of a Concrete Music* (1952) are particularly valuable for beginners, both as a source reading for the origins of *musique concrète* and as a conceptual guide to sonic experimentation. They document Schaeffer's own beginnings in the art of composing with "the field of noises," and in places, they reveal an explicitly didactic purpose—for instance, when Schaeffer notes down his desire "to provide essential pointers in my research for possible successors."[27] There are even hints of constructivist and pragmatist tendencies in his claim that "the listener cannot know an object unless he is capable of reproducing it, making it as if for the first time."[28] This challenge considerably raises the stakes for our initial proposition that "anyone can make music with a laptop" by introducing the prospect of direct compositional modeling. The idea recapitulates, too, a standard approach to teaching harmony and counterpoint, transposed here from literate to sonic inscription.

In observing and following Schaeffer's tracks in working with sound, what will students discover? Perhaps most striking is Schaeffer's experimental spirit. He emphasizes direct, empirical contact with sound that nonetheless remains informed by his prior knowledge of music, visual culture, philosophy, and science.[29] His trial-and-error process leads from playing bells, whirligigs, and other objects (housed in the radio studio for sound effects), through a failed experiment with organ pipes damaged during the war, to manipulating shellac discs. When he migrates from the studio to the sound booth, sound reproduction equipment becomes the instrument that makes *musique concrète* possible. In describing this process, he brings an attention to sonic materials that is instructive for students, encouraging sensitivity to the timbre and developmental potential of sounds in the instruments available to them. The idea of an "instrument" is the first of four thematic areas in the text that I explore in some detail.

Instruments and Materials

We encounter a series of largely obsolete tools, techniques, and materials, including shellac discs, the record cutter, "locked grooves," magnetic tape, the *phonogène*, and the *potentiomètre d'espace*. Schaeffer's interaction with these materials invites inquiry into the relationship between creative expression and instruments. It directs attention as well to the distinctive sonic signatures of these tools in the *Cinq études de bruits* (1948) and the *Symphonie pour un homme seul* (1949–50), among other works. Considering instrumentality and technological mediation in their own experience, students may compare these tools with the affordances of modern computing devices, Electronic Digital Instruments (EDIs), DIY instruments, and synthesizers.

One difference worth pondering is the experience of tactility. For Schaeffer, it was a prime source of creative invention and distinguished his approach from that of *elektronische Musik*, as he wanted "direct contact with sound material, without any electrons getting in the way."[30] He discovered his technique in "touching" recorded bell sounds—that is, in physical contact with the recording medium: "Separating the sound from the attack was the generative act."[31] As their first step in using a sound editor or DAW, students may imitate this act by manipulating the envelope of a bell sample, in the process learning about the concept of a sound envelope. This type of initiatory experiment and the more complex explorations that follow will ideally involve students in second-order observations about their process, developed through journals written in dialogue with Schaeffer's and through peer discussion.

In thinking about tactility and digital interfaces, research in media archaeology and critical organology, including Magnussun's work cited previously, will be of obvious value.[32] The versatility of computers makes them invaluable as pedagogical tools, yet their capacity to incorporate and even to "universalize" distinct forms of sonic production poses the risk of flattening out essential differences among instruments. The prevalence of computers and screens, in fact, may be one of the reasons for the growing interest in critical organology, as John Tresch and Emily I. Dolan have argued.[33] This research reflects an awareness that instruments enable unique artistic forms and expressions—indeed, students should be encouraged to think about the kinds of music that sampling and DAWs cannot produce, as well as the irreplaceable properties of records and magnetic tape. The lesson, in part, is that losing contact or familiarity with instruments diminishes both historical and aesthetic understanding. What this loss entails is implicit in Jacques Attali's observation that "Each instrument, each tool, theoretical or concrete, implies a sound field, a field of knowledge, an imaginable and explorable universe."[34] It is often unfeasible and at times impossible to access original equipment such as recording lathes and shellac discs, let alone a *phonogène*; in their absence, virtual emulations that model distinctive physical layouts, as well as historical and archival information, may at least indicate their affordances. Évelyne Gayou and Daniel Teruggi have provided this kind of historical perspective of the intersection of technology and composition at the GRM, beginning with Schaeffer and continuing into the early 2000s.[35]

In his contribution to this volume, Marc Battier treats the GRM as one of several case studies in advocating for the study of instruments and collaborations between composers and engineers within specific environments (chapter 3). Conditions at the GRM also impacted musical practices in China: Annie Yen-Ling Liu and Yang Yinuo discuss how Zhang Xiaofu and Xu Shuya, prominent composers who studied in Paris, relayed techniques from the GRM into Chinese electroacoustic music (chapter 11).

Contributors who inquire into technological affordances within other domains include Rishabh Rajan (on Skrillex's transformation of synthesis techniques in dubstep and the role of EDIs in a course of study involving electronic dance music; chapter 4), Lucy Ann Harrison (on interactive sound in video games and other immersive environments; chapter 5), and V. J. Manzo (on diverse applications of algorithmic processes, including video games and computer-generated instrumental music; chapter 6). Marian Mazzone explores computational processes in new media, which artists are using to redefine the "material composition" of their work and the concept of the "composer" (chapter 12). The theme is also a major focus of Raul Masu and Fabio Morreale's account of maker communities and hacking cultures, in which they promote the use of open, user-modifiable technologies in instruction (chapter 9).

Agency

Materials and objects assert themselves throughout Schaeffer's process: his journals are punctuated by frequent drifts of agency between humans and objects, and "objects" themselves drift in their identities. They first reveal themselves through their resistance to creative assertion.

For instance, initial attempts to manipulate sound with magnetic tape recorders provoked frustration and pointed up the (surprising) advantages of records. Schaeffer describes how malfunctioning tape machines turned the studio into a "battlefield" in which his collaborators fought against the machines.[36] He observes on another occasion that performers struggled with "zanzis" and whirligigs when playing from a score designed "to impose order on everything," writing that "the objects had resisted"; using similar language, but shifting from these physical objects to the "sound" object, Schaeffer later describes how "the object resists, it won't play, it sets into a wearisome sameness, it imposes."[37] The importance of touch in the encounter with recorded bells is mirrored in live presentation. When he describes the first public concert of *musique concrète*, Schaeffer expresses concerns about the potential negation of the human performer in sound diffusion by machines. He judges that the "imperceptible hand movements" with which he had controlled the amplitude of playback had been inadequate; he is seeking out an "interpretative space" in this new art form as it crosses into the domain of live performance.[38]

In their experiments, students may test whether forms of agency—not only resistances but also desires and quirks—belong to their computer interfaces, software, and sonic materials. Encountered in the guise of a "source reading," Schaeffer's most compelling expression of this nonhuman agency may strike students as rather outlandish. The passage has a metaphysical tinge that echoes the writings of E. T. A. Hoffmann and Arthur Schopenhauer: "the miracle of concrete music . . . is that, in the course of experimentation, things begin to speak by themselves, as if they were bringing a message from a world unknown to us and outside us," a message that involves "the secret correspondence between man and the world, to which music is one of the keys."[39] Experientially, when students engage with their instruments in intensive struggle, creative play, and dialogue, they may confirm Schaeffer's otherwise improbable insight into the agencies of "things." Passages like these also provide instructors with links to previous critical discourse about music—here, the opportunity to trace Schaeffer's ideas back to nineteenth-century German aesthetics, including E. T. A. Hoffmann's account of Beethoven's instrumental music and the concept of absolute music, which will inform the distinction Schaeffer draws between the "abstract" and the "anecdotal" I discuss later.

The resistance and desires of objects point to themes of nonhuman agents in actor-network theory (ANT) as well as research in new materialism.[40] Kate Galloway draws from ANT in her analysis of nonhuman actors and the "assemblage" in a work of sound art that memorializes the mule deer within Indigenous lands as a "spiritual mediator" (chapter 10). Patti Kilroy connects the decentering of the autonomous subject through multiple agencies to posthumanist theory, applying the concepts of hybrid identities, distributed cognition, and mutation to the analysis and documentation of live performance with electronics (chapter 8).

Manzo's survey of algorithmic processes likewise inspires reflection on human agency, creativity, and aesthetic response.

Collaboration and Community

Schaeffer's perspectives on instruments and agencies were shaped by a collaborative network, which included the material and institutional resources of Paris Radio, engineers such as Jacques Poullin, performers, and composers such as Pierre Henry and Pierre Boulez. In his call for "adherents" among "not only musicians, painters, and artists in general but also physicists, psychologists, and serious researchers in the field of aesthetics," Schaeffer expresses an aspect of the emerging concept of postmodernism then developing in cybernetics and information theory.[41]

This interest in collaboration sets a model for establishing a "community of practice" among students.[42] Paired work on projects, for instance, may take the Schaeffer-Henry partnership of the early 1950s as inspiration. Such collaborative experiences and communities are of critical value for amateurs in electronic music production, given that they often work "with the help of machines and without the encumbrances of humans," as Thomas Turino puts it.[43] Turino stresses the potential isolation of practitioners of "studio audio art" by distinguishing it from the fields of "participatory performance" and "presentational performance," whose social mediations are more pronounced and direct. By conceiving a class as a community of makers and interpreters, we can model contexts of social feedback for electronic music (such as festivals and online discussion forums): these include demos of works-in-progress, peer discussion at multiple stages of the process, sharing projects online and making them available for download, and responding to and analyzing completed artifacts produced by peers.

Representation, Abstraction, and the "Anecdotal"

Making music within a community of peers brings questions of communication and meaning to the forefront. In following Schaeffer's process, students encounter his struggle between musical abstraction and representation. The difficulty is rooted in the material itself. The "anecdotal" quality of concrete sounds, which typically carried referential associations, required fragmentation and decontextualization, which Schaeffer described as "the effort to abstract the noise from its dramatic context and raise it to the status of musical material."[44] The tension and effort involved with this aesthetic aim mark nearly every juncture of his process and lend a new, technological inflection to long-standing debates about absolute music.

Whether reducing sound to mere fragments or working with larger shapes and gestures, Schaeffer faced considerable difficulties in generating

coherent forms over time. He expresses this challenge with an admira-
bly blunt question: "Can concrete music hang together, and how can it
be made to develop?"[45] Reading the journals as one would a letter by
Mozart or a concert review by E. T. A. Hoffmann, this question would
likely inform a study of Schaeffer's compositional process and offer direction for listening and analysis. These are by no means passive activities,
yet in using Schaeffer's journals in the way I am suggesting here, I have
found that this issue is entirely transformed in significance for students
when they understand and experience it in terms of their own production, seeking to discover and fashion relationships among sounds to create perceptually meaningful forms.

Like these formal issues (and related to them), representation is experienced by students as a creative decision rather than as a property to be
recognized only in another work. Empirical study of acousmatic and sample-
based music instruction has in fact documented strong student interest in
allusiveness and narrative over abstraction.[46] Such preferences may partly
reflect formative musical experiences that associate sound with narrative
content in popular music, film, and other media. Appropriating and hacking
Schaeffer's key term, students may choose to create "real" (*concrète*) music
that registers their personal experience and may include sounds they have
recorded for documentary purposes. Parallel exploration of field recordings, soundwalks, and soundscape composition is an obvious move here, as
is study of Luc Ferrari's recuperation and embrace of the "anecdotal."

As for the question of large-scale formal development, the guidance
offered by the journals may prove to be insufficient. Schaeffer's methods
at this stage remained tentative. Where intuition and experimentation
founder, analyzing and imitating preexisting works may suggest viable
strategies at different levels of scale. A particular benefit of direct creative
modeling is that it demands careful listening, similar to the type popular
musicians use when learning songs "by ear"—what Lucy Green has characterized as "purposive listening."[47] Too exclusive a focus on modeling,
however, risks imposing an external style onto students and negating the
value of self-expression in their creative work.[48]

Questions of representation, structure, and meaning figure prominently
in Andrew Selle's contribution, which presents an analytical method for
beginners inspired by Schaeffer's theory of "reduced listening" in the
Treatise on Musical Objects (chapter 2). Shifting from an aesthetic mode
to broader questions of identity and cultural values, I would like to highlight the arguments of two chapters already briefly mentioned. In counterpoint with her discussion of Indigenous sound art, Galloway examines
the political and ecological meanings of "extractive electronic music" as
exemplified by soundscape compositions that erase or evade the meanings of the contested sites they purportedly document. Liu and Yang
investigate the concept of a "Chinese model" of electroacoustic music

that prioritizes reference over abstraction; they discuss how composers such as Zhang Xiaofu brought techniques from the GRM and other practices into dialogue with the sonic cultures of Beijing opera, Indigenous peoples, and Buddhist and Taoist philosophy and ritual.

The Digital Vernacular

Experimenting with concrete or "real" music has an appealing resonance with educational movements prioritizing student inquiry, problem-solving, and the experiential source and relevance of "real-world" projects. Sampling, for instance, is both materially and culturally accessible as one of the many forms of "'redactive' creativity" and "digital participation" in youth culture identified by Nicholas Cook.[49] These acts of appropriating and remixing have a family resemblance to shaping imaginary worlds within *Second Life*, creating and spreading memes through various platforms, and sharing edited and remixed videos on YouTube. All of these activities constitute what we might now call the "digital vernacular" to describe the fallout of the "digital revolution," whose effects have become increasingly unremarkable and tacit—at least when our devices work and when we do not have the uncanny sense that algorithms are beginning to "speak by themselves," to invoke Schaeffer again.[50] Sampling is also intuitive from a listening perspective, both from its frequent use in recorded music and in the way we use recordings by controlling their repetition, selection, and playback speed.[51] In this sense, listening is itself a sampling practice that normalizes collage-like juxtapositions that are translatable into compositional acts.

Creative experimentation, hacking electronics, navigating through interactive and immersive sound environments, expanding and decolonizing the spaces of electronic music: these and other topics in *Teaching Electronic Music* open perspectives that help clarify the situation we as instructors find ourselves in and indicate ways of moving forward with our students. My concern in this introduction has been with the place of participatory forms of digital culture at the ends of historical narratives and in the potential experience of students as they weave in and out of our classrooms. The pragmatist philosopher and theorist of experiential education, John Dewey, posed a question about art and aesthetics that seems apt for these issues in the age of digital musicking: "How is it that the everyday making of things grows into the form of making which is genuinely artistic?"[52] I have suggested that the experience of following Schaeffer's itinerary with contemporary tools and materials offers a way of experimenting with possible answers to this question. Students test the hypothesis that anyone can make music with a laptop, to be sure, but they are also testing a more fundamental thesis—that in musicking, *making* and *knowing* are actions in necessary and perpetual relay.

Notes

I would like to thank Jim Davis, Robert McClure, and my colleagues Marian Mazzone and Michael O'Brien for their many helpful comments on an earlier version of this essay.

1. Richard Taruskin and Christopher H. Gibbs, *The Oxford History of Western Music: College Edition*, 2nd ed. (New York and Oxford: Oxford University Press, 2019) and J. Peter Burkholder, Donald Jay Grout, and Claude V. Palisca, *A History of Western Music*, 10th ed. (New York and London: W. W. Norton, 2019); for the sake of convenience, I will refer to Burkholder as the author of the Norton textbook.
2. J. Peter Burkholder and Claude V. Palisca, *Norton Anthology of Western Music*, vol. 3: *The Twentieth Century and After*, 8th ed. (New York and London: W. W. Norton, 2019).
3. The exclusion of fixed-medium electronic works in the anthology accompanying the Taruskin-Gibbs textbook is largely congruent with its 'literate thesis,' whereas Burkholder's pluralism admits them alongside traditionally notated works. Their presence calls attention to the contrast, even friction, between literate and aural modes of transmission as they involve analytical method and detail. This dialogue between forms of transmission extends to examples of blues and jazz represented by recordings, sheet music, lead sheets, and transcriptions—types of sources also included in the Oxford anthology.
4. Joanna Demers, *Listening through the Noise: The Aesthetics of Experimental Electronic Music* (Oxford and New York: Oxford University Press, 2010), 167–8.
5. For a succinct overview of the GRM's history, consult Marc Battier, "What the GRM Brought to Music: From Musique Concrète to Acousmatic Music," *Organised Sound* 12, no. 3 (2007): 189–202, as well as other articles in this special issue of *Organised Sound* devoted to the GRM. A comprehensive history is offered in Évelyne Gayou, *Le GRM, Groupe de recherches musicales: Cinquante ans d'histoire* (Paris: Fayard, 2007).
6. Burkholder et al., *A History of Western Music*, 959 and 1006.
7. Taruskin and Gibbs, *The Oxford History of Western Music*, 823–6. The Beatles seem enshrined as a locus classicus of this relay; see, for instance, Thomas Turino, *Music as Social Life: The Politics of Participation* (Chicago and London: University of Chicago Press, 2008), 84–5; and Jennifer Iverson, *Electronic Inspirations: Technologies of the Cold War Musical Avant-Garde* (New York: Oxford University Press, 2019), 198–9. Iverson cites the group as one of many examples of the "migration" of techniques from studios and research institutions into vernacular music, film, TV, Spectralism, New Complexity, and minimalism.
8. After describing the emergence of electronic music in the 1940s–60s, Burkholder states the principle directly: "Electronic music, whether played in concert or distributed in the form of recordings for private listening, attracted a relatively small, devoted audience without gaining broad popularity. Yet it became a potent tool in music for film and television, and most of the music produced today, especially popular music, uses technology developed by the pioneers of electronic music." Burkholder et al., *A History of Western Music*, 945.
9. Georgina Born, "On Musical Mediation: Ontology, Technology and Creativity," *Twentieth-Century Music* 2, no. 1 (2005): 26.
10. Born, "On Musical Mediation," 25.
11. These issues are also explored and documented in Georgina Born and Christopher Haworth, "From Microsound to Vaporwave: Internet-Mediated Musics, Online Methods, and Genre," *Music and Letters* 98, no. 4 (2017): 601–47.

12. The term is inspired by Born's account of relayed creativity; Brian Kane uses it in describing the "relay and transformation of a practice as it encounters a shift in media" in his "Relays: Audiotape, Material Affordances, and Cultural Practice," *Twentieth-Century Music* 14, no. 1 (2017): 66.

13. For a discussion oriented around electronics as a "medium," see Peter Manning, *Electronic and Computer Music*, 4th ed. (New York: Oxford University Press, 2013), 481–91.

14. Taruskin and Gibbs, *The Oxford History of Western Music*, 863.

15. Taruskin and Gibbs, *The Oxford History of Western Music*, 847. The disruptive impact of electronic music is more strongly characterized in the volume of *The Oxford History of Western Music* from which the college edition derives: "electronic music . . . produced the first fundamental alteration of the relationship between composition and notation in a thousand years, pointing the way (not that anyone was looking for it then) toward musical 'postliteracy.' This will be a big theme, in fact the biggest, in the closing chapters of this book." Richard Taruskin, *The Oxford History of Western Music*, vol. 5: *Music in the Late Twentieth Century* (Oxford and New York: Oxford University Press, 2010), 52. Taruskin's characterization of the potential consequences of this shift—left out of the college edition—is that digital modes of production and dissemination "may eventually render musical literacy, like knowledge of ancient scripts, superfluous to all but scholars" (509–10).

16. Burkholder et al., *A History of Western Music*, 994. The point is emphasized by an extended narrative excursus entitled "Music Technology for Everyone" (996–7).

17. Burkholder et al., *A History of Western Music*, 1011. With slight modifications, this passage also concludes the last several editions of the textbook.

18. Born, "On Musical Mediation," 28.

19. Christopher Small, *Music, Society, Education* [1977] (Middletown, CT: Wesleyan University Press, 1996), 218.

20. Thor Magnusson, *Sonic Writing: Technologies of Material, Symbolic, and Signal Inscriptions* (New York and London: Bloomsbury Academic, 2019), 241. One may explore the potential ramifications of Magnusson's proposal by taking current NASM guidelines and imagining how the skills enumerated as "Essential Competencies" and "Relevant Competencies for Area Programs" in the Bachelor of Music in Music Technology could productively migrate into program descriptions for performance, composition, and music history and literature, which at present include only scattered references to electronic media and computing. For these competencies, see NASM, *National Association of Schools of Music Handbook 2019–20*, 2020, 111–13.

21. Magnusson, *Sonic Writing*, 241.

22. Magnusson, *Sonic Writing*, 241.

23. Recent exceptions include Joseph Auner, *Music in the Twentieth and Twenty-First Centuries* (New York and London: W. W. Norton, 2013) and Tim Rutherford-Johnson, *Music after the Fall: Modern Composition and Culture since 1989* (Oakland, CA: University of California Press, 2017).

24. Leigh Landy, *Making Music with Sounds* (New York and London: Routledge, 2012); Andrew R. Brown, *Music Technology and Education: Amplifying Musicality*, 2nd ed. (New York and London: Routledge, 2015); and Andrew Hugill, *The Digital Musician*, 3rd ed. (New York and London: Routledge, 2019). Landy's list of recommended readings gives a historical perspective of pedagogical applications of *musique concrète* beginning in the early 1970s, including Terence Dwyers, *Composing with Tape Recorders: Musique Concrète for Beginners* (London and New York: Oxford University Press, 1971). See Landy, *Making Music with Sounds*, 200–1. More specialized and advanced sources that nonetheless offer much of value to introductory

courses include Trevor Wishart, *On Sonic Art*, ed. Simon Emmerson, 2nd ed. rev. (Amsterdam: Harwood Academic, 1996); Adrian Moore, *Sonic Art: An Introduction to Electroacoustic Music Composition* (New York and London: Routledge, 2016); and Curtis Roads, *Composing Electronic Music: A New Aesthetic* (Oxford and New York: Oxford University Press, 2015).

25. We report on these experiences in Bill Manaris and Blake Stevens, "Connecting Music and Computer Science: An Interdisciplinary Learning Community for First-Year University Students," in *Performing Arts As High-Impact Practice*, ed. Michelle Hayford and Susan Kattwinkel (Cham, Switzerland: Palgrave Macmillan, 2018), 68–82, and Bill Manaris, Blake Stevens, and Andrew R. Brown, "JythonMusic: An Environment for Teaching Algorithmic Music Composition, Dynamic Coding, and Musical Performativity," *Journal of Music, Technology & Education* 9, no. 1 (2016): 33–56.

26. Landy discusses "sample-based" music within this paradigm in his "Re-Composing Sounds . . . and Other Things," *Organised Sound* 24, no. 2 (2019): 130–8.

27. Pierre Schaeffer, *In Search of a Concrete Music*, trans. Christine North and John Dack (Berkeley, Los Angeles, and London: University of California Press, 2012), 47 and 78.

28. Schaeffer, *In Search of a Concrete Music*, 164; he specifies that he is invoking an idea of Paul Valéry's.

29. The translators note that among various meanings, *concrète* suggests "palpable, nontheoretical, and experiential," as well as "real-world." Another crucial word in Schaeffer's account is the noun *expérience*, which means both "experience" and "experiment." See the "Translators' Note," in Schaeffer, *In Search of a Concrete Music*, xii–xiii.

30. Schaeffer, *In Search of a Concrete Music*, 7.

31. "Où réside l'invention? Quand s'est-elle produite? Je réponds sans hésiter: quand j'ai *touché* au son des cloches. Séparer le son de l'attaque constituait l'acte générateur. Toute la musique concrète était contenue en germe dans cette action proprement créatrice sur la matière sonore." Pierre Schaeffer, *À la recherche d'une musique concrète* (Paris: Éditions du seuil, 1952), 16. See Schaeffer, *In Search of a Concrete Music*, 8.

32. Recent musicological perspectives on media archaeology appear in Alexander Rehding, convenor, "Colloquy: Discrete/Continuous: Music and Media Theory after Kittler," *Journal of the American Musicological Society* 70, no. 1 (2017): 221–56.

33. John Tresch and Emily I. Dolan, "Toward a New Organology: Instruments of Music and Science," *Osiris* 28 (2013): 279.

34. Jacques Attali, *Noise: The Political Economy of Music*, trans. Brian Massumi (Minneapolis and London: University of Minnesota Press, 1985), 133.

35. Gayou, *Le GRM*, and Daniel Teruggi, "Technology and Musique Concrète: The Technical Developments of the Groupe de Recherches Musicales and Their Implication in Musical Composition," *Organised Sound* 12, no. 3 (2007): 213–31.

36. Schaeffer, *In Search of a Concrete Music*, 89.

37. Schaeffer, *In Search of a Concrete Music*, 16–17 and 165.

38. Schaeffer, *In Search of a Concrete Music*, 61 and 65.

39. Schaeffer, *In Search of a Concrete Music*, 91–2.

40. See Benjamin Piekut, "Actor-Networks in Music History: Clarifications and Critiques," *Twentieth-Century Music* 11, no. 2 (2014): 191–215; on materialism, ANT, and object-oriented ontology, see Christoph Cox, *Sonic Flux: Sound, Art, and Metaphysics* (Chicago and London: University of Chicago Press, 2018).

41. Schaeffer, *In Search of a Concrete Music*, 105.

42. The term is associated with the work of Etienne Wenger in *Communities of Practice: Learning, Meaning, and Identity* (Cambridge: Cambridge University Press, 1999) and is applied to maker and hacker communities by Masu and Morreale in Chapter 9.
43. Turino, *Music as Social Life*, 79.
44. Schaeffer, *In Search of a Concrete Music*, 24.
45. Schaeffer, *In Search of a Concrete Music*, 81.
46. Anna-Marie Higgins and Kevin Jennings, "From Peering in the Window to Opening the Door: A Constructivist Approach to Making Electroacoustic Music Accessible to Young Listeners," *Organised Sound* 11, no. 2 (2006): 179–87; on the links between sampling and accessibility, see also Landy, "Re-Composing Sounds."
47. Lucy Green, *Music, Informal Learning and the School: A New Classroom Pedagogy* (Aldershot, UK and Burlington, VT: Ashgate, 2008), 6.
48. Jeffrey Martin emphasizes the importance of real-world examples and personal "authenticity" in secondary school contexts in his "Toward Authentic Electronic Music in the Curriculum: Connecting Teaching to Current Compositional Practices," *International Journal of Music Education* 30, no. 2 (2012): 124. Research on technology-based music classes at the secondary level is informative about the types of prior experiences students may bring to college music classes; see David Brian Williams, "The Non-Traditional Music Student in Secondary Schools of the United States: Engaging Non-Participant Students in Creative Music Activities through Technology." *Journal of Music, Technology and Education* 4, nos. 2–3 (2012): 131–47. For an account of college-level pop ensembles that also addresses the connection between personally relevant repertoire and student engagement, see Justin Patch, "The Case for Pop Ensembles in the Curriculum: Amateurism, Leadership, Civics, and Lifelong Learners," in *College Music Curricula for a New Century*, ed. Robin D. Moore (New York: Oxford University Press, 2017), 115–33.
49. Nicholas Cook, "Digital Technology and Cultural Practice," in *The Cambridge Companion to Music in Digital Culture*, ed. Nicholas Cook, Monique M. Ingalls, and David Trippett (Cambridge and New York: Cambridge University Press, 2019), 16–17.
50. I borrow the expression "digital vernacular" from James Stevens and Ralph Nelsen, *Digital Vernacular: Architectural Principles, Tools, and Processes* (New York and London: Routledge, 2015).
51. François Delalande, "The Technological Era of 'Sound': A Challenge for Musicology and a New Range of Social Practices," *Organised Sound* 12, no. 3 (2007): 256. This is just one aspect of the much broader impact of recording on musical production surveyed in Mark Katz, *Capturing Sound: How Technology Has Changed Music*, rev. ed. (Berkeley, Los Angeles, and London: University of California Press, 2010).
52. John Dewey, *Art as Experience* [1934] (New York: Perigee, 2005), 11.

Selected Bibliography

Attali, Jacques. *Noise: The Political Economy of Music.* Translated by Brian Massumi. Minneapolis and London: University of Minnesota Press, 1985.
Auner, Joseph. *Music in the Twentieth and Twenty-First Centuries.* New York and London: W.W. Norton, 2013.
Battier, Marc. "A Constructivist Approach to the Analysis of Electronic Music and Audio Art: Between Instruments and Faktura." *Organised Sound* 8, no. 3 (2003): 249–55.

Battier, Marc. "What the GRM Brought to Music: From Musique Concrète to Acousmatic Music." *Organised Sound* 12, no. 3 (2007): 189–202.

Bell, Adam Patrick. *Dawn of the DAW: The Studio as Musical Instrument*. New York: Oxford University Press, 2018.

Born, Georgina. "On Musical Mediation: Ontology, Technology and Creativity." *Twentieth-Century Music* 2, no. 1 (2005): 7–36.

Born, Georgina, and Christopher Haworth. "From Microsound to Vaporwave: Internet-Mediated Musics, Online Methods, and Genre." *Music and Letters* 98, no. 4 (2017): 601–47.

Brown, Andrew R. *Music Technology and Education: Amplifying Musicality*. 2nd ed. New York and London: Routledge, 2015.

Burkholder, J. Peter, Donald Jay Grout, and Claude V. Palisca. *A History of Western Music*. 10th ed. New York and London: W.W. Norton, 2019.

Burkholder, J. Peter, and Claude V. Palisca. *Norton Anthology of Western Music*. Vol. 3: *The Twentieth Century and After*. 8th ed. New York and London: W.W. Norton, 2019.

Burnard, Pamela, ed. *Developing Creativities in Higher Music Education: International Perspectives and Practices*. London and New York: Routledge, 2014.

Cook, Nicholas, Monique M. Ingalls, and David Trippett, eds. *The Cambridge Companion to Music in Digital Culture*. Cambridge and New York: Cambridge University Press, 2019.

Cox, Christoph. *Sonic Flux: Sound, Art, and Metaphysics*. Chicago and London: University of Chicago Press, 2018.

Delalande, François. "The Technological Era of 'Sound': A Challenge for Musicology and a New Range of Social Practices." *Organised Sound* 12, no. 3 (2007): 251–8.

Demers, Joanna. *Listening through the Noise: The Aesthetics of Experimental Electronic Music*. Oxford and New York: Oxford University Press, 2010.

Dewey, John. *Art as Experience* [1934]. New York: Perigee, 2005.

Gayou, Évelyne. *Le GRM, Groupe de recherches musicales: Cinquante ans d'histoire*. Paris: Fayard, 2007.

Green, Lucy. *Music, Informal Learning and the School: A New Classroom Pedagogy*. Aldershot, UK and Burlington, VT: Ashgate, 2008.

Greher, Gena R., and Jesse M. Heines. *Computational Thinking in Sound: Teaching the Art and Science of Music and Technology*. Oxford and New York: Oxford University Press, 2014.

Haddon, Elizabeth, and Pamela Burnard, eds. *Creative Teaching for Creative Learning in Higher Music Education*. London and New York: Routledge, 2016.

Higgins, Anna-Marie, and Kevin Jennings. "From Peering in the Window to Opening the Door: A Constructivist Approach to Making Electroacoustic Music Accessible to Young Listeners." *Organised Sound* 11, no. 2 (2006): 179–87.

Holmes, Thom. *Electronic and Experimental Music: Technology, Music, and Culture*. 6th ed. New York and London: Routledge, 2020.

Hugill, Andrew. *The Digital Musician*. 3rd ed. New York and London: Routledge, 2019.

Iverson, Jennifer. *Electronic Inspirations: Technologies of the Cold War Musical Avant-Garde*. New York: Oxford University Press, 2019.

Justice, Sean. *Learning to Teach in the Digital Age: New Materialities and Maker Paradigms in Schools*. New York: Peter Lang, 2016.

Kane, Brian. "Relays: Audiotape, Material Affordances, and Cultural Practice." *Twentieth-Century Music* 14, no. 1 (2017): 65–75.

Kane, Brian. *Sound Unseen: Acousmatic Sound in Theory and Practice*. Oxford and New York: Oxford University Press, 2014.

Katz, Mark. *Capturing Sound: How Technology Has Changed Music*. Rev. ed. Berkeley, Los Angeles, and London: University of California Press, 2010.

Landy, Leigh. *Making Music with Sounds*. New York and London: Routledge, 2012.

Landy, Leigh. "Re-Composing Sounds . . . and Other Things." *Organised Sound* 24, no. 2 (2019): 130–8.

Landy, Leigh. *Understanding the Art of Sound Organization*. Cambridge, MA and London: The MIT Press, 2007.

Magnusson, Thor. *Sonic Writing: Technologies of Material, Symbolic, and Signal Inscriptions*. New York and London: Bloomsbury Academic, 2019.

Manaris, Bill, and Blake Stevens. "Connecting Music and Computer Science: An Interdisciplinary Learning Community for First-Year University Students." In *Performing Arts as High-Impact Practice*, edited by Michelle Hayford and Susan Kattwinkel, 68–82. Cham, Switzerland: Palgrave Macmillan, 2018.

Manaris, Bill, Blake Stevens, and Andrew R. Brown. "JythonMusic: An Environment for Teaching Algorithmic Music Composition, Dynamic Coding, and Musical Performativity." *Journal of Music, Technology & Education* 9, no. 1 (2016): 33–56.

Manning, Peter. *Electronic and Computer Music*. 4th ed. New York: Oxford University Press, 2013.

Martin, Jeffrey. "Toward Authentic Electronic Music in the Curriculum: Connecting Teaching to Current Compositional Practices." *International Journal of Music Education* 30, no. 2 (2012): 120–32.

Moore, Adrian. *Sonic Art: An Introduction to Electroacoustic Music Composition*. New York and London: Routledge, 2016.

Moore, Robin D., ed. *College Music Curricula for a New Century*. New York: Oxford University Press, 2017.

Móricz, Klára, and David E. Schneider, eds. *Oxford Anthology of Western Music*. Vol. 3: The Twentieth Century. 2nd ed. New York and Oxford: Oxford University Press, 2019.

NASM. *National Association of Schools of Music Handbook 2019–20*, 2020. Accessed September 2, 2020. https://nasm.arts-accredit.org/wp-content/uploads/sites/2/2020/01/M-2019-20-Handbook-02-13-2020.pdf.

O'Neill, Susan A., and Deanna C. C. Peluso. "Using Dialogue and Digital Media Composing to Enhance and Develop Artistic Creativity, Creative Collaborations and Multimodal Practices." In Burnard, *Developing Creativities in Higher Music Education: International Perspectives and Practices*, 115–26.

Patch, Justin. "The Case for Pop Ensembles in the Curriculum: Amateurism, Leadership, Civics, and Lifelong Learners." In Moore, *College Music Curricula for a New Century*, 115–33.

Piekut, Benjamin. "Actor-Networks in Music History: Clarifications and Critiques." *Twentieth-Century Music* 11, no. 2 (2014): 191–215.

Rehding, Alexander, convenor. "Colloquy: Discrete/Continuous: Music and Media Theory after Kittler." *Journal of the American Musicological Society* 70, no. 1 (2017): 221–56.

Rinsema, Rebecca M. *Listening in Action: Teaching Music in the Digital Age*. London and New York: Routledge, 2017.

Roads, Curtis. *Composing Electronic Music: A New Aesthetic*. Oxford and New York: Oxford University Press, 2015.

Rutherford-Johnson, Tim. *Music after the Fall: Modern Composition and Culture since 1989*. Oakland, CA: University of California Press, 2017.

Schaeffer, Pierre. *In Search of a Concrete Music*. Translated by Christine North and John Dack. Berkeley, Los Angeles, and London: University of California Press, 2012.

Schaeffer, Pierre. *À la recherche d'une musique concrète*. Paris: Éditions du Seuil, 1952.

Schaeffer, Pierre. *Treatise on Musical Objects: An Essay across Disciplines*. Translated by Christine North and John Dack. Oakland, CA: University of California Press, 2017.

Small, Christopher. *Musicking: The Meanings of Performing and Listening*. Middletown, CT: Wesleyan University Press, 1998.

Small, Christopher. *Music, Society, Education* [1977]. Middletown, CT: Wesleyan University Press, 1996.

Stevens, James, and Ralph Nelsen. *Digital Vernacular: Architectural Principles, Tools, and Processes*. New York and London: Routledge, 2015.

Taruskin, Richard. *The Oxford History of Western Music*. Vol. 5: Music in the Late Twentieth Century. Oxford and New York: Oxford University Press, 2010.

Taruskin, Richard, and Christopher H. Gibbs. *The Oxford History of Western Music: College Edition*. 2nd ed. New York and Oxford: Oxford University Press, 2019.

Taylor, Timothy D. *Strange Sounds: Music, Technology, & Culture*. New York and London: Routledge, 2001.

Teruggi, Daniel. "Musique Concrète Today: Its Reach, Evolution of Concepts and Role in Musical Thought." *Organised Sound* 20, no. 1 (2015): 51–9.

Teruggi, Daniel. "Technology and Musique Concrète: The Technical Developments of the Groupe de Recherches Musicales and Their Implication in Musical Composition." *Organised Sound* 12, no. 3 (2007): 213–31.

Tresch, John, and Emily I. Dolan. "Toward a New Organology: Instruments of Music and Science." *Osiris* 28 (2013): 278–98.

Turino, Thomas. *Music as Social Life: The Politics of Participation*. Chicago and London: University of Chicago Press, 2008.

Wenger, Etienne. *Communities of Practice: Learning, Meaning, and Identity*. Cambridge: Cambridge University Press, 1999.

Williams, David Brian. "The Non-Traditional Music Student in Secondary Schools of the United States: Engaging Non-Participant Students in Creative Music Activities through Technology." *Journal of Music, Technology and Education* 4, nos. 2–3 (2012): 131–47.

Wishart, Trevor. *On Sonic Art*. Edited by Simon Emmerson. 2nd ed. rev. Amsterdam: Harwood Academic, 1996.

Part I
Analytical, Descriptive, and Creative Strategies

1 Then and Now

A Practical Guide for Introducing Electronic Music

Robert McClure

The terms acousmatic, electroacoustic, electronic, techno, soundscape, *musique concrète*, EDM, *elektronische Musik*, tape music, and synthesis all have at least one thing in common: they all refer to music created using some kind of electronic technology. Yet they are not interchangeable. Some refer to technique. Some refer to genre. Some have a historical basis. As technology becomes faster, cheaper, and more accessible, more students are engaging actively with music technology and electronic music. A primary tool for creating music, a Digital Audio Workstation (DAW), comes built into every Apple computer, tablet, and phone. Many music technology "freeware" programs are also readily downloadable. YouTube hosts hundreds of hours of content in the form of tutorials and "how-to" videos from enthusiastic users and software companies. The days of cutting and splicing tape are over, yet many of the same techniques and principles remain. With music technology so readily available, students need guidance in connecting the past with the present.

Students in universities and conservatories face a complex, even contradictory situation: they are surrounded by a popular musical culture in which sampling and other electronic techniques are the norm, while their formal music studies privilege concert music and score-based literacy and musicianship. Concert music performance has a homogenizing effect on sound production. From a very early age, musicians are taught "good" technique from "bad" technique. Unique sounds from vocalists or instrumentalists are largely excised from the scope of performance and, thus, the scope of composition. For example, whistle tones, multiphonics, and a breathy tone might be eliminated from a young flutist's performative practice in the name of "good" technique. In an interview with Tara Rodgers, the composer and performer Pamela Z has addressed this issue in terms of vocal technique:

> I do think it's really interesting that in Western classical music, when you study with a bel canto teacher, they're very interested in having you go after what's considered to be a correct sound—like looking for a certain tone color that is the right way to sing. And when you

get involved in more experimental types of singing, or other, broader views of it, you find that there are all these other colors that you have and can use—and it's not right and wrong, it's just different colors.[1]

In studying and producing electronic music, the "good sound" vs. "bad sound" dichotomy should be reframed as desired sound and undesired sound, given a certain set of criteria specific to the genre of music involved.

Most concert music, furthermore, is mediated through notation. Composers do not work with specific sounds but rather with a generic set of symbols and instructions for others to produce sound. Igor Stravinsky identified "two states of music: potential music and actual music," referring to the notated score and the performance or interpretation of this score, respectively.[2] Notation needs to be not only clear but also universal enough to be realized by not just a single musician with unique skills but rather a generic musician with the set of "good" technical skills. It has only been in the later twentieth century and continuing into the present that composers and performers have been pushing the boundaries of their respective fields with regard to sound production, timbre, and technique. While a direct causal link between the advent of electronic music and the exploration of acoustic sound production (for instance, in "extended techniques") would be difficult to prove, the fact that these two streams of research and creativity coincided is not surprising. Many composers who work in the field of electronic music also compose acoustic works and works that blend the two worlds together. Each practice informs the other.

Electronic music has afforded composers the opportunity to explore diverse sounds apart from what Pierre Schaeffer described as "preconceived sound abstractions" by using sounds that are unique to a single place, time, event, object, or even person.[3] The ultimate sonic distinguishing factor of each person is arguably the voice. The human voice, with its seemingly endless modifications and combinations of sounds, is perhaps one of the most complex instruments ever developed, with 7.8 billion distinct expressions at this moment. This number rises as more voices are recorded and archived. While much of notated solo, vocal chamber, and choral music demands that each individual voice produce only a select number of these possible sounds in a homogenous manner, electronic music allows composers and musicians to explore voices in all their diversity.

This chapter is framed around developing a student project that uses the human voice and software to bring methods of electronic sound production to life, lifting the veil on what was once only an insider's skill. It seeks to demystify the basic techniques of electronic music through an explanation of terms and techniques linked to pieces from the field's origins to the present, with the goal of informing students' creative work and establishing a foundational knowledge of several key aspects of electronic music. This survey demonstrates connections between past and present electronic music techniques and seeks to expand knowledge of the field by including recently composed electronic music. The experiential mode of instruction proposed here allows for a deeper understanding of music that permeates nearly all facets of our technology-infused lives.

Exploring Practices and Genres of Electronic Music

Many of the techniques used in contemporary electronic music originated in traditions such as *musique concrète* and *elektronische Musik*. To build a toolbox of techniques students can use in creating sound-based compositions, they should explore the history of electronic music to understand the origins of these techniques and how composers have used them creatively. The section that follows introduces these major traditions through selected works that illustrate specific sound production and modulation techniques centering on the human voice, followed by a more detailed examination of specific techniques. In addition to offering models of sound modulation through landmark works, this section reviews the basic terminology describing the genres of electronic music.

At the most general level, "electronic" and "electroacoustic" are broad terms that encompass music that uses electronic, as opposed to acoustic, means of sound production. This may be accomplished through live performance on electronic instruments such as synthesizers, generators, other sound-producing circuits, and digitally processing an acoustic source or playback of electronically produced or processed sound via loudspeakers. "Electronic music" is possibly broader than "electroacoustic" and can include, in addition to all forms of art music, various genres within popular music that use electronic elements such as synthesizers and digital signal processing (DSP). The same cannot be said of "electroacoustic music," as the term has become more associated with art music than popular music. Despite this small difference, "electronic" and "electroacoustic" have been used interchangeably as the parent genre for all subsequent generations of music produced using electronic means.

The main practices for students to explore in preparing to undertake their projects are the genres of early magnetic tape music, acousmatic music, soundscape composition, music for instrument(s) and fixed media, live or interactive electronic music, and popular music created electronically. I will consider each in turn.

Magnetic Tape Music

Electronic music composed with magnetic tape covers the broad category of electronic music that was performed via playback over loudspeakers. As the overwhelming majority of electronic music being composed today is done so in the digital realm, magnetic tape compositions are largely a thing of the past. This should not be confused with recorded acoustic music disseminated through tape playback. Rather, composers used the mechanics and material of magnetic tape by cutting, splicing, reversing, degrading, delaying, and altering the playback speed of the sonic material captured on tape to create their compositions. Two distinct and com-peting methods of composing electronic music are identified within this category: *musique concrète* and *elektronische Musik*, the first centered in Paris at the Radiodiffusion-Télévision Française (RTF), and the second in Cologne at the Westdeutscher Rundfunk (WDR). For a brief period in the infancy of electronic music's history, the two studios' methods and materials could not have been more distinct. Both of these early methods may be combined with one or more instruments/voices for the ubiquitous "instrument and tape" work.

Musique Concrète

Musique concrète, which originated in the work of Pierre Schaeffer in the 1940s at the RTF and later with the Groupe de Recherches Musi-cales (GRM), is based on the manipulation of recorded sound. Schaeffer emphasized the role of real, as opposed to abstract, sounds in the practice:

> I have coined the term *Musique Concrète* for this commitment to compose with materials taken from 'given' experimental sound in order to emphasize our dependence, no longer on preconceived sound abstractions, but on sound fragments that exist in reality and that are considered as discrete and complete sound objects, even if and above all when they do not fit in with the elementary definitions of music theory.[4]

Although many other composers throughout the twentieth century would use the term *musique concrète* to describe their music (with varying accu-racy), other terms such as "acousmatic music" have replaced it, as the methods and materials of electronic composition have relaxed from the strict meaning that this term once carried.

Because the practice is based on recorded sound, the voice figures prom-inently and in diverse ways in many classic works of *musique concrète*. The pioneering work of Halim El-Dabh, *The Expression of Zaar* (1944), was produced before Schaeffer developed the concept and practice of *musique concrète* in Paris; it uses high-pass filtering techniques to isolate the upper frequencies of a choir singing in a religious ceremony in Cairo, Egypt. Pierre Schaeffer and Pierre Henry's *Symphonie pour un homme seul* (1949–50) explores a wide range of vocal expressions, including humming, laughing, and singing; a particularly effective excerpt to illus-trate these diverse vocalizations is mvt. 4, "Erotica." Pierre Henry's *Varia-tions pour une porte et un soupir* (1963) is an expert demonstration of tape modulation techniques based on samples of a door squeaking and a human sigh; listeners may reflect on how human and nonhuman sounds interact and overlap, depending on the specific modulation techniques used by Henry.

Luciano Berio's *Thema (Omaggio a Joyce)* (1958) is a masterful work utilizing Cathy Berberian's voice reciting from the Sirens chapter of James Joyce's novel *Ulysses*. Berio applies classic tape techniques (varispeed, playback direction, cutting/splicing, etc.) to transform the original spoken text into a wide array of gestures and textures. Berio was studying onomatopoeic poetry with Umberto Eco at the time of this composition, a fact made more interesting when several moments of *Thema* are closely examined.[5] After the text is read by Berberian, the opening of the work offers several incredible examples of what I will term "electroacoustic onomatopoeia."[6]

Beginning at 2:17, a short phrase juxtaposes the words "fife" (from "fifenote") and "flutes." This short phrase contains a tremolo effect on "flutes" that was likely created by cutting and splicing several copies of "flu" together. Berio speaks about this process of using multiple copies of sounds spliced together in an interview with Barry Schrader.[7] The tremolo on "flutes" brings to mind the technique of flutter-tonguing, a common extended technique for the flute and other wind instruments, one Berio makes extensive use of in his *Sequenza I* for solo flute, also from 1958. With "flute," Berio creates a sound similar to one that could be created with a flute. Using electroacoustic techniques, Berio has furthered the possibilities of onomatopoeia by reapplying the effects of sound to the word that describes the sound.

At 2:45, Berio again engages "electroacoustic onomatopoeia" with his treatment of the word "blooming." "Blew," "blue," "bloom," "bloo," and "blooming" all appear in the original text and recording. Using these homonyms and the technique of splicing multiple copies of sounds together, Berio proceeds through the phonetic sounds of the word "blooming" until the final complete word is heard at 2:52. Just as a bud would unfurl to become a flower, the word "blooming" aurally blooms! This is quite possibly the most technologically and musically impressive moment in the early history of tape music.

Elektronische Musik

In almost direct opposition to *musique concrète*, *elektronische Musik* was composed onto magnetic tape using audio oscillators such as sine and sawtooth wave generators, white noise generators, and ring modulators as its sound sources, as well as an array of audio filters. Composers employed both additive and subtractive synthesis to create dynamic spectromorphologies from the otherwise sterile sound sources. It was pioneered by three men working at the WDR between 1949 and 1951:

Dr. Werner Meyer-Eppler (physicist and information theorist), Herbert Eimert (composer and musicologist), and Robert Beyer (sound engineer).

Karlheinz Stockhausen's *Studie II* (1954) displays this classic approach to *elektronische Musik* through additive synthesis, filtering, reverberation, and tight control of attack and decay.[8] Due to the profound influence the Cologne studio had on the NHK studio in Tokyo, Makoto Moroi and Toshirō Mayuzumi's work *Shichi no Variation* (7 Variations) (1956) contains many of the same features. Stockhausen's *Gesang der Jünglinge* (1956) fused *musique concrète* and *elektronische Musik*, as it used electronic sounds and recordings made by a boy soprano, Josef Protschka. Particular attention should be paid to Stockhausen's use of space through the application of reverb, volume, and panning applied to the vocal and synthetic sounds alike. Stockhausen's vocal sound gestures mirror the complexity of his synthetic gestures as the work showcases a technological mastery in an extended duration that distinguishes it from the early experimentations and studies produced at the WDR.

Fixed Media

Fixed media is the modern-day successor to "magnetic tape music," as the sounds are still fixed in time as they were on tape, but now the transmission medium is variable, including tape, DAT, CD, Mini Disc, mp3, and the current relevant methods such as WAVE, Audio Interchange File Format (AIFF), and other lossless digital formats. Two practices that emerged from early tape music are still in use today: "acousmatic music" and "soundscape composition." Furthermore, as a successor to magnetic tape music, the vast category of "instrument and fixed media" music can be distinguished from both acousmatic and soundscape music.

Acousmatic Music

Acousmatic music refers to electroacoustic music composed of sounds that are temporally fixed on a playback medium to be performed via loudspeakers/headphones without the intervention of a live performer.[9] The practice is a modern descendant of *musique concrète* without the historical, stylistic, or material limitations of its predecessor.[10] In acousmatic music, original sound sources are invisible. The listener only interacts with sounds projected through loudspeakers without visual feedback as to the sound's original source or cause. This is a striking contrast to how audiences have interacted, both aurally and visually, with music since its inception.

Pauline Oliveros' *Bye Bye Butterfly* (1965), an example of "tape composition" in the United States, samples Puccini's *Madama Butterfly* to contrast operatic vocal techniques with a performance captured to tape of wailing oscillators using tape delay. *Arturo* (1998) by Elainie Lillios features the voice of a tarot card reader as the primary sonic material that is manipulated in myriad ways, including filtering, pitch alteration, delay, granulation, and many others. My own work in collaboration with poet Alix Anne Shaw, *untangle my tongue* (2011), uses whispered (Hilary Purrington) and spoken (Shaw) versions of the text. In a nod to Luciano Berio's *Thema (Omaggio a Joyce)*, certain words like "cicadas" and "stuttering" are manipulated to sound like the sound the word is describing, recalling "electroacoustic onomatopoeia." Jon Fielder's *Think* (2017) explores a friend's temporary schizophrenic breakdown through the sonic manipulation of bits of text taken from the friend's social media accounts during the episode. Text is jumbled in both the acoustic performance and later in the electronic procession to create a disorienting sonic landscape. Students may also want to explore Trevor Wishart's *Tongues of Fire* (1992–94) and Paul Rudy's *Thema: Omaggio* (2002) for examples of pieces using nonsung/spoken vocal sounds and a diverse array of signal processing methods.

Soundscape Composition

The term "soundscape" as it applies to electroacoustic music is most often associated with environmental sounds or, rather, sounds that are recorded without intervention from the recording engineer or performer. The composer Barry Truax labeled this type of acousmatic music "soundscape composition" and argued that "the original sounds must stay recognisable and the listener's contextual and symbolic associations should be invoked for a piece to be a soundscape composition."[11]

While soundscape composition is most often associated with the World Soundscape Project and the pioneering work of R. Murray Schafer, the use of field recordings as unaltered musical material was also present, although discouraged, at the GRM with Luc Ferrari's *Presque Rien no. 1 'Le lever du jour au bord de la mer'* (1967–70).[12] Hildegard Westerkamp's *Kits Beach Soundwalk* (1989) features soft and calming narration by the composer that guides the listener through the background soundscape. Luc Ferrari's *Far West News* (1998–99) uses the voice as both narration and sonic material, drawing from recordings made on a trip across the southwest region of the United States. Most recently, the experimental hip-hop group Clipping ("clipping.") has used soundscape techniques on their 2019 album *There Existed an Addiction to Blood* with tracks such as "Run for Your Life," in which the majority of background sounds are recorded city sounds that have been either looped to create rhythms or left unaltered. The final track on this album is an 18-minute soundscape cover of Annea Lockwood's *Piano Burning* (1968).

Instrument and Fixed Media

A piece combining instrument(s) or voice(s) with fixed media often has a written score that may or may not contain a notated fixed media part that gives cues to the performer(s). The difference between the generically labeled "instrument and fixed media" category and "instrument and tape" is a matter of medium. Many works are still mislabeled as using "tape" when no magnetic tape was used in the production or playback of the work. The following representative compositions include works with both fixed media and tape.

Milton Babbitt's *Philomel* (1964), for soprano and tape, furthers the tradition of combining synthesized and vocal sounds that began with Stockhausen's *Gesang der Jünglinge* (1956) by using the RCA Mark II Sound Synthesizer to process prerecorded vocal sounds to tape that sonically and narratively interact with the live soprano. Jon Christopher Nelson's *They Wash Their Ambassadors in Citrus and Fennel* (1994) is a more modern take on vocal sampling and synthesis. The voice is chopped, distorted, pitch shifted, and vocoded in the fixed media track against a performance that utilizes the entire range of vocal possibilities. Listeners would not be at fault in thinking that these electronic manipulations were happening in real time. Nelson's piece was created just before processing and sampling of a live performer became computationally available and more prevalent.

Live or Interactive Electronic Music

While live electronics have been incorporated in musical performance since the advent of electronic instruments such as the theremin, ondes Martenot, and later with the Buchla synthesizer and the Sal-Mar Construction, it is now commonplace for a composer to run various kinds of live electronics from their laptop computer. Composers frequently combine live DSP of a live source and/or real-time synthesis with fixed media playback to create vast and varied sound worlds. The electronics are typically run from a computer music programming language that simultaneously processes the digital signal and provides control to move from one electronic state to another. Programs such as Max, SuperCollider, Pure Data (Pd), RTcmix, and Ableton Live facilitate live interaction with the performer, whether the performance involves an acoustic instrument, voice, or electronic controller. While DSP has become the norm, the tactility and charm of analog electronics still holds great appeal. Music for acoustic instruments mediated with microphones, interfaces, and computers—as well as music for electronic instruments such as analog synthesizers, controllers, and no-input mixers—is beginning to blur the lines of this already vaguely defined category of electronic music. Liveness is the important factor.

Although originally written for different pieces of hardware that are now obsolete, Kaija Saariaho's *NoaNoa* (1992), for flute and electronics, now runs in Max and combines reverb, sampling of the flute, and whispered text from the performer to create a weightless piece that never seems to touch the ground. Jenn Kirby's *Phonetics* (2017), for voice and GameTrak controller with Max, allows the performer to physically manipulate the sound of their voice with delay, pitch shifting, and reverb using the hacked Playstation GameTrak controller. This controller allows the performer's body to become a more integral part of the performance. Kristopher Bendrick's *Semi-Human/Semi-Sentient* (2019), for voice, QuNeo controller, no-input mixer, fixed media, and live video processing, continues this theme of the body, as a small camera is pointed directly into the performer's mouth as grunts, moans, glottal stops, and other nonsung vocal sounds are combined with harsh and aggressive electronics. Students can usefully compare *Semi-Human/Semi-Sentient* with Wishart's *Tongues of Fire* (1992–94).

Popular Music Created Electronically

Electronics have made perhaps the biggest impact on popular music. If you turn on the radio . . . wait. The radio? If you open your favorite music streaming platform today, numerous artists employ techniques developed in the electronic music studio. Electronic instruments, sounds, and manipulations permeate a wide swath of popular music that exceeds the obvious genres of electronica and EDM.

Radiohead's "Everything in its Right Place" (*Kid A*, 2000) achieves a constantly varying playback direction of its opening vocal melody through the use of a playback scrubber. The genre-blurring Icelandic artist Björk consistently uses electronics and electronic processing techniques in her songs. "Mouth's Cradle" (*Medúlla*, 2004) employs a sequenced vocal sample using Musical Instrument Digital Interface (MIDI) for its opening ostinato as well as reversed vocal melodies as accompaniment to the verses. This "all vocal" album is a fantastic resource for students to explore how a creative artist uses the voice in myriad ways. "Hide and Seek" (2005) by Imogen Heap features a single vocal melody harmonized through the process of vocoding. "Woods" (*Blood Bank*, 2009) by Bon Iver is another highly inventive repurposing of technology, as it again seems to feature a single vocal melody that is being harmonized, although singer Justin Vernon recorded every track individually and applied extreme pitch correction using Auto-Tune. Finally, "First of the Year (Equinox)" (*More Monsters and Sprites*, 2011) by Skrillex features a reversed, rearranged, and pitch-shifted vocal melody in addition to the completely electronic surrounding track.

Making Electronic Music: Foundational Tools and Techniques

There is more access to the tools necessary to create electronic music today than ever before. Between freeware, built-in programs, and web-based resources, many of the past hurdles placed before students have been removed, opening up the possibility of a direct, experiential under-standing of electronic music. Despite the enormous leap in technology from the first years of working with tape to now, many of the techniques have remained the same. This section outlines some of the relevant meth-ods of sound manipulation still in use and how those have been updated or have led to other DSP techniques.[13] I also cite particularly effective uses of these techniques in specific works for instructors to consider including as examples in lectures or class discussions.

Digital Audio Workstation

Replacing the multitrack tape recorder, a Digital Audio Workstation (DAW) is the primary software for making fixed electronic music. Notable DAWs currently available are Logic Pro X, Pro Tools, Ableton Live, Digi-tal Performer, Reaper, Cubase, GarageBand, and many others.[14] While Logic and GarageBand (a lite version of Logic) are specific to the OS X platform, most other DAWs have cross-platform functionality. Although each DAW has a unique look and layout, the fundamentals of working with a DAW are mostly universal. Instructors and students have a wealth of knowledge at their fingertips in the form of online video tutorials that describe the basic functionality and workflow of using a particular DAW, including how to implement the DSP effects, described later. Typically, a simple search engine query like "reverse playback Reaper" will produce the necessary answer in either video or written form. Instructors and stu-dents can make use of these free resources away from the classroom.

Cutting and Splicing (Temporal Editing)

What was once an arduous process of physically manipulating tape with an *editing block*, *razor blade*, *splicing tape*, and *leader tape* has become simple, fast, and, most importantly, nondestructive. Any faulty edit can be recovered since DAWs do not work with the original sound files but rather with aliases referencing original sound files. This technique enables composers to rearrange audio by juxtaposing and layering sounds that previously had no relationship.

Students can experiment with editing a sound's attack or decay char-acteristics. Effective models of this technique include Björk's "Mouth's Cradle" (*Medúlla*, 2004), whose opening ostinato sounds more like a synthesizer due to her editing of the vocal attack of the sung pitches. Bernard Parmegiani creates a one-note etude playing with timbre in his creative editing of many unique sound sources in the movement "Acci-dents/Harmoniques" from his masterwork *De Natura Sonorum* (1975).

A more recent form of sound editing is granulation or granular synthe-sis, wherein a sound is split into microsound "grains" and played back at more or less random times. Using granulation, Curtis Roads identified new sound mesostructures such as streams and clouds, as well as new morphologies such as coalescence, evaporation, points of attraction and repulsion, and transmutations and morphogenesis.[15] With this technique, composers can use sound as the fundamental material for creating completely new gestures and textures. Through close and dynamic control of the parameters of granulation, the composer sculpts with sound. Iannis Xenakis first used analog granular synthesis in his work *Analogique A et B* (1958–59) for string orchestra and tape.[16] More recent acousmatic examples include Horacio Vaggione's *24 Variations* (2001), Elainie Lillios's *Listening Beyond . . .* (2007), and my own work, *in excess* (2017).

Nathaniel Haering's work *Medical Text p. 57* (2017), for voice and live electronics, makes effective use of granular synthesis among several other live effects such as delay, reverb, filtering, and triggered fixed-media playback to augment a virtuosic vocal performance that features singing, speaking, shouting, humming, stuttering, breathing, vocal frying, and nearly every other manner of using the human voice to make sound. With its focus on the voice, the piece is a compelling successor to Luciano Berio's *Thema (Omaggio a Joyce)*, pushing what could once only be done in the studio into the live performance domain.[17]

Reverse Playback

Through reverse playback, the composer immediately doubles the number of sounds in their library. The reverse envelope is not a naturally occurring sound and is thus quite recognizable when employed. Percussive attacks with natural decays are easily susceptible to this playback manipulation, as the decay transforms into a crescendo. The Beastie Boys' "Paul Revere" (*Licensed to Ill*, 1986) is a prime example of combining forward and backward playback directions to create a rhythm track. Countless pop artists and producers have made use of reversed percussion sounds in their tracks as a subtle sound preceding a percussive hit to add emphasis. As previously mentioned, Radiohead uses a playback scrubber to alter the playback direction and starting points of a vocal melody in the song "Everything in Its Right Place" (*Kid A*, 2000).

Varispeed Playback

Composers experimented with playback speed to alter pitch on both tape players and phonograph turntables. Speed and pitch are linked through the following equation: $s = 2^{(x/12)}$ where s = playback speed and x = the number of semitones to transpose. For example, to raise the pitch of a sound by one octave, the playback speed must be doubled ($2 = 2^{(12/12)}$). Using turntables, test tone records, and varispeed playback, John Cage created a siren effect in his piece *Imaginary Landscape No. 1* (1939). This effect is also how the voices were created for the cartoon *Alvin and the Chipmunks*. This kind of effect is also used in Kesha's song "TiK ToK" (2009) at 1:35 on the word "down," as the speed and pitch of the word are rapidly decreased—a clear example of electroacoustic text painting in a pop song.

Today, pitch and speed have been decoupled and can be manipulated separately, a technique made possible by fast Fourier transform (FFT), through time stretching and pitch shifting. Maggi Payne's *Sferics* (2016) utilizes sounds recorded by NASA from the Voyager 1 and 2 spacecrafts that were then time stretched up to twenty times their original duration. One of the most striking pitch manipulations to sound in the recent past has been the invention of the Auto-Tune plugin by Antares. Originally designed for pitch correction on vocal recordings, artists like T-Pain and Kanye West and the band Bon Iver have used Auto-Tune creatively to modify their vocal timbre and capabilities. Irish composer Alex Dowling's album *Reality Rounds* (2020) utilizes Auto-Tune on four live vocalists to create stunning microtonal textures on seemingly digital voices. The "King of Thumbs" movement is a wonderful example from this innovative work.[18]

Tape Loops (Looping)

Before magnetic tape came to be the prominent medium, loops were created with lock grooves in phonograph discs.[19] Later, splicing a length of tape end to end to play in a perpetual loop became a fundamental tape technique. Perhaps the most famous and obvious use of tape loops is Steve Reich's first experiments with phasing in *It's Gonna Rain* (1965) and *Come Out* (1966). As a prominent popular music method, companies such as Boss, DigiTech, Line 6, Electro-Harmonix, and others have developed stand-alone looper pedals that can create several layers of loops that sync together. The musician/comedian Reggie Watts has made looping central to his beatboxing/singing/comedy act; numerous examples are available on YouTube, including a TED Talk.[20]

Composer and video artist Dan Tramte started working with loops as both a commentary on our social media-driven lives and a subtle rebellion against composition professors urging students to avoid exact repetition.[21] In *degradative interference* (2014) for table-top electric guitar, vine video, pedals, and objects, Tramte works directly with social media materials in the form of Vine videos of a guitar played with various objects used to create nontraditional guitar sounds. Looping videos or parts of videos, Tramte creates a perpetually shifting, rhythmic backdrop against which the live guitarist executes many noise-based gestures.

Filtering (Equalizer)

Filters, which amplify and attenuate frequencies, are a powerful tool for creating timbral manipulations. DAWs have a number of different equalizer (EQ) and filtering options, including low pass, high pass, band pass, resonant, comb, and others. Dynamic control of filter parameters such as cutoff or center frequency, Q factor, and gain can drastically modify a sound's timbral characteristics. The second part of Éliane Radigue's *Trilogie de la Mort*, *Kailasha* (1991), uses filtering dynamically to produce slowly evolving timbres and even melodies stemming from the ARP 2500 synthesizer. Jean-François Laporte's *Mantra* (1997) features analog filtering, created as Laporte slowly moved his microphone around an ice rink compressor utilizing polyvinyl chloride (PVC) pipes to act as resonant filters. Resonant filter banks can be particularly powerful in modifying timbre. Using a resonant filter bank, plastic sounds made through crumpling, stretching, and popping were modified to resemble sounds closer to plexiglass and wooden materials in my work *in excess* (2017).

Tape Echo or Delay (Multitap Delay)

Tape echo or delay can be accomplished by threading tape through multiple tape machines or using a tape player with multiple play heads. Sounds pass through the play heads at times determined by the physical length by which the play heads or tape machines are separated.[22] Pauline Oliveros utilized long tape delays in her work *I of IV* (1966). In the digital realm, the variation in time separation between delay taps accounts for a number of effects, including reverb, chorus, flanging (below 25 milliseconds), and echo or delay.[23] The opening of Trevor Wishart's *Imago* (2002) is a brilliant example of using delay with feedback. The entire piece is made from a 1-second sound of two whisky glasses clinking together and is a sonic masterclass in the myriad possibilities of sonic manipulation and variation. My work *in excess* (2017) includes a collection of sounds that use reverse delay made by reversing a sound, applying delay with feedback, and then reversing it again to create a crescendo.

Reverb

Reverberation was applied to sounds in several different ways in the tape era, including transducers and pickups attached to metal springs and plates and/or recording the reverberation response of a sound played back in a physical space.[24] In 1961, Dr. Manfred R. Schroeder developed the first digital reverb algorithm at Bell Telephone Laboratories.[25] Now, every DAW comes equipped with digital reverb, and numerous third-party plugins are available. These reverbs include replications of spring and plate reverb, convolution with impulse responses, and physical models of simulated spaces. More than just an audio effect, reverb, in combination with EQ and volume, allows the composer to control the virtual spatial qualities of their sounds. Curtis Roads has also suggested more creative uses of reverb that include pitch-shifted reverberation chords.[26] Using reverb and reverse playback is an effective method of creating spatial motion from far to near. Reverb, like every other sonic manipulation, should be applied creatively and purposefully.[27]

Project Prompt

To synthesize the historical and technical excursions above, students may create a sound-based work that reflects a knowledge of these practices and traditions. This project was designed with a general student (as opposed to music major) in mind. However, the project can easily be adapted for noncomposition music students or even composers. Formal, stylistic, and technical limitations may be placed on students with less experience to focus their creativity within a small window.

1) Compose a 2- to 4-minute acousmatic work for stereo fixed media in a DAW.
2) Sound sources: your voice or sounds made using your mouth, lips, tongue, etc.[28]
3) Record your vocal sounds through one of the following:

   a) Your cell phone using a voice memo; this is the most accessible method, yet recording quality will vary.
   b) Portable hand-held digital recorder such those made by Zoom, TASCAM, or Sony; some institutions may have a digital equipment checkout library with this equipment.
   c) A microphone/interface/computer system; consider partnering with your institution's media program, recording studio, or other department that may have access to this equipment if it is not housed in the music area.

4) DSP techniques available:

   a) Classic "tape" techniques

      i) Cutting/slicing (temporal editing)
      ii) Reverse playback
      iii) Varispeed playback (pitch/speed shifting)
      iv) Filtering (EQ)
      v) Looping
      vi) Reverb
      vii) Delay
      viii) Multitrack playback (layering)
      ix) Volume
      x) Panning

5) Compositional techniques to consider:

   a) Cause and effect

      i) With no visual source causing sounds to occur, develop an aural system whereby a sound's appearance, activity, change, or disappearance can be linked to another adjacent or overlapping event in the composition.

b) Layering

   i) Foreground, middle ground, background

c) Space

   i) Use a combination of volume, panning, EQ, and reverb to alter the listener's perception of space and depth in the stereo field, aiding in creating layers.

d) Structure and form

   i) Sections—phrases—gestures—motives—individual sounds.

6) Render/bounce your finished composition to a .wav or .aiff file.

Note: For students who have some experience with electronic music, challenge them to include the following DSP techniques:

Granulation
Resonant filter banks
Time stretching
Pitch shifting

Depending on the particular DAW students use, some of these effects may be included as plugins. For others, third-party plugins may be necessary. YouTube, software tutorials and forums, and search engine queries are the first place to discover pertinent techniques relative to the student's specific DAW.

Notes

1. Tara Rodgers, *Pink Noises: Women on Electronic Music and Sound* (Durham, NC and London: Duke University Press, 2010), 218.
2. Igor Stravinsky, *Poetics of Music in the Form of Six Lessons* (New York: Vintage, 1947), 121.
3. Pierre Schaeffer, *In Search of a Concrete Music*, trans. Christine North and John Dack (Berkeley, Los Angeles, and London: University of California Press, 2012), 14.
4. Schaeffer, *In Search of a Concrete Music*, 14. With "preconceived sound abstractions," Schaeffer is referencing traditional methods of composing with abstract pitches and rhythms to be realized later into sound by a singer or instrumentalist. I should note that although *musique concrète* is associated with "tape music," the first several compositions falling under this term by Schaeffer and Henry were composed and performed using turntables and gramophone discs rather than magnetic tape.
5. Barry Schrader, *Introduction to Electro-Acoustic Music* (Englewood Cliffs, NJ: Prentice-Hall, 1982), 179.
6. At least two recordings are available for this piece. The recording referenced here is found on Luciano Berio, *Many More Voices*, BMG Classics 09026-68302-2, 1998, CD. The only difference among the recordings is the addition of the recorded source material preceding the work.

7. Schrader, *Introduction to Electro-Acoustic Music*, 181.
8. Thom Holmes, *Electronic and Experimental Music: Technology, Music, and Culture*, 6th ed. (New York and London: Routledge, 2020), 241.
9. Such performances may involve a sound engineer who spatially diffuses the sound over a multichannel array of loudspeakers; this type of spatial "performance" does not alter the original musical material fixed on the medium.
10. Francis Dhomont surveys the emergence of the term in his "Is There a Québec Sound?," *Organised Sound* 1, no. 1 (1996): 23–5. For an in-depth discussion of the concept of the "acousmatic," see Brian Kane, *Sound Unseen: Acousmatic Sound in Theory and Practice* (New York: Oxford University Press, 2016).
11. Barry Truax, "Soundscape Composition as Global Music: Electroacoustic Music as Soundscape," *Organised Sound* 13, no. 2 (2008): 105; see also idem, "Soundscape, Acoustic Communication and Environmental Sound Composition," *Contemporary Music Review* 15, no. 1–2 (1996): 54 and 63.
12. See John Levack Drever, "Soundscape Composition: The Convergence of Ethnography and Acousmatic Music," *Organised Sound* 7, no. 1 (2002): 22.
13. For a detailed list of digital signal processing effects, see Curtis Roads, *Composing Electronic Music: A New Aesthetic* (Oxford and New York: Oxford University Press, 2015), 130–4.
14. Audacity, while a fine sound editor, does not have the same functionality as the other DAWs on this list and should not be considered for the project proposed in this chapter, despite its availability and attractive price point (free).
15. Roads, *Composing Electronic Music*, 308–12.
16. See Curtis Roads, *The Computer Music Tutorial* (Cambridge, MA: The MIT Press, 1996), 169.
17. "72: Live From SEAMUS 2018," on "Adjective New Music Lexical Tones," podcast with Robert McClure, April 15, 2018, accessed January 20, 2020, https://soundcloud.com/lexical-tones/72-live-from-seamus2018-1.
18. "122: Alex Dowling," on "Adjective New Music Lexical Tones," podcast with Robert McClure, February 10, 2020, accessed June 25, 2020, https://soundcloud.com/lexical-tones/122-alex-dowling.
19. Holmes, *Electronic and Experimental Music*, 218.
20. "Reggie Watts Disorients You in the Most Entertaining Way," YouTube video, 9:43, May 25, 2012, www.youtube.com/watch?v=BdHK_r9RXTc.
21. "27: Dan Tramte," on "Adjective New Music Lexical Tones," podcast with Robert McClure, February 13, 2017, accessed January 20, 2020, https://soundcloud.com/lexical-tones/27-dan-tramte.
22. Richard Orton, *Electronic Music for Schools* (Cambridge: Cambridge University Press, 1991), 38–9.
23. Alessandro Cipriani and Maurizio Giri, *Electronic Music and Sound Design: Theory and Practice with Max*, vol. 2 (Rome: ConTempoNet, 2014), 210.
24. Roads, *Composing Electronic Music*, 243.
25. Roads, *Composing Electronic Music*, 247.
26. Roads, *Composing Electronic Music*, 257.
27. As an experiment, try this: record a short spoken sentence. Make a reversed version of this sound file. Apply a long reverb that only affects the final syllable in the reversed sound file. Render/bounce the reverb-affected sound file, including the reverb tail, and reverse it again. The first syllable will now ramp up from a quiet, wet sound to a louder, dry sound.
28. Students may explore a theoretical framework of how to use their voices compositionally in Andreas Bergsland, "The Maximal-Minimal Model: A Framework for Evaluating and Comparing Experience of Voice in Electroacoustic Music," *Organised Sound* 18, no. 2 (2013): 218–28.

Selected Bibliography

Bergsland, Andreas. "The Maximal-Minimal Model: A Framework for Evaluating and Comparing Experience of Voice in Electroacoustic Music." *Organised Sound* 18, no. 2 (2013): 218–28.

Berio, Luciano. *Many More Voices*. BMG Classics 09026–68302-2, 1998. CD.

Bernstein, David W., John Rockwell, and Johannes Goebel. *The San Francisco Tape Music Center: 1960s Counterculture and the Avant-Garde*. Berkeley: University of California Press, 2016.

Caux, Jacqueline. *Almost Nothing with Luc Ferrari: Interviews*. With Texts and Imaginary Autobiographies by Luc Ferrari. Translated by Jérôme Hansen. Berlin and Los Angeles: Errant Bodies Press, 2012.

Cipriani, Alessandro, and Maurizio Giri. *Electronic Music and Sound Design: Theory and Practice with Max*. Vol. 2. Rome: ConTempoNet, 2014.

Collins, Nick, and Julio d'Escriván, eds. *The Cambridge Companion to Electronic Music*. 2nd ed. Cambridge: Cambridge University Press, 2017.

Dhomont, Francis. "Is There a Québec Sound?" *Organised Sound* 1, no. 1 (1996): 23–8.

Drever, John Levack. "Soundscape Composition: The Convergence of Ethnography and Acousmatic Music." *Organised Sound* 7, no. 1 (2002): 21–7.

Hettergott, Alexandra. "Human Voice Treatment in Various Types of Electroacoustic Music." *Proceedings of the International Computer Music Association*, 1999, 557–60. Accessed June 18, 2020. http://hdl.handle.net/2027/spo. bbp2372.1999.470.

Holmes, Thom. *Electronic and Experimental Music: Technology, Music, and Culture*. 6th ed. New York and London: Routledge, 2020.

Howe, Hubert S. *Electronic Music Synthesis: Concepts, Facilities, Techniques*. New York: W.W. Norton, 1975.

Iverson, Jennifer. *Electronic Inspirations: Technologies of the Cold War Musical Avant-Garde*. New York: Oxford University Press, 2019.

Kane, Brian. *Sound Unseen: Acousmatic Sound in Theory and Practice*. New York: Oxford University Press, 2016.

Lucier, Alvin. *Music 109: Notes on Experimental Music*. Middletown, CT: Wesleyan University Press, 2014.

Orton, Richard. *Electronic Music for Schools*. Cambridge: Cambridge University Press, 1991.

Roads, Curtis. *Composing Electronic Music: A New Aesthetic*. Oxford and New York: Oxford University Press, 2015.

Roads, Curtis. *The Computer Music Tutorial*. Cambridge, MA: The MIT Press, 1996.

Rodgers, Tara. *Pink Noises: Women on Electronic Music and Sound*. Durham, NC and London: Duke University Press, 2010.

Schaeffer, Pierre. *In Search of a Concrete Music*. Translated by Christine North and John Dack. Berkeley, Los Angeles, and London: University of California Press, 2012.

Schaeffer, Pierre. *Treatise on Musical Objects: An Essay across Disciplines*. Translated by Christine North and John Dack. Oakland, CA: University of California Press, 2017.

Schrader, Barry. *Introduction to Electro-Acoustic Music*. Englewood Cliffs, NJ: Prentice Hall, 1982.

Stockhausen, Karlheinz. *Stockhausen on Music: Lectures and Interviews*. Compiled by Robin Maconie. London and New York: M. Boyars, 2000.

Strange, Allen. *Electronic Music*. Dubuque, Iowa: W.C. Brown, 1972.

Stravinsky, Igor. *Poetics of Music in the Form of Six Lessons*. New York: Vintage, 1947.

Truax, Barry. "Soundscape, Acoustic Communication and Environmental Sound Composition." *Contemporary Music Review* 15, no. 1–2 (1996): 49–65.

Truax, Barry. "Soundscape Composition as Global Music: Electroacoustic Music as Soundscape." *Organised Sound* 13, no. 2 (2008): 103–9.

Weber-Lucks, Theda. "Electroacoustic Voices in Vocal Performance Art: A Gender Issue?" *Organised Sound* 8, no. 1 (2003): 61–9.

Wörner, Karl H. *Stockhausen: Life and Work*. Translated by Bill Hopkins. Berkeley: University of California Press, 1976.

2 Parametric Analysis
An Early Tool for Analyzing Electronic Music

Andrew Selle

When I first tried to teach electronic music analysis to a group of under-graduate music theory students, I came to the realization that there were not a lot of approachable analytical methods for students (and scholars) who were either new to analysis or new to electronic music. Many methods required either specialized knowledge of electronic music, production, and processes or advanced theoretical and analytical frameworks that many students simply do not have. In response, I set out to create an analytical methodology that requires no technical knowledge or experience and that ultimately focuses on the *listening experience itself*. What I arrived at was a process that I call "parametric analysis," and I have found it to be a useful tool. In this chapter, I first present a detailed discussion of the methodology as it might be undertaken individually in the classroom. I then undertake a model analysis of a work by Jean-Claude Risset to demonstrate the efficacy of this methodology. Finally, I suggest some other works that might be analyzed with this strategy in the classroom.

First Listenings: The Phenomenological Experience

The first step I suggest we take when analyzing electronic music, like any analysis, is to listen to the piece in its entirety. The function of this initial listening (as well as any subsequent initial listenings) is to get a broad, general sense of the piece. While this stage is important in all forms of musical analysis, it is especially important for our purposes, given that most works of electronic music do not translate to an appreciable musical score. Even for those works that do have a score, there is certainly a question as to whether or not that score helps the analyst understand the listening experience in any meaningful or accurate way. When I am teaching this type of analysis, I find it important to make the distinction early on that the score, even in more traditional forms of music-making, is only an *approximation*, a set of instructions, and not a representation of the actual sounding experience of the work. Once students realize that even traditional music notation leaves many aural qualities of music absent (such as timbre, texture, and space), I often find that they are quite eager to leave it behind. At this stage of initial listening, we will not be actively analyzing; we may not be able to help but form conceptions of what the analysis might look like, but above all we will seek to engage the work in a manner as true to the concept of "reduced listening" as possible.[1] In other words, we will listen to the piece for its own qualities without considering any sort of formal or syntactical systems at play. At this point in the analysis, we may want to make some descriptive notes based on our hearing and experience with the work, but we will make analytical judgments later. If we were to permit analytical concerns to enter into our listenings, it could easily (and likely would) color the judgments that we are to make later. Although what I am proposing is a hybrid form of analysis, in the sense that it fuses subjective experience and analytical observation, it is important not to let either side encroach on the territory of the other. The phenomenological experience is meant to provide the raw data that we will be working with, and we should thus allow the subjective experience to happen without being tainted by the expectation of objective confirmation at a later stage in the process.[2]

Once the initial listenings have been completed, and a general sense of the piece has been gained, we will undertake a series of self-reflective listenings. By self-reflective, I mean that we will listen to the piece while paying attention to our own experience of the work and the ways in which it directs our listening. For example, we might notice that we hear certain moments of a work as particularly marked for consciousness, or similarly that particular stretches of the piece require more effort to actively focus our listening on than others.[3] It is not important at this stage of the process to ask or answer the question as to *why* our experience of the piece is such, but rather just to note that it *is*. Again, it is crucial not to inject the objective side of our hybrid process into the subjective. So, for example, we might say, "At 3:30 in the piece, there is a sudden change in the quality of the piece," or "that moment really draws our attention." These statements reflect our experience in listening to the piece. However, a statement like, "At 3:30 in the piece, there is a clear formal articulation," presupposes the function of that moment. At this point in the analytical process, we are only reflecting on the phenomenological experience of listening; therefore, we should still avoid imposing analytical evaluations that are under the purview of later steps.

Staking Out the Parameters

Once the initial and self-reflective listenings have been completed, the next step is to identify the work's salient sonic parameters that may have guided the listening experience in the previous steps. For instance, if we heard a striking moment that caught our attention, we might now ask what it was about that moment that drew us to it. Perhaps there was a sudden change in a specific timbral quality, maybe the texture became much more dense or sparse, or there may have been a sudden change in register, etc. Of course, there is no comprehensive list of what sonic parameters are possible. We might identify some convenient starting points, such as Leigh Landy and Robert Weale's "Something to Hold on to Factors," or Jan LaRue's SHMRG (Sound, Harmony, Melody, Rhythm, and Growth) categories, which are umbrella groups for many different identifiable sonic parameters.[4] It is obviously not possible to provide a comprehensive list of all possible parameters, but some of the most recurrent and important ones that I have found through teaching this method and through my own analysis include the following:

1. Pitch (specific frequencies or relative "highness" and "lowness")
2. Tessitura (general ranges that passages seem to emphasize)
3. Dynamics (overall intensity, gradual/sudden changes, etc.)
4. Harmonic density (how many layers of sound, how condensed)
5. Attack (onset) density (rate of articulation, density of articulation, grouping, etc.)
6. Timbral qualities (brightness, glitchiness, noisiness, etc.)
7. Spatial concerns (distance, placement in the stereo field)
8. Oppositions of sound types (pitched vs. unpitched, metallic vs. wood, etc.)

Ultimately, it is up to each analyst to determine which sonic parameters he or she is able to hear and track. Some listeners may simply not be attuned to listening for harmonic density, for instance, and it will thus never be something that draws their attention when listening to a work. This is an acceptable and expected situation that arises from an analytical methodology rooted in subjective experience. I personally use (and suggest that others use) colloquial/informal terms when referring to audible sonic parameters or characteristics. Because we necessarily speak of all musical and auditory experience through embodied metaphor in the first place, it makes sense to speak of sounds in terms of their relative brightness and dimness, for example, rather than to speak about their harmonic spectra in technical terms. I think we intrinsically understand descriptions of the subjective experience of hearing much more easily than we do the technical. It may be worthwhile from a pedagogical standpoint to examine the question of whether or not an overly technical description of sounding events in electronic music is itself useful. Though I suggest that it is not the preferred method of description, certain listeners and groups of listeners may find the opposite and gravitate toward this mode of listening.

Parametric Listening and Analysis

Once we have identified any sonic parameters that appear important, salient, or functional in the work being examined, we will then undertake a series of parametric listenings. A parametric listening involves listening to the piece while only paying attention to one specific sonic parameter that has been identified in the previous step. It is an even further reduced-listening procedure, mentally bracketing out not only physical or semantic concerns but also any sonic qualities that we might call extraparametric. If we are doing a parametric listening focused on harmonic density, for instance, that is the only sonic quality that we will be concerned with; we will not pay attention to any of the other salient parameters that we have identified, as they will each get their own series of parametric listenings. As the parametric listening is occurring, we will continually note the relative parametric intensity on a scale of 1–5. In the previous example of harmonic density, a parametric intensity of 1 might be our perception of the least possible harmonic density within the confines of this piece, whereas 5 would be reserved for the most harmonically dense possibilities. The remaining middle three intensity values thus represent the exact perceptual middle and values that lean toward one pole or another. (It should be noted that the reversal of these poles will have no effect on the actual outcome of the analysis, so they could easily be swapped for one another.) As we hear changes in the parametric intensity of the particular parameter that we are listening to, we will plot the changes on a timeline that has a horizontal line for each value from 1 to 5.

Although it resembles a musical staff, the relative "highness" and "lowness" does not necessarily correspond to pitch; rather, it indexes relative proximity to the polar extremes of the sonic parameter. While it is certainly possible to adapt the system such that it has more discrete levels of parametric intensity (seven levels, nine levels, etc.), I find that having five levels allows for accurate measurement (insofar as it agrees with my subjective hearing) without having to labor over which intensity value is really "correct." In other words, it is quite simple to have to make a choice between a polar extreme, leaning toward one extreme, or exactly in the middle (the five intensity options). However, in a system with more discrete intensities, we may have to debate with ourselves about the perceived value. For example, whether or not a specific moment was really a value of five or six on a seven-point scale is much more difficult to quantify. Subjective interpretation accordingly becomes more complex as the range of possible values increases.

We will also have to determine how many time intervals to include on the graph and how compactly to space them, as there is only so much horizontal space that we can reasonably comprehend. The goal, after all, is to get a relatively comprehensive image of each sonic parameter that can be grasped with little study. For example, if the piece being examined is only 4 minutes long, it might make sense to have a time marker every 10 seconds. However, if the piece is not 4 minutes but maybe 40 minutes long, tracking parametric intensities at intervals of 10 seconds is probably not practical. Furthermore, it makes logical sense that longer and larger pieces might have larger structural segments; it would not at all be unusual for a large work to contain formal units that are many minutes in duration, whereas a very short work will likely contain smaller units. Ultimately, all choices will have a different balance between resolution and practicality, and therefore, it may be preferable to work with different time intervals depending upon the piece being examined.

Of course, there is no way to guarantee that any two analysts will arrive at exactly the same parametrical graph, even if they have chosen to examine the same parameter with the same timeline intervals. Just as two listeners may grasp onto vastly different sonic parameters when listening to a piece, so too would we expect differences in their listenings to the same parameter. This is inherent in the subjective nature of the procedure. One would certainly expect any two listeners to hear movement in the same "direction" toward or away from one of the parametric poles, however. If Listener A perceives a relative intensity change from one to four, and Listener B hears the same change as moving from one to three, two to four, two to five, etc., they essentially agree on the fundamental behavior of the parameter. If two listeners were to disagree on the direction of the parameter, then at that point they might each wish to re-listen and evaluate their hearing again.

The completion of the graphs initiates the objective phase of our hybrid analytical procedure. While the process of listening, reflecting on our listening, choosing sonic parameters, and graphing those parameters engages with the subjective experiential side, once that is complete, we will begin to make observations about the raw "data" we have collected. This data represents the listener's subjective experience in listening to the music; any analysis of it necessarily integrates the subjective with the objective, the entire goal of the process. One of the most obvious uses for these graphs is to look at each of them individually to see if we can identify recurring trajectories of parametric intensity (what I will call a *parameter-motive*). We may find, for instance, that specific formal units of a piece are defined in relation to the initialization and completion of a specific parameter-motive, allowing us to make observations not only about the cohesion of formal segments but also about the function of specific sonic parameters. Furthermore, we could also speak about the form of a work in relation to each specific parameter based on what we observe in the intensity data. Formal segments might be strongly defined by individual parameters based on their intensity values or parameter-motives, for example.

We are also able to look beyond individual parametric intensity graphs and compare them with one another. One of the most important things that we will be able to see by comparing multiple graphs is the extent to which they agree in terms of a piece's form and segmentation. If we see many different graphs that imply formal breaks or marked moments within the same temporal span, we might be able to speak with greater confidence about the form of the work, or at least support our formal readings. However, if we see intensity graphs that are considerably different from one another, this may lead us to suspect that either the form of the work is not so clear or else that perhaps the work being considered manifests its form in a different way. This is by no means to say that even if one were to get the forms of all the parametric intensity graphs to agree with one another, that this *is* the form of the work. Rather, the implication would be that the particular listener doing the analysis *experiences* the form of the work in this way. Remember that the raw data with which we begin the observation process already has subjectivity built into it, so any analysis that we perform on that data is inherently interpretive.

Not only can we look at intensity graphs individually and comparatively, but it will also be useful to create composite graphs that consider some or all of the individual graphs completed for a particular piece. Depending upon the piece, this could provide us with a variety of information. One thing we will track, for instance, is the composite change in parametric intensities throughout any given span of time, which could indicate moments that are likely points of formal segmentation or that at the very least are strongly marked for consciousness. When we see multiple parameters that undergo sudden shifts in intensity levels all at the same time, this might lead us to conclude that such a point has occurred. Similarly, when we observe musical segments that are relatively static in the composite, this will usually indicate a cohesive unit or segment. Ultimately, what any composite analyses reveal about a piece is largely dependent upon the piece itself and our experience in listening to it.

My approach to segmenting electronic music into discrete formal units will largely utilize two different types of graphs, the Parametric Intensity Graph and Value-Change (VC) Graph. Before we begin analyzing works of electronic music using these graphs, an explanation of their derivation is first necessary. Remember that the data in these graphs is not necessarily raw or empirical in the scientific sense, but rather, the graphs attempt to model the listening experience of a given piece. Thus, the observations made about them as well as the data itself should be understood as based on an inherently subjective process.

The Parametric Intensity Graph is essentially a way to measure a specific parameter on a scale of 1–5. Any scale could be chosen, but I have found that 1–5 provides a convenient array of values that represent a parameter being at an extreme (1 or 5), leaning toward an extreme (2 or 4), and somewhere in the middle of the two extremes (3). This graph can help us see both individual trajectories of specific parameters and sudden shifts within those parameters that might help us suggest syntactical units or segmentation points. The VC Graph is a way of measuring the absolute change in a parameter's intensity value over a certain period of time, somewhat akin to the concept of the derivative in calculus. I use two numbers to describe these graphs: the first refers to how large a span of time is being considered, and the second tells us how often we are sampling values. In other words, a "15–5" graph (which I have found to be the most useful) means that we are considering the past 15 seconds of music at every 5-second interval. These graphs have a way of smoothing out the data as well as showing not just how a parameter is changing over time but also the absolute intensity of the change.

We will also utilize composites of these graphs, especially the VC Graphs. The native listening experience of any given piece of music is not necessarily focusing on one parameter, but rather it is experiencing all sonic parameters either simultaneously or as they increase and decrease in salience. It is analytically useful for us to separate out one parameter at a time to study its behavior, but by making a composite of all salient parameters, we create a model that is closer to the experience of hearing a work. There are certainly inherent problems with "adding" intensities across multiple parameters. Although logistically it makes sense to say that a perceived change in intensity of one in two different parameters might equal a composite intensity change of two, the process of perception is not so black-and-white. For instance, would a composite intensity change of two across multiple parameters be perceived the same as an intensity change of two in a single parameter? The answer to this question might be "probably not," but we will not be comparing single parametric intensities to composite parametric intensities. Rather, I believe that the composite graphs show where different parameters are working together to effect a strong sense of change (and thereby formal coherence) in the mind of the listener. To this end, I propose that local maximum values in composite parametric intensity change may signal formal boundaries, whereas moments of little/no change or consistent change might signal formal units or segments.

Let us now consider an analytical case study so that we may examine the possible outcomes of a parametric-style analysis. I will then briefly present additional works that I have found to be useful for introducing this methodology and for analyzing with students of various levels of expertise.

Case Study: Jean-Claude Risset, *Sud* (1985)

Jean-Claude Risset's *Sud* is an interesting case study for the analysis of electronic music in that it seems to project a relatively clear surface-level extra-musical narrative (presenting a natural soundscape of water, waves, birds, insects, etc.), while at the same time it has a deceptively complex underlying musical structure. The work thus raises the issue of what the analyst might do when the essence of a piece, what the listener might perceive that the piece is "about," collides with the desire to talk about musical form, structure, and syntax. Giselle Ferreira offers a semiotic analysis of the work:

> [T]he listener is not presented with an idyllic soundscape, beyond the reach of human intention, untouched. The contact between a natural

element and imagined human artefacts suggests nature modified by human will and action. Indeed, *Sud* may be perceived as an encounter between human imagination and nature in two of its most powerful symbols: the sea, which is alluded to through the sounds of the waves, and the forest, which is alluded to through the sounds of its inhabitants. . . . These symbols are brought together not according to an aesthetics of *collage*, but through an exploration of the essence of the environmental sounds, which are either modified or recreated with different substances. . . . In appealing to symbols so widespread in different cultures, *Sud* is pregnant with ontological meanings and symbolic connotations.[5]

It is true that *Sud* is inherently full of symbolic meaning, and I believe that just about any listener would hear this or could be easily directed toward it without much convincing. However, what does this extramusical interpretation say about the form or structure of the work? Ferreira uses this extramusical information to inform her analysis of the structure of the first movement, basing each section on the *types of sounds* present. While looking at the work in this manner may produce satisfying analytical results, we might wonder what would happen if the analysis were to be based in a reduced-listening approach rather than an extramusical approach. In other words, how would our understanding of the piece change if we decided to bracket out all extramusical information and focus only on the sounds present in the piece for their own sake?

Let us consider the results of a parametrical approach to the second movement of *Sud*. I have selected this movement not only because it is much less written about than the first and third movements, but because I also believe that it is more difficult than these movements to analyze, especially in terms of extramusical associations. As Ferreira notes,

> The second movement explores several elements introduced previously and incorporates new aspects inherent in a predominantly aural discourse. . . . Unlike the introductory movement, environmental recordings are seldom perceived, and the whole movement is endowed with a distinctly abstract quality.[6]

Thus, in the absence of any sort of extramusical program, we must rely on our own experiences and perceptions when listening to the music in order to discern possible formal segments and syntactical functions.

After multiple listenings to the second movement of this work, I took note of a number of sonic parameters that seemed to guide my listening experience and direct me toward marked moments in the movement. For the purposes of this analysis, I selected four parameters. There is theoretically no limit to how many parameters can be examined, and the analyst may choose more or fewer depending upon the work being considered. In the case of *Sud*, the most salient sonic parameters in terms of my listening experience were the amount of *overall noise* present, *harmonic density* (the amount of sounds and sound objects layered on top of one another), the *tessitura* into which most of the salient sound objects fall, and the overall quality of *brightness* present throughout the work. First, let us consider each sonic parameter individually and how it might contribute to the formal segmentation of the piece. Remember that the values I am tracking are my own personal experiences. I do not propose that there is an objectively "correct" value at any given time for any particular sonic parameter; rather, these values represent my own subjective listening. Figures 2.1–2.4 show my graphs for the parameters I chose.

For the sake of space, I encourage you to consider each of these individually and comparatively, but I will only provide a fraction of the observational depth that one might find. If we consider Figures 2.1, 2.2, and 2.4,

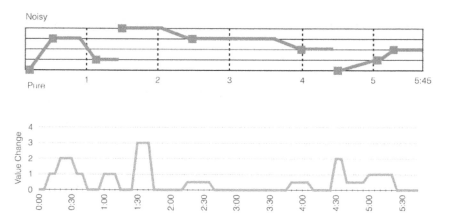

Figure 2.1 Jean-Claude Risset: *Sud*—Parametric Intensity Graph and 15–5 VC Graph for overall noise

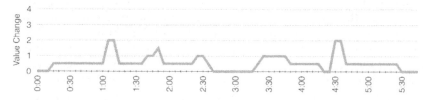

Figure 2.2 Jean-Claude Risset: *Sud*—Parametric Intensity Graph and 15–5 VC Graph for harmonic density

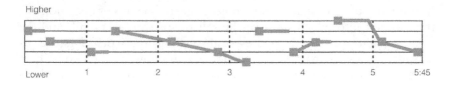

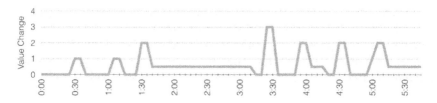

Figure 2.3 Jean-Claude Risset: *Sud*—Parametric Intensity Graph and 15–5 VC Graph for tessitura

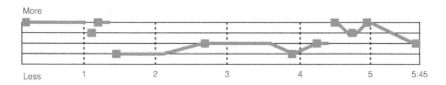

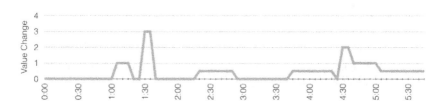

Figure 2.4 Jean-Claude Risset: *Sud*—Parametric Intensity Graph and 15–5 VC Graph for brightness

for instance, both the Parametric Intensity Graphs and the VC Graphs all seem to suggest an overall segmentation into three distinct parts, while Figure 2.3 (tessitura) is a bit at odds with this analysis. Likewise, even though Figures 2.2 and 2.4 agree with each other in terms of the number of segments, they do not necessarily agree in terms of the trajectory of intensity within each of those segments. Figure 2.2 shows more of an arched structure, whereas Figure 2.4 shows a more stepped structure. Similar observations can be made regarding other parameters, both as examined here and that might be examined in one's own listening.

Figure 2.5 shows the composite VC Graph for all four parameters that I have examined in this discussion. By examining the composite graph, we can see how each of these parameters interacts with one another to

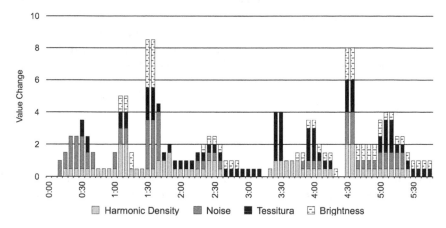

Figure 2.5 Jean-Claude Risset: *Sud*—15–5 VC composite

suggest formal segmentation points as well as which parameters are most involved in those points.

The composite 15–5 VC Graph for these four parameters shows strong agreement that the moments surrounding 1:30 and 4:30 are the strongest candidates for formal boundaries. In addition, it also shows other local maxima across all four parameters that may suggest marked moments of transition or interest within a segment such as the seconds following 1:00 or the span from 5:00 to 5:30. These are lower level maxima and are, therefore, not considered primary candidates for segmentation points, either due to their relatively low value compared to overall maxima (the maximum at 2:30, for example) or because of their close proximity to another higher value (such as the maximum right after 1:00). Similarly, while a local maximum occurs right before 3:30, we should be careful to note that this value is almost entirely composed of intensity change in the tessitura parameter, whereas the other maxima present throughout the graph are all composed of all four parameters. This is not to say that the change in tessitura around 3:30 should disqualify it from any sort of formal consideration, but simply that this is a fundamentally different type of composite change than the rest of the maximum values. While the composite VC Graph may help us determine how many distinct formal units we might hear, it tells us nothing about the function of these units, how they relate to each other, which ones might be similar to or different from one another, etc. For that, I think that the composite graph is most useful when combined with an examination and comparison of individual parametric intensity graphs, as we have already done.

Given the examination of the individual and composite graphs, we can suggest larger formal structures and organizations. For example, I do not think it would be a stretch to suggest that this particular movement is **ABA** or **ABA'** in terms of its form, given the interaction between parameters to effect moments of stylistic change. Though the choice about which parameters to listen to is initially subjective (based on the experience during the initial listenings), the resulting analysis is more object oriented based on those parameters. I find that the resulting analysis is, at the very least, critical, repeatable, and a good springboard for further analytical discourse in the realms of form, structure, musical syntax, and the ways in which other types of analyses (graphic, technological, etc.) might interact with the phenomenological.

Further Examples for Analysis

Now that we have seen what a model analysis of a work might look like, I will share some further works that I have found to be useful for analytical practice with my students as well as a brief description and highlights for each.

> **John Chowning, *Stria* (1977):** This work is usually one of the first that I present to my students. Because of its nature as a computer-generated work primarily using FM synthesis techniques, it quickly encourages students to abandon traditional notions of extramusical associations and to focus instead on a reduced-listening strategy for analysis. Whereas some works feature more recognizable sounds (like *Sud*, that I consider here), this work will strike many students, especially those completely new to this style of music, as more foreign, and thus perhaps a bit more inherently difficult to comprehend. For this piece, I like to start with four parameters: brightness, dynamics, harmonic density, and onset/attack density, all of which I have found to be approachable in analysis. Different groups of students will necessarily gravitate toward different parameters, of course.[7]
>
> **György Ligeti, *Artikulation* (1958):** This is another work that I have found to be exceptionally useful at an early stage in learning this analytical process. Not only is it an absolute classic in the field of electronic music (which allows the instructor to discuss concerns of history, literature, technology, etc.), but students always seem to come away from this piece with clear analytical thoughts. It also provides the opportunity to compare the resulting analysis to the graphic score that was created for the work, further extending the discussion about the utility of scores in the medium. In my own analyses, I have found the following parameters to be the most useful: onset/attack density, location in the stereo field (L/R), "glitchiness" of the sounds, and the perceived distance of the sounds. In my experience, students also tend to focus on pitch as well as the timbral opposition between metallic and nonmetallic sounds as useful parameters.

Jonty Harrison, *Klang* (1982): This is a slightly more difficult work, although still quite approachable. It is effective for analysis for a number of reasons. First, it draws from a small, consistent world of metallic sounds, and there is ample information about the creation, recording, and manipulation of these sounds.[8] Second, the composer suggests a "clear" formal outline of the piece, and I have found it to be very rewarding to analyze the structure of the work as the class perceives it and then to compare it with what the composer says the structure is. (This offers a great opportunity to delve into Roland Barthes' questions about authorship in his essay "The Death of the Author" and what they mean to us as analysts.[9]) When I analyze this work, I gravitate toward the parameters of tessitura/register, harmonic density, and the timbral opposition between raw and processed sound recordings. Students tend to lean toward the various *qualities* of metallic sounds, given that the piece is composed almost entirely of metal. All of these parameters have proven fruitful in the classroom.

Elainie Lillios, *Threads* (1998): A more difficult work among the pieces listed here, *Threads* is much more active both from a technical and from an experiential standpoint. The opening 30 seconds alone feature some of the most intense changes in parametric intensity that I have come across, and my composite graphs for this work are often slathered with many different moments of intense change. I have found that students enjoy debating the structure and syntax of this work, but it is definitely one to leave for a later project. Some specific parameters that I have found to be particularly useful include tessitura, density (both harmonic and attack/onset), dynamics, resonance, and the opposition between pitched and unpitched sounds.

From Parameters to Structures

Parametric analysis is a tool that I have found to be a useful and approachable way to analyze a work of electronic music not based on some extramusical association or abstract concept but rather *through the experience of listening*. As a result, not all analysts will necessarily arrive at the same conclusions, but each listening and analysis provides a starting point for meaningful, critical dialogue about the structure and behavior of electronic music. In my own work, these parametric-based analyses have often served as a point of departure for discussions about structure at lower levels, including the behavior and syntax of specific sounds, units, and sound objects at the micro level, suggesting phrase- and form-functional uses for specific types of processing to create larger structures, and even examining ways in which an examination of a piece in a reduced-listening analytical framework such as parametric analysis can interact with and inform an extramusical semantic analysis. Students have often used their analyses to discuss the deployment of specific sounds or types of sound in relation to a perceived larger structure (especially in works like *Artikulation* and *Klang*). They also tend to be very interested in being able to articulate and describe the overall forms of specific works, an undertaking to which this methodology certainly lends itself. (I once had a contingency of students argue that *Artikulation* was *clearly* in sonata form, for example, a conclusion they arrived at completely through this methodology.) Ultimately, I believe that by examining not just the work itself but also the *experience* of listening to the work, students, teachers, and scholars at all levels are able to come away with something meaningful and unique about any work of electronic music.

Notes

1. A term originating from Pierre Schaeffer, "reduced listening" is essentially a way of listening wherein listeners only pay attention to the *sonic qualities* of what they are hearing, attempting to bracket out all concerns of meaning, structure, or association. See Pierre Schaeffer, *Treatise on Musical Objects: An Essay across Disciplines*, trans. Christine North and John Dack (Oakland, CA: University of California Press, 2017).
2. Briefly, phenomenological inquiry revolves around the intersection between consciousness and experience. Schaeffer draws on Husserl's notion of the *epoché*, the process of removing inherent biases and assumptions about the nature of the experience being examined, so that the viewer (or listener, in our case) understands the phenomenon in terms of its own properties. Inherent to this process, and to reduced listening, is the idea of repetition. See the studies by Clifton, Ferrara, and Lewin listed in the bibliography for a more in-depth discussion of phenomenological concerns. Lewin in particular offers insights into a phenomenologically-based analysis of more traditional acoustic works.
3. From a phenomenological and semiotic perspective, "markedness" refers to standing out as special, unusual, or otherwise important.
4. Leigh Landy, "The 'Something to Hold on to Factor' in Timbral Composition," *Contemporary Music Review* 10, no. 2 (1994): 49–60; Robert Weale, "The Intention/Reception Project: Investigating the Relationship between Composer Intention and Listener Response in Electroacoustic Compositions" (PhD diss., De Montfort University, 2005); idem, "Discovering How Accessible Electroacoustic Music Can Be," *Organised Sound* 11, no. 2 (2006): 189–200; Jan LaRue, *Guidelines for Style Analysis*, 2nd ed. (Sterling Heights, MI: Harmonie Park Press, 2011).
5. Giselle Martins dos Santos Ferreira, "A Perceptual Approach to the Analysis of J.C. Risset's *Sud*: Sound, Structure and Symbol," *Organised Sound* 2, no. 2 (1997): 104.
6. Ferreira, "A Perceptual Approach to the Analysis of J.C. Risset's *Sud*," 100.
7. For further information about *Stria*, consult the special Fall 2007 issue of the *Computer Music Journal* entitled "The Reconstruction of *Stria*."
8. Detailed notes from the composer about *Klang* can be found in various sources; ElectroCD has a conveniently formatted version: https://electrocd.com/en/oeuvre/13799/Jonty_Harrison/Klang.
9. Roland Barthes, "The Death of the Author," in *Image-Music-Text*, trans. Stephen Heath (London: Fontana, 1977), 142–8.

Selected Bibliography

Barthes, Roland. *Image-Music-Text*. Translated by Stephen Heath. London: Fontana, 1977.

Chion, Michel. *Sound: An Acoulogical Treatise*. Translated by James A. Steintrager. Durham, NC: Duke University Press, 2016.

Clifton, Thomas. *Music as Heard: A Study in Applied Phenomenology*. New Haven: Yale University Press, 1983.

Demers, Joanna. *Listening through the Noise: The Aesthetics of Experimental Electronic Music*. New York: Oxford University Press, 2010.

Ferrara, Lawrence. "Phenomenology as a Tool for Musical Analysis." *The Musical Quarterly* 70, no. 3 (1984): 355–73.

Ferreira, Giselle Martins dos Santos. "A Perceptual Approach to the Analysis of J.C. Risset's *Sud*: Sound, Structure and Symbol." *Organised Sound* 2, no. 2 (1997): 97–106.

Harrison, Jonty. "Klang." https://electrocd.com/en/oeuvre/13799/Jonty_Harrison/Klang.

Kane, Brian. *Sound Unseen: Acousmatic Sound in Theory and Practice*. New York, NY: Oxford University Press, 2014.

Koffka, Kurt. *Principles of Gestalt Psychology*. London: Routledge & Kegan Paul Ltd., 1962.

Köhler, Wolfgang. *Gestalt Psychology: An Introduction to New Concepts in Modern Psychology*. New York: Liveright Publishing Corp., 1947.

Landy, Leigh. "The 'Something to Hold on to Factor' in Timbral Composition." *Contemporary Music Review* 10, no. 2 (1994): 49–60.

LaRue, Jan. *Guidelines for Style Analysis*. 2nd ed. Sterling Heights, MI: Harmonie Park Press, 2011.

Lewin, David. "Music Theory, Phenomenology, and Modes of Perception." *Music Perception* 3, no. 4 (Summer 1986): 327–92.

Schaeffer, Pierre. *Treatise on Musical Objects: An Essay across Disciplines*. Translated by Christine North and John Dack. Oakland, CA: University of California Press, 2017.

Selle, Andrew. "Experiencing Sound: A Hybrid Approach to Electronic Music Analysis." PhD diss., Florida State University, 2018.

"The Reconstruction of *Stria*." *Computer Music Journal* 31, no. 3 (Fall 2007).

Weale, Robert. "Discovering How Accessible Electroacoustic Music Can Be: The Intention/Reception Project." *Organised Sound* 11, no. 2 (August 2006): 189–200.

Weale, Robert. "The Intention/Reception Project: Investigating the Relationship between Composer Intention and Listener Response in Electroacoustic Compositions." PhD diss., De Montfort University, 2005.

3   Analyzing Electronic Music

Uncovering the Original Conditions of Production

Marc Battier

After over seventy years of an existence rich in innovations, electronic music remains an elusive object for analysis. Numerous attempts have been made, including several quite elaborate systems of representation and paradigmatic fragmentation, but many of these methods have been unable to convince the musical and the musicological communities, so that, in turn, new approaches keep arriving.

For many, because a large fraction of electronic music production is purely aural and lacks scores, works in this domain are considered with the same regard as recordings of non-notated extra-European music or of improvisations. To compensate for the lack of scores, some sort of visual representation is considered necessary before any serious analysis can take place. Indeed, musical analysis has traditionally given a large place to aural perception, and it is understandable that when notation does not exist, a system of representation can be invented in its place to give analysis precious temporal and spectral information.

At present, this general approach, which is based on hearing, has developed through the use of research in the domains of signal analysis and perception. The scientific world of acoustics, signal processing, and psychoacoustics has identified a large number of sound descriptors. Music analysts have taken advantage of these recent discoveries by integrating them into graphical representations. Furthermore, once the audio recording, descriptors, and representation are juxtaposed in a software program, other digital tools can be applied to further investigate aspects of a piece or to compare several versions of the same piece. Software such as Pierre Couprie's EAnalysis, an annotation tool that is able to incorporate the data output of analysis software such as Sonic Visualiser, can be coupled with other methods to make the use of descriptors meaningful within the framework of a musical analysis. This field of research has progressed rapidly during the past few years.

However, electronic music can hardly be compared with recordings of other forms of non-notated music. This is because composers have usually paid significant attention to specific aspects made possible by the use of artificial sounds and electronic technology, including timbre, morphology, time behavior, texture, and other parameters. All of these categories have taken on new meaning in the development of this music. This is why musicologists and students in musicology should gain some familiarity with the technologies of electronic and computer music. This type of knowledge is particularly important in approaching specific works. The conditions under which a composer produced a piece are quite relevant in providing information about the material and its processing, as well as the treatment of space and the possibilities and limitations of the technology at the time of production.

This chapter illustrates how an understanding of the conditions in which a piece was realized informs the meaningful analysis of electronic music. These conditions become guides to delve into the creativity of composers facing particular environments. What were the choices available to composers, how familiar with the technology were they, were there assistants to help guide them, and if so, how did these conditions shape their work? Questions like these, and many more, address the production aspect of a piece of electronic music and go beyond the description of its sonic surface. Along these lines, the chapter also considers some of the analytical approaches outlined earlier.

Electronic Music and Its Ever-Shifting Environments

When Pierre Schaeffer embarked on a systematic quest to define methods of turning noises into musical sounds in 1948, no one could have guessed that *musique concrète* would lead to a major field of musical creation. Before the birth of electronic music in Paris, there had been many isolated attempts at introducing noises into the orchestra. As early as 1913, the Italian Futurists envisioned ways to create machines (in fact realized by Luigi Russolo with his *intonarumori*) that would mimic the sounds and noises of modern city environments: the roars of the tramways and the trains, the rumbles and hisses of factories, and the trepidation of urban life. Edgard Varèse translated the modern urban environment of his adopted home of New York City by exploring new expressive possibilities of percussion instruments as well as sirens in *Ionisation* (1931). Varèse also explored the potential of setting up a research laboratory that would help composers experiment with new sonic possibilities, including electronic sounds. Although his efforts may not have received support from existing laboratories, it was one of the first attempts to link music, science, and technology.

In his work at French Radio in the 1940s, Schaeffer inhabited a space that allowed for just this type of sonic experimentation. He devised techniques of processing sounds closely derived from his use of phonograph records, given that for the first few years, magnetic tape recorders were unavailable in the Paris studio. These techniques included speed change, time reversal by playing the disc backward, and above all the practice of the "closed loop" (*sillon fermé*), which occurs when the stylus goes back and repeats the same passage, whose duration is around 1 second. It may occur on damaged records, but here it was intentional, as repetition, for Schaeffer, tended to obliterate the semantic or referential content of the recording.

As soon as the studio became equipped with tape recorders, Schaeffer, with the engineer Jacques Poullin, conceived a device to transpose recorded sounds: the *phonogène*, which is a modified tape recorder designed to produce musical results. It could be operated with a twelve-note keyboard, or, in another version, with a lever that could continuously vary the speed. The effect of the keyboard *phonogène* can be heard in Schaeffer's 1958 work *Étude aux allures*. At 2 minutes into the piece, a passage is entirely produced by the device: a resonance is variously transposed to create a sort of melody at times interrupted by percussion sounds. Listening to this passage, it is easy to imagine Schaeffer playing the keyboard of his *phonogène* (Figure 3.1).

Figure 3.1 Pierre Schaeffer at the *phonogène*

The *phonogène* is described in patents obtained by Schaeffer in France, the United States, and Germany. Schaeffer also mentions it in his 1952 book, *À la recherche d'une musique concrète* (*In Search of a Concrete Music*).[1] Its effects are also documented in letters from Pierre Boulez to John Cage, as Boulez was a student of Schaeffer in 1951–52 and composed two short studies in the radio studio.[2] They were subsequently premiered at a festival of electronic music in May 1952 in Paris (see Figure 3.2). The impact of the technology available in the studio was essential: Boulez played with the various ratios of transposition allowed by the *phonogène*, which he described in great detail in these letters. The audio quality of his two studies is not high, but the explanation of the use of the studio equipment enables the listener to understand how these pieces were conceived and realized. Only an understanding of the technology used by Boulez can reveal the compositional processes of these two short studies. This remark can be applied to the study of most electronic music, if one wants to go beyond a vague description of what is heard.

The collaboration in the Paris studio between an engineer (Poullin) and a composer (Schaeffer) is emblematic of the collaborative environments

Figure 3.2 "Deux concerts de musique concrète," May 21 and 25, 1952, in the festival "L'Œuvre du XXème siècle"

in other studios. As composers were introduced to new technological surroundings, it became important to provide them with personnel who could
understand musical issues and, at the same time, operate the various electronic devices in a creative manner. During the 1950s, in the electronic music
studios in Cologne and Milan, it was radio technicians who provided this
service. In fact, the Italian composer Luciano Berio who, with Bruno Mad-
erna, created the Studio di Fonologia Musicale at Milan Radio in 1955,
wrote a memorandum intended for invited composers in which he exhorted
them to work with the technicians, because only they could operate the
machines. Composers brought musical ideas, and technicians realized them
and inscribed them on magnetic tape, the recording medium of the time.
In fact, film footage from the studio at the end of the 1950s shows that in
reality, composers took a more active part in experimentation. In creating
electronic music, new ideas and inspiration often come from direct contact
with devices. However, the technology of the time was not designed initially
for musicians; the machines were conceived for the radio. They were expensive, delicate, complicated, and required trained technicians to maintain and
operate them, so Berio's recommendation was not far-fetched. During the
1950s, there were few possibilities for composers to create electronic music;
in Europe as well as in Japan, they often had to use radio studios, because
it was only there that suitable equipment was available. In order to fully
understand the works that were realized in this early period of the field, it is
critically important to study these environments. For instance, because the
devices available in a radio studio were not conceived to be used creatively
by composers, technicians and sometimes scientists, such as Alfredo Lietti in
Milan, designed specific machines for musical use.

In addition to the *phonogène*, another important device created for
musicians during the 1950s is the tempophone, which was realized for
the Cologne studio and the Swiss studio of Gravesano. It allowed the
pitch of recorded sounds to be transposed without changing their duration. This is because if a sound is played by a disc player at 45 rpm,
changing the speed to 33 rpm will transpose the sound down but will also
dilate the time, so that everything becomes slower and lower. To avoid
this, Anton Springer designed first a time regulator to achieve the effect
of transposing a sound without changing its duration and then a time and
pitch regulator to manipulate the duration and the pitch of a recorded
sound independently, with alterations of up to 25%. This can be heard
quite clearly in a piece by Herbert Eimert, *Epitaph für Aikichi Kuboyama*
(1958–62), in which some sounds seem stretched, an effect obtained by
the use of the tempophone.

In North America, electronic music developed more slowly because of
the lack of national radio stations, which were common in other parts
of the world. Brave composers had to either use a private studio, such as
John Cage, who worked in the studio of Louis and Bebe Barron in New
York City to compose his *Williams Mix* in 1952, or set up a studio in a

university, as Vladimir Ussachevsky and Otto Luening did at Columbia University the same year.

Differences between the technical equipment available in America and that of other countries contribute to explaining the various routes taken by composers. It was in the United States and Canada that the first synthesizers were conceived, apart from some experiments in Russia that were only discovered later. Their rapid diffusion contributed to a trend toward "mixed music," in which electronic sounds are mixed with live instruments. While "tape music," or music composed on a recording medium, was still practiced (and still is), mixed music was produced by composers who did not specialize in electronic music but who could find electronic music studios in their institutions.

The implantation of studios in universities in North America had another side effect. It was in the United States that computer music emerged. Although originally conceived in an industrial research institution by Max Mathews—the Bell Telephone Laboratories in New Jersey—it was further developed in universities that were equipped with large computers: MUSIC IVB (1967) and MUSIC 360 (1969) at Princeton University, MUSIC 11 at MIT (1973), and Cmusic at the University of California, San Diego (1980). In Europe, access to computers for creative work was much more limited and only started to appear in a few places during the 1970s, but it spread rapidly. It was in France, for instance, that the Max programming environment, now used all over the world, was first designed and used in 1987.

The possibilities and limitations offered by studio equipment at any given time should be taken into account when approaching a historical work of electronic music, as new technologies appeared frequently and altered the modes of production. This is easier said than done, as documentation from the time is scarce: many documents were discarded when they became obsolete by the lack of space to house them, or simply because they had been replaced by more recent ones. Thus, a large fraction of knowledge of past environments cannot be retrieved. Fortunately, some publications offer snapshots of the technical equipment of the main studios at a given moment of their history.[3] Some devices were thoroughly described, and documentation can also be found in patent offices, which are now frequently accessible online. This is the case with Schaeffer and Poullin's *phonogène* and, of course, for many electrical and electronic musical instruments of the first half of the twentieth century. Scholars nonetheless struggle to locate pertinent documents, as was the case for Jo Langton Hutton, who sought to understand the working environments of the four composers she studied in her doctoral dissertation.[4] As these composers were from different countries and times, understanding their equipment proved to be a challenge.

These examples show that the environments in which composers work to create electronic music, be it with tape recorders or with computers, is ever-changing. This makes it even more important to assess the technology available at any given time, not forgetting the stylistic milieu in which musicians evolved. For instance, we may extend beyond the formative period of the Groupe de Recherches Musicales (GRM) in the 1950s to consider how evolving studio technology and practices have shaped the work of subsequent composers in the studio:

From the 1960s to the 1970s, composers at the GRM became liberated from Schaeffer's strict requirements of making short studies that experimented with musical objects. For instance, Luc Ferrari became interested in sonic landscapes and recordings that were only minimally edited—a departure from the notion of the Schaefferian sound object. The arrival of analog synthesizers in the studio brought about significant changes, including François Bayle's replacement of the old musical object with the notion of the sound image made of flowing energy, a concept that can be clearly heard in Bernard Parmegiani's groundbreaking work, *De Natura Sonorum* (1975). Along the same lines, Guy Reibel became attracted to live interaction with "sound bodies" and even wrote about them and the creation of instruments.[5] His work *Variations en étoile 2* (1969), for percussion and tape, is an effective example of this interactive approach.

The GRM became equipped with a mini-computer Digital PDP11 in the late 1970s. Rather than using existing software such as MUSIC V, it was decided to develop programs closer to the practice of composers in the studio. The principle of processing sound through a variety of effects allowed composers, until then working with magnetic tape and analog gear, to access and make use of digital techniques. Eventually, a digital sound processor, Syter, was built and used by many before its algorithms became a set of plugins (GRM Tools), now widely used in electroacoustic music. The digital approach marked a departure from work with analog magnetic tapes: it created new practices and sonic materials, yet it retained a particular attention to the quality of sounds inherited from a long-standing GRM tradition.

Repertoire

It is also important for those who aim at studying and teaching electronic music to know the repertoire as much as possible. When I was a student in the 1970s, this was a difficult task, as this music was rarely available on recordings, and these were few and far between. Now, by using the World Wide Web, a wealth of music can be easily accessed. Exploring the repertoire can be facilitated by consulting databases listing musical works in certain areas or within a given period. For instance, British musician and musicologist Hugh Davies made a comprehensive compilation of works up to 1967 in his *Répertoire international des musiques électroacoustiques/International Electronic Music Catalog*, published by the ephemeral *Electronic Music Review* and reprinted by the MIT Press

(1968), now available online.[6] For Latin-American electronic music, it is recommended to consult the collection gathered by Ricardo Dal Farra at the Langlois Foundation in Montreal.[7] For East Asia, the EMSAN database lists music from China, Japan, and South Korea.[8] Maintained in Germany, the International Documentation of Electroacoustic Music is a user-generated, collaborative database of works.[9]

Advent of Live Electronic Music

If the production of electronic music in the 1950s was rather sparse, it was in part because of limited access to equipment. This situation triggered the development of analog synthesizers during the 1960s, when individual musicians and composers working in schools or in private centers turned to engineers to help create affordable electronic music systems that, in essence, could replace the expensive machines used in radio stations and research universities. On the East Coast of the United States, for instance, Herbert Deutsch, a professor at Hofstra University, asked Robert Moog, known for his production of theremins, to develop an affordable system with basic electronic music components such as voltage-controlled oscillators and a voltage-controlled amplifier. This happened in 1964, and it marked the beginning of the development of the successful Moog modular synthesizers.

On the West Coast at around the same time, Morton Subotnick and Ramón Sender, two composers affiliated with the San Francisco Tape Music Center (SFTMC), approached a young engineer, Donald Buchla, to conceive and build a comprehensive system. The goal was to come up with something that would spare composers from having to spend hours cutting and splicing magnetic tape, as was the case at that time given the center's struggle to acquire suitable equipment and its reliance on tape manipulation to create works. Buchla provided a complete system, which he called the Modular Electronic Music System. Although it was also based on voltage-controlled modules, it was quite different from the Moog synthesizers, as shown in a 1966 advertisement pamphlet (Figure 3.3). It had a variety of synthesis and, above all, processing units, such as a ring modulator and a frequency shifter, a voltage-controlled mixer, a number of different sound generators, a sequencer, and a unique touch-sensitive keyboard. Another unit, the "proximity detector," allowed for the connection of antennas for gestural control in the manner of the theremin. Buchla's device was clearly meant for studio work as well as for real-time performance on stage.

The unique sound quality of the Buchla system can be heard in Morton Subotnick's early electronic works. When the SFTMC moved to Mills College in 1966, he left for New York City, where he was commissioned to compose full-length pieces for LP releases. He exclusively used his Buchla system to compose *Silver Apples of the Moon* (1967), *The Wild*

THE MODULAR
ELECTRONIC
MUSIC SYSTEM

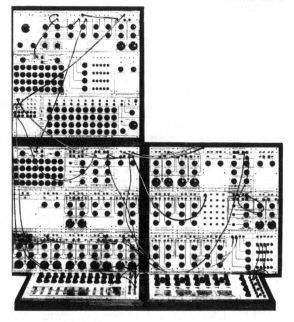

Figure 3.3 Buchla pamphlet, 1966

Bull (1968), and *Touch* (1969). Other pieces followed, all of an experimental nature.

The structural differences between the Moog synthesizers of the first years and the Buchla systems explain why they fit different types of music. The former was quickly adopted by pop and jazz artists, while the latter appealed to adventurous and experimental sound designers and composers such as Suzanne Ciani, who, like Subotnick, remained faithful to the Buchla systems after discovering them in the late 1960s.

The Case of John Chowning's *Stria*

A scholar who has studied in depth the original conditions of production of computer music is the Italian musicologist Laura Zattra. The reader will find in the bibliography some of her publications that deal with this question. Zattra applies philological techniques to the analysis of extant computer music scores and program listings. A striking example of her work can be found in her study of John Chowning's *Stria*, a computer-generated work realized at Stanford University's Center for Computer Research in Music and Acoustics (CCRMA) in 1977. Neither of the two recordings of the work was perfect in Chowning's judgment, and he expressed the wish to recreate a version closer to his initial intention. Zattra begins her article by describing her methodology:

> This article starts from the assumption that musicology needs methods borrowed from philology for studying computer music. The analysis of the creative and revision process that John Chowning carried out in the realization of *Stria* (1977) is made possible by textual criticism and interpretation based on digital and audio sources, sketches, and oral communications.[10]

In the same issue of the *Computer Music Journal*, two researchers, Olivier Baudouin and Kevin Dahan, describe their recreations of *Stria*. Each author started with archives provided by the composer, consisting of fragments of program listings written in an obsolete language, SAIL (Stanford Artificial Intelligence Language), and portions that were generated by MUSIC 10, a version of Max Mathews' MUSIC IV written for the Digital PDP 10 computer at Stanford. As Chowning puts it,

> It is a story of . . . how they rehabilitated a piece of music given a program with some missing code and missing data, two different sound recordings, and my memory (aided by fading notes and drawings) of what I had done more than 30 years ago.[11]

The task for Baudouin and Dahan was thus very difficult. Despite the composer's help, they faced conflicting program listings written in an old language derived from ALGOL. This is where Zattra's philological approach is revealed to be effective, as they had to find the versions that seemed to correspond to the recordings of the piece. Chowning evokes these difficulties and this philological method by describing

> their carefully analyzing my not-very-clean code written in an old language, . . . carefully analyzing the existing recordings and inferring what I must have done so they could faithfully recreate a critical lost version of the program and its data—and finally, creating *Stria* anew.[12]

For this project, Baudouin used the popular Python programming language and Csound (a popular sound synthesis language derived from MUSIC IV) for the sound generation. To understand the sound synthesis listings written in MUSIC 10, he used a manual I wrote in 1982 for that language when I was at IRCAM, the music research institute founded in Paris by Pierre Boulez in the 1970s. In his article, Baudouin describes the necessary trade-offs caused by the differences in the languages used at Stanford then and those of today. Dahan took another route and, after careful analysis of the extant sources, chose to transcribe the SAIL code into the Ruby language, and the MUSIC 10 scores into Csound. One notable problem Dahan encountered was the lack of reliable sources for the ending of the piece. He had to resort to musicological analysis to find a suitable solution, which seems to have worked, as it is this version that Chowning often prefers when performing *Stria*.

The reconstruction of *Stria* illustrates the difficulties in salvaging older computer sources to port (or adapt) them to latter-day software. It also shows that for pieces created with computers, care has to be taken to keep the program listings and scores. This is rarely the case, however, and Zattra has shown through her philological work that this presents a significant obstacle in studying older pieces. From the 1960s to the 1980s, most musical works created with computers were programmed. Composers used flavors of MUSIC IV (such as MUSIC 360, MUSIC 10, MUSIC 11, or, as of 1985, Csound), or MUSIC V and its newer incarnation, CMUSIC. During the 1990s, approaches to computing started to change in favor of real-time systems that involved a dose of interaction. Hence, written programs became more elusive, as one could change parameters on the fly with gestures. Although it was still possible to preserve traces of all the actions, doing so was rare. Experimentation, fine-tuning, and changes to the programs were frequent, such that it became increasingly difficult to keep track of the final versions of works. With software like Max and Kyma, real-time interactive approaches no longer required writing lines of code.[13] Programs that do rely on lines of instructions, such as SuperCollider or Csound, which are both real-time programs in current use, opened the door to live coding, a popular practice in which musicians write instructions that are immediately converted into sounds.[14]

Music combining instruments and electronics (mixed music) started to depend on real-time devices during the 1980s, with machines such as GRM's Syter and IRCAM's 4X. At the same time, the arrival of the Musical Instrument Digital Interface (MIDI) technology, which was conceived in the mid-1980s as a real-time way of controlling digital synthesizers through keyboards or computers, allowed for the rapid development of gestural control systems, including gloves, motion sensors, video and infrared capture of movements, and so on.[15] These systems rarely leave written traces, and composers must find innovative ways to notate the actions in their scores.

Computer Music Designers

The problems that arose with the progress of computer music toward real-time interactive systems have made the documentation of recent pieces quite delicate. To approach these challenges, a number of elements in addition to audio or video recordings can be useful. First and foremost, many composers are still helped in their creative work by musical assistants or computer technicians. This is the case at IRCAM: while this institute encourages young composers to learn techniques such as Max for real-time operations and sound synthesis software elaborated at IRCAM and OpenMusic for computer-assisted composition operations, a number of older composers invited to create pieces have been provided with musical assistants, as was the case with the British composer Jonathan Harvey in his work at the institute.

For many years, these assistants were called "tutors," but today they are known as "computer music designers" (in French, *réalisateurs en informatique musicale*). Zattra has studied their role and practices, which is an important step toward understanding their function as creative partners of the composer, even if, in the end, the latter is solely responsible for the work. Places where musical assistants had a determinant role can be traced back to Cologne in 1958, when Karlheinz Stockhausen worked on his piece *Kontakte*, for four-channel tape, piano, and percussion. He was assisted in the studio by Gottfried-Michael Koenig, who later moved to establish a computer music studio in the Netherlands and developed an influential practice of computer-assisted composition. The role of assistants was also quite important in the case of Italian composer Luigi Nono, who was for some time director of the Milan studio and produced a number of complex pieces involving real-time processing of sounds, including multichannel spatialization.

The Visualization of Music

One of the earliest software programs designed for the visualization of electronic music was made around 1994 at the instigation of François Bayle, then director of the GRM. Its name, Acousmographe, is derived from the concept of "acousmatic music," the term chosen by Bayle for tape music that has no visual component. The absence of visual stimuli was a potential barrier for people who were not accustomed to electronic music performed from tape, including students. A graphical representation of the events in a work, which of course did not have a score, helped listeners follow its narrative. The Acousmographe software offered, from its debut, a palette of signs, shapes, and colors that the analyst could annotate with text. A cursor moves in time so that it is always possible to know exactly the visual position of what is played. This software, twenty-five years later, is still produced and made available by the Institute national de l'audiovisuel (INA), the parent company of the GRM. The set of graphical shapes is quite extensive and enables the user to place graphical elements corresponding to what is heard on a time window and to add textual annotations. Figure 3.4 is an illustration of a graphical analysis of a piece by François Bayle, "Polyrythmie," a movement from the larger composition *Vibrations composées* (*Composed Vibrations*, 1973–74).

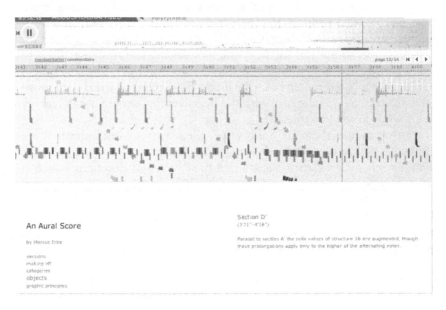

Figure 3.4 Acousmographe representation of François Bayle, "Polyrythmie," from *Vibrations composées*, 1973–74

Another visualization approach was developed by French researcher Pierre Couprie, currently a professor of music at the University of Evry. His first program, iAnalyse, was designed in a way similar to the Acousmographe. Programmed for the Apple Macintosh, and now freely distributed on the App Store, this program also offers a large gamut of graphical shapes and the ability to add textual notes (see Figure 3.5 for a representation of an excerpt from Parmegiani's *De Natura Sonorum*). Any kind of music can be entered into it. If a piece has a score, the pages can be added, so that the music flows with the score.

Couprie created a second program, EAnalysis, derived from the first and with added capabilities. It was commissioned by De Montfort University in Great Britain and was mostly aimed at creating visual illustrations of electronic music. Although no longer being developed or updated, a particularity of this program is that the display can be arranged in horizontal layers, each one receiving a different type of information, although everything is shown in sync with the music. For instance, one layer may display a sonogram, and another may receive annotations and comments; the program is also able to read analyses produced by the British program Sonic Visualiser, IRCAM's Audiosculpt, GRM's Acousmographe, and even Avid Pro Tools sessions. A typical use of EAnalysis is to display analyses that show various sound descriptors produced by AudioSculpt or Sonic Visualiser. In any case, as with any software, the user must verify the program's compatibility with their own computer system.

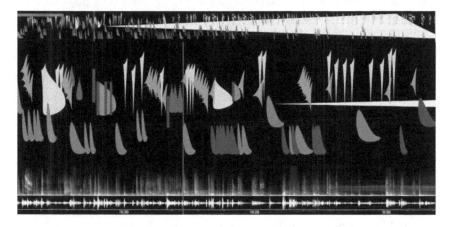

Figure 3.5 Representation of "Ondes Croisées" by Bernard Parmegiani realized
    by Pierre Couprie

Whether the animation produced by Acousmographe or iAnalyse is
analytical or descriptive, having a visual representation, possibly with textual or graphical annotations, is an effective way to introduce electronic
music to any audience, particularly one with no previous knowledge of
it. This approach may go against the idea of acousmatic music, which
consists precisely in sound diffusion without visuals. One may respond,
however, that to ensure the proper impact of acousmatic music, certain
conditions have to be met: the quality of the diffusion, preparation of
the audience, and, possibly, prior verbal presentation, as is often the case.
These conditions may not always be possible to meet, particularly when
presenting this music to young audiences, for whom visuals will certainly
assist in listening. Animations may reinforce the abstract sounds coming
out of the loudspeakers and provide visual cues to guide perception.

Conclusion

Access to teaching tools for electronic music has been rendered easier
through the vast amount of music available on the internet, although not
necessarily with the required audio quality. These include archives, databases, and websites of resources, including Ubuweb[16] and the various sites
gathered by Barry Truax in the Sonic Research Studio.[17] With many other
documents accessible online, as well as published books on electronic
music (some of which can be considered excellent), it is possible to gather
sufficient information for teaching. In addition, digital humanities tools
such the visualization software presented here help in creating dynamic
and vibrant presentations. In the end, of course, listening to as many pieces
as possible and having students get acquainted with them are musts.

Especially critical is an understanding of the conditions of production. Knowing which technology was available where and when a piece was produced and how the composer possibly found innovative workarounds with the inherent limitations of the devices informs our way of listening to electronic music. It does not take away any of the charm, poetry, and interest of the music, but it gives us a more thorough grasp of how it was composed. In this respect, publishing a complete score has given access to Karlheinz Stockhausen's second electronic study, *Studie II* (1954), by highlighting the realization process.[18] One can understand the obstacles of producing a piece from sine waves with a rigorous compositional lay-out under difficult conditions: the Cologne studio was not designed for Stockhausen's approach, and he had to fight for his ideas of composing from only sine waves, when the studio was equipped with expensive electronic keyboard instruments, Harald Bode's Melochord, co-designed with Werner Meyer-Eppler, and Friedrich Trautwein's Monochord, that both produced rich spectra. This was precisely what Stockhausen rejected, as he wanted to compose the sound themselves.[19] Not having proper equipment was a huge challenge, and yet this study became a landmark of the electronic music repertoire. If a detailed score had not been made available, it would certainly not have had the impact it has had. Indeed, Stockhausen is one of the few composers to have produced scores for his electronic works: some are aimed at describing the production process, as with *Studie II*, or are realization scores, as with *Kontakte* (1958–60), *Telemusik* (1966), and *Oktophonie* (1991), to mention only some tape pieces.

All of the aids offered today by digital tools and ready access to documentation and the repertoire make it possible to gather a wealth of information on electronic music. This information encourages us to have a critical view of the existing literature that recounts its history, as some popular books are not exempt from approximations and mistakes carried over from previous writings. Our knowledge of the development of electronic music is now much more informed thanks to thorough research that has emerged over the past few years. Electroacoustic music studies is now an established field, and we can be hopeful that it will lead to a better understanding of what motivated composers of the past as well as those of the present.

Notes

1. Pierre Schaeffer, *In Search of a Concrete Music*, trans. Christine North and John Dack (Berkeley, Los Angeles, and London: University of California Press, 2012), for instance at 174 and 181.
2. See Jean-Jacques Nattiez, ed., *The Boulez-Cage Correspondence*, trans. Robert Samuels (Cambridge: Cambridge University Press, 1993), 181ff.
3. See, for instance, *Répertoire international des musiques expérimentales: studios, œuvres, équipements, bibliographie* (Paris: Service de la recherche de la Radiodiffusion-Télévision française, 1962).

4. Jo Langton Hutton, "Beyond the Instrumental: Systems, Objects and Space in the Work of Beatriz Ferreyra, Teresa Rampazzi, Éliane Radigue and Delia Derbyshire" (PhD diss., University of Surrey, 2020).
5. Guy Reibel, *L'homme musicien: musique fondamentale et création musicale* (Aix-en-Provence: Edisud, 2000).
6. Hugh Davies, *International Electronic Music Catalog*, accessed November 13, 2020, https://archive.org/details/InternationalElectronicMusicCatalog/mode/2up.
7. Ricardo Dal Farra, "Latin American Electroacoustic Music Collection," accessed November 13, 2020, www.fondation-langlois.org/html/e/page.php?NumPage=556.
8. EMSAN (Electroacoustic Music Studies Asia Network) Project, accessed November 13, 2020, www.ums3323.paris-sorbonne.fr/EMSAN/.
9. "International Documentation of Electroacoustic Music," (EMDoku), accessed November 13, 2020, www.emdoku.de/en.
10. Laura Zattra, "The Assembling of *Stria* by John Chowning: A Philological Investigation," *Computer Music Journal* 31, no. 3 (2007): 38.
11. John Chowning, "*Stria*: Lines to Its Reconstruction," *Computer Music Journal* 31, no. 3 (2007): 23.
12. Chowning, "*Stria*: Lines to Its Reconstruction," 23.
13. For Max, consult Alessandro Cipriani and Maurizio Giri, *Electronic Music and Sound Design: Theory and Practice with Max 8* (Rome: ConTempoNet, 2019), and for Kyma, consult Jeffrey Stolet, *Kyma and the SumOfSines Disco Club* (Self-published, n.p., 2011).
14. See Richard Boulanger, ed., *The Csound Book: Perspectives in Software Synthesis, Sound Design, Signal Processing, and Programming* (Cambridge, MA: The MIT Press, 2000).
15. Marcelo Wanderley and Marc Battier, *Trends in Gestural Control of Music* (Paris: IRCAM, Centre Pompidou, 2000) [electronic book].
16. "UbuWeb," accessed November 13, 2020, https://ubu.com/.
17. "The Sonic Research Studio," accessed November 13, 2020, www.sfu.ca/sonic-studio-webdav/.
18. Karlheinz Stockhausen, *Studie II, Score* (Kürten: Stockhausen Verlag, 1954), www.stockhausen-verlag.com.
19. Elena Ungeheuer and Oliver Wiener, "Between Mass Media, Entertainment Electronics and Experimental Music: Harald Bode's Melochords in the Intersection of Many Interests," *Musique, Images, Instruments* 17 (2018): 166–91.

Selected Bibliography

Battier, Marc. "Describe, Transcribe, Notate: Prospects and Problems Facing Electroacoustic Music." *Organised Sound* 20, no. 1 (2015): 60–7.
Battier, Marc. "*Nuo Ri Lang* by Zhang Xiaofu." In *Between the Tracks: Musicians on Selected Electronic Music*, edited by Miller Puckette and Kerry L. Hagan, 174–93. Cambridge, MA and London: The MIT Press, 2020.
Battier, Marc, and Kenneth Fields, eds. *Electroacoustic Music in East Asia*. London and New York: Routledge, 2020.
Baudouin, Olivier. "A Reconstruction of *Stria*." *Computer Music Journal* 31, no. 3 (2007): 75–81.
Boulanger, Richard, ed. *The Csound Book: Perspectives in Software Synthesis, Sound Design, Signal Processing, and Programming*. Cambridge, MA: The MIT Press, 2000.

Chadabe, Joel. *Electric Sound: The Past and Promise of Electronic Music.* Upper Saddle River, NJ: Prentice Hall, 1997.

Chowning, John. "*Stria*: Lines to Its Reconstruction." *Computer Music Journal* 31, no. 3 (2007): 23–5.

Cipriani, Alessandro, and Maurizio Giri. *Electronic Music and Sound Design: Theory and Practice with Max 8.* Rome: ConTempoNet, 2019.

Dahan, Kevin. "Surface Tensions: Dynamics of *Stria*." *Computer Music Journal* 31, no. 3 (2007): 65–74.

Erickson, Robert. *Sound Structure in Music.* Berkeley: University of California Press, 1975.

Langton Hutton, Jo. "Beyond the Instrumental: Systems, Objects and Space in the Work of Beatriz Ferreyra, Teresa Rampazzi, Éliane Radigue and Delia Derbyshire." PhD diss., University of Surrey, 2020.

Nattiez, Jean-Jacques, ed. *The Boulez-Cage Correspondence.* Translated by Robert Samuels. Cambridge: Cambridge University Press, 1993.

Puckette, Miller, and Kerry L. Hagan, eds. *Behind the Tracks: Musicians on Selected Electronic Music.* Cambridge, MA and London: The MIT Press, 2020.

Reibel, Guy. *L'homme musicien: musique fondamentale et création musicale.* Aix-en-Provence: Edisud, 2000.

Répertoire international des musiques expérimentales: studios, œuvres, équipements, bibliographie. Paris: Service de la recherche de la Radiodiffusion-Télévision française, 1962.

Schaeffer, Pierre. *In Search of a Concrete Music.* Translated by Christine North and John Dack. Berkeley, Los Angeles, and London: University of California Press, 2012.

Stolet, Jeffrey. *Kyma and the SumOfSines Disco Club.* n.p., 2011 [self-published].

Teruggi, Daniel. "Technology and Musique Concrète: The Technical Developments of the Groupe de Recherches Musicales and Their Implication in Musical Composition." *Organised Sound* 12, no. 3 (2007): 213–31.

Ungeheuer, Elena, and Oliver Wiener. "Between Mass Media, Entertainment Electronics and Experimental Music: Harald Bode's Melochords in the Intersection of Many Interests." *Musique, Images, Instruments* 17 (2018): 166–91.

Wanderley, Marcelo, and Marc Battier. *Trends in Gestural Control of Music.* Paris: IRCAM, Centre Pompidou, 2000. Electronic book.

Zattra, Laura. "The Assembling of *Stria* by John Chowning: A Philological Investigation." *Computer Music Journal* 31, no. 3 (2007): 38–64.

Zattra, Laura. "The Identity of the Work: Agents and Processes of Electroacoustic Music." *Organised Sound* 11, no. 2 (2006): 113–18.

Zattra, Laura. "Symmetrical Collaborations: Jonathan Harvey and His Computer Music Designers." *Nuove Musiche* 4 (2018): 29–57.

Zattra, Laura, and Nicolas Donin. "A Questionnaire-Based Investigation of the Skills and Roles of Computer Music Designers." *Musicae Scientiae* 20, no. 3 (2016): 436–56.

4 Sound Design and Compositional Process in Skrillex

From Minimalism and FM Synthesis to Dubstep

Rishabh Rajan

What are students listening to these days? Is there any academic value to the popular styles of music they prefer? These may be questions we ask in relation to EDM, a category that comprises hundreds of electronically produced subgenres. Casting aside personal preferences and preconceived notions, it is difficult to overestimate the rise and importance of this genre of music in the past decade. What used to be exclusively an underground scene with performances at private venues, abandoned warehouses, and even pirate radio stations is now very much part of contemporary music and culture. Electric Daisy Carnival (EDC), one of the most popular electronic dance music festivals, attracted 450,000 people across three days in 2019.[1] There is no doubting the popularity of this music, but looking beyond the superficiality of raves, parties, and hard drugs associated with EDM music festivals, I feel that it is important to analyze the composition and production of this music to understand its widespread appeal: in identifying the key elements that make this style of music resonate with the new generation, we can also uncover traces of minimalism and a sound synthesis technique originating in advanced research shaping the production of dubstep.

Producing EDM does not require extensive musical training, as demonstrated by the plethora of untrained but successful EDM producers such as Burial (William Emmanuel Bevan, b. 1979), so there is little adherence to classical structures or forms per se. The stylistic idiom of producers such as Burial emerged alongside the rise in affordability and mobility of computers that could run Digital Audio Workstation (DAW) applications like Ableton Live and Logic Pro. The majority of the techniques developed and pioneered in these forms of EDM resulted either from experiments within the software or from a lack of musical training on the part of the composer/producer. For example, Burial produced his entire debut album *Burial* (2006) using Sound Forge, a two-track audio editor that does not have a musical grid, quantization, or other seemingly necessary tools to aid in the compositional process.[2] Successful EDM producers have developed their own unique approaches to composition through trial and error. Analyzing EDM music with the hope of developing a blueprint, therefore, can be futile or at the very least difficult. However, analysis of a variety of compositions from varied producers within the broad category of EDM can lead to the discovery of some common traits underlying specific subgenres. For example, in House and Techno, placing the kick drum on every downbeat is common and is known as a "four-on-the-floor" pattern.[3] In Trap, by contrast, the kick drum's amplitude is elongated to act like a bass tone, making it unnecessary to even have a separate bass part. A comparison of many tracks across different EDM subgenres reveals that simplicity in harmonic movement and consistency in rhythm are two of the most common elements linking together multiple subgenres.

Throughout the 2010s, popular music was infused with elements of electronic music.[4] Simplified chord progressions with minimal tension notes and repeating harmonies were common, which facilitated the blending of electronic techniques and styles. Rihanna and Katy Perry, who each had seventeen Billboard number one singles from 2010 to 2019, are two artists who have fused pop with electronic elements. They have worked with electronic music producers such as Dr. Luke (Lukasz Sebastian Gottwald), Max Martin, Calvin Harris, Stargate (Tor Erik Hermansen and Mikkel Storleer Eriksen), and, more recently, Skrillex (Sonny Moore).[5] Skrillex, a dubstep producer, is one of the most prominent names in contemporary EDM and is, to some extent, responsible for the influx of electronic music in mainstream pop music in the 2010s. Dubstep originated as an EDM subgenre in the late 1990s in the United Kingdom, and it is known for its minimalist treatment of melody and harmony, its syncopated rhythms, and the prominence of undulating sub-bass frequencies that were highly popular in the clubs where the music was played. Skrillex's EP *Scary Monsters and Nice Sprites* (2010) played a major role in popularizing this underground genre and won him multiple Grammy awards in 2012. The success of this EP saw the rise in popularity of dubstep, with the music being used in Hollywood films and video game soundtracks.[6]

My focus in this chapter is Skrillex's dubstep composition "Scary Monsters and Nice Sprites" from the 2010 EP of the same name. With the release of "Scary Monsters and Nice Sprites," Skrillex redefined the genre, straying from the hermetic standard tropes of dubstep by using more prominent melodies performed on synthesizers, interspersed with androgynous vocal phrases and mid-frequency heavy bass lines that take center stage.[7] I provide a pedagogically oriented analysis of the composition and sound production techniques of this track, hoping to create a framework for studying and legitimizing the importance of EDM in academic courses. In the chapter's conclusion, I briefly discuss the role of EDM as a subject area in the EDI program at the Berklee College of Music.

Song Form

The compositional structure of "Scary Monsters and Nice Sprites" is somewhat unusual, with unconventional measure groupings for its sections, although the different sections are fairly short in this 4-minute track. I have delineated a timeline indicating when each section is heard (see Figure 4.1). The following are the four sections, and references to them in my analysis will be italicized for clarity:

> *Lead*—Monophonic synth melodic phrase
> *Vocal*—Manipulated vocal recordings
> *Bass*—Heavy bass part as the foreground instrument
> *Outro*—Unprocessed voice with piano accompaniment

The song is in the key of G minor, with a repeating progression of E♭ major, F major, and G minor, a common ♭VI, ♭VII, and i progression. The harmony remains largely static, as this chord progression repeats through most of the track. In EDM and specifically dubstep, harmonic changes are not typically relied upon to create atmosphere, dynamics, and/or movement. This is an ideal example of one underlying framework that is generally followed by producers of EDM.[8] Not unlike the music of Philip Glass, Terry Riley, and other minimalist composers, EDM relies heavily on minimal harmonic progression and shifts the listener's focus to other compositional elements such as rhythm, timbre, and short repeating motifs. In "Scary Monsters and Nice Sprites," there is one slight change in the chord progression. The harmony completely cuts out during the *Bass* section as well as in some parts of the *Outro*. This may be compared to an NC ("no chord") section in a score where either there is no clear harmony or the harmony is implied. In the case of "Scary Monsters and Nice Sprites," however, the actual harmony of the *Bass* section is ambiguous, as the focus is more on sound design than on harmonic contrast. We do not hear any accompaniment, and the only instruments in the section are the drums and the heavily distorted and conspicuous bass pattern.

The form of "Scary Monsters and Nice Sprites" is unusual at first glance, yet its highly repetitive structure is characteristic of EDM. You will notice that the *Lead* section, which is two measures long, almost always occurs right after the *Bass* section, which is six measures long. A two-measure section is uncommon in most EDM genres. The more common formula works off of multiples of four measures. Another way to look at the six-two sectional grouping is to consider the entire *Bass* section as eight measures long, with the last two being a response to the heavy distorted bass with a relatively mellow synthesized lead melody, quite similar to a call and response section. Typically, the Blues call and response form will have equal

0:00	0:28	0:41	0:51	0:55	1:05	1:09	1:19	1:23	1:33	1:46
Lead (16)	Vocal (8)	Bass (6)	Lead (2)	Bass (6)	Lead (2)	Bass (6)	Lead (2)	Bass (6)	Lead (8)	Vocal (8)

2:00	2:10	2:14	2:24	2:28	2:38	2:42	2:52	3:05	3:19
Bass (6)	Lead (2)	Bass (6)	Lead (2)	Bass (6)	Lead (2)	Bass (6)	Lead (8)	Vocal (8)	Outro (24)

Figure 4.1 Timeline of Skrillex, "Scary Monsters and Nice Sprites"

measures on both sides; for example, an eight-bar section featuring the drums could be immediately followed by eight bars of a guitar solo. This even sharing of measures through call and response has a long tradition in genres featuring improvisation, yet Skrillex throws us off by presenting a six-two grouping: six measures of the *Bass* are followed by two measures of the *Lead* within the standard eight-bar section. The improvisational element of a call and response is suggested by the fact that every time the *Bass* section is stated, there is a subtle variation in the rhythmic structure and sound design of the bass instrument. Of course, this layout is not literally improvisational, as the parts are designed and composed beforehand, and there is minimal use of live improvisation in the production process. The *Lead* section is also identical every time it is heard. This alternation between the *Bass* and *Lead* sections with the six-two pairing is not followed throughout the entire song. Right at the beginning of the track and at 1:33 and 2:52, we hear the *Lead* section as an entire eight-measure section (doubled to sixteen measures in the opening), independent of the *Bass* section. There is a high probability that the first two measures of the *Lead* section were edited out and pasted to occur right after the *Bass* section. In the DAW environment, splicing sections of a composition and moving them around in an arrangement timeline is fairly simple. Another reason this may be true is that the *Lead* section melodic phrase is identical every time it is heard, except in the two-measure version, where the phase is still identical, just incomplete.

Sound Design

To understand the complexity of dubstep and specifically Skrillex's work, it is necessary to delve more deeply into its sound design processes. Much of the compositional process in the subgenre focuses on sound design for the bass instruments. Developing new and unique bass timbres that can make an entire track stand out is one of the primary goals in dubstep music.

In the late 2000s, the most common sound synthesis and design technique practiced by producers of EDM was subtractive synthesis, in which a harmonically rich waveform such as a sawtooth or a square wave is run through a filter and shaped to produce new and interesting sounds. This technique has been the foundation of electronic music since the late 1960s with the invention of the Moog modular system. A relatively newer synthesis technique made widely available in the early 1980s, FM synthesis (frequency modulation synthesis), also plays an important role in dubstep. Skrillex skillfully used FM synthesis to create his signature bass sounds in "Scary Monsters and Nice Sprites" without having a strong underlying grasp of the sound design principles of FM synthesis. FM synthesis has a rich history in both academic research and popular music, and it is worth going back and tracing the early days of this synthesis technique to better understand Skrillex's use of it and its popularization in modern dubstep.

FM Synthesis was discovered by John Chowning while working at the research facility at Stanford University in the late 1960s. Chowning was experimenting with synthetically produced vibrato (modulation of one audio rate oscillator with another sub-audio rate oscillator) using sine waveforms (see Figure 4.2 for the spectrum analysis of a sine waveform). In his experiments, Chowning noticed that when increasing the depth of modulation on the first oscillator, his ears could still track the instantaneous pitch of the oscillator, but when he increased the rate of the second oscillator along with the depth of modulation, he could no longer aurally track the instantaneous pitch and heard a completely new and rich spectrum instead of the original sine waveform (see Figure 4.3 for the spectrum analysis of an FM tone).[9] Chowning's discovery led to developments in FM synthesis and the discovery of a multitude of synthetically

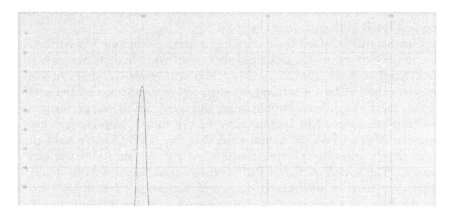

Figure 4.2 Tonal spectra of note G1 sine-wave tone

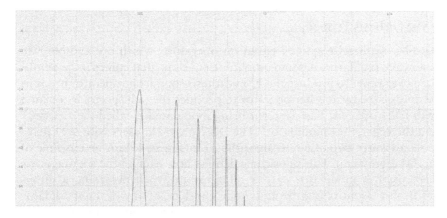

Figure 4.3 Tonal spectra of note G1 being modulated by another sine wave at the same frequency

generated tones that could to a certain extent mimic acoustic and real-world instruments such as flutes, brass, marimbas, violins, basses, and pianos. This discovery eventually led to the development of the first commercially produced FM synthesizer, the Yamaha DX7, in 1983. The DX7 was one of the first fully digital, sixteen-voice polyphonic, commercially available keyboard synthesizers that also had Musical Instrument Digital Interface (MIDI) capability. MIDI, a digital communications protocol for musical instruments, was in its infancy and would eventually become a standard in synthesizers released after 1984. Musicians of the time did not have access to synthesizers that could produce the wide variety of timbres made possible by the DX7. The sonic landscape of contemporary pop music produced in the United States and the United Kingdom was transformed by the Yamaha DX7, which became a ubiquitous part of its sound. The "E. Piano 1" preset, which emulated the sound of a Fender Rhodes electric piano, was used on 61% of No. 1 hits on the pop, country, and R&B Billboard charts in 1986.[10]

Yamaha and Stanford University had a stranglehold on FM synthesis due to their patent on the technique, but other synth manufacturers tried their hand with variations, notably Casio with their CZ series of synthesizers that utilized a technique called phase distortion. By the early 1990s, the FM synthesis bubble burst and most producers, performers, and even audiences had become tired of the sound. Notable jazz keyboardist Mitchel Forman commented that the DX7 "doesn't have the same depth, warmth or expressiveness" of the Fender Rhodes electric piano.[11] The sound of digital FM synthesis could seem notably "cold" when compared to other synthesizers and instruments that utilized analog synthesis. The "warmth" of analog instruments was attributed to the physicality involved with sound generation, whereas digital synthesizers use a series of computer-generated 0s and 1s.

FM Synthesis Primer

An FM synthesis engine is based on operators, which are audible rate sine-wave oscillators with an amplitude envelope that controls the amplitude over time. To produce the FM synthesis sound, one operator needs to be modulated by another operator to produce the rich spectra associated with FM synthesis. The operator being modulated is called the "carrier," and the other, the "modulator." The DX7 provided users with six operators and thirty-two different algorithms (see Figure 4.4 for an example of an FM algorithm). The algorithms defined how each of the six operators were used in modulator–carrier relationships, each providing a different timbre. Controlling the amplitude envelope of any of the modulator operators created a change of timbre over time. The modulator operator's amplitude envelope could also be controlled with the keyboard MIDI velocity to create real-time dynamics. One of the key aspects of FM synthesis was the mathematical relationship between the frequencies of

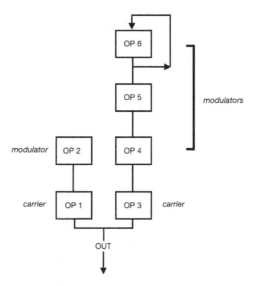

Figure 4.4 DX 7 FM algorithm #1

various operators. If an integer ratio was maintained between the operators in use, the result would always lead to harmonically pleasant tones,
whereas noninteger ratios would lead to dissonant sounds.

The FM patent held by Stanford University and Yamaha expired in
1995. In 2002, a music software development company, Native Instruments, created a software plug-in version of the original Yamaha DX7
and called it FM7.[12] The software worked directly inside a DAW and
provided the composer with all the capabilities of the original keyboard
synthesizer on a personal computer. The Yamaha DX7 was notoriously
difficult to program, and most users would resort to using its built-in pre-
sets. Remember "E. Piano 1"? The graphical user interface of the Native
Instruments FM7 made it much easier to use and program. In 2007,
Native Instruments updated the program to FM8, adding new features
such as an audio effects section, an arpeggiator, and, most importantly,
additional waveforms aside from the standard sine-wave shape.

Skrillex used Native Instruments FM8 to create his signature bass
sounds for "Scary Monsters and Nice Sprites." It is quite incredible to
witness the depth and variety of FM synthesis, spanning from the mellow
electric piano in pop ballads of the 1980s to the harsh, sonically destructive tones of dubstep bass sounds of the 2010s.[13] How is it possible that
one synthesis technique provided such variety in tonal design? How is it
that no one prior to Skrillex in 2010 had discovered the extreme capabilities of FM synthesis? Can we attribute some of this inventiveness to
Skrillex's lack of formal musical training and to the "trial-and-error"
approach to composition and sound design typical of EDM producers?

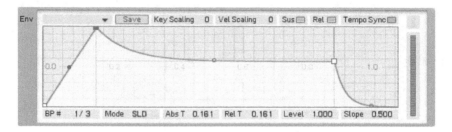

Figure 4.5 Amplitude envelope editor in Native Instruments FM8

The sound of FM synthesis was mostly extinct by the early 2000s, and we can attribute its resurgence to Native Instrument's software design. The inclusion of additional waveforms in the operator section in FM8 made it possible to create a wider variety of tones.[14] Creating change over time in FM8 was also fairly straightforward, as the user could graphically edit the multiple point amplitude envelope (see Figure 4.5).

Skrillex has commented on the sound design elements in "Scary Monsters and Nice Sprites," mentioning in interviews that he designed most of his signature bass sounds using Native Instruments FM8.[15] One underlying principle from the early days of FM synthesis was the mathematical relationship established between the frequencies of the carrier and modulator operators. There needs to be a whole number relationship between the operator and modulator's pitch in order to get a harmonically pleasing result. The common ratio values used were 2:1, 3:2, 1:1, etc. A fractional value other than 0.5 would typically lead to an inharmonic tonality that may or may not be consistent across a wide set of notes. Whole number values always produce a harmonic tonality that is consistent across the entire keyboard range. As an example, if we play middle A = 440 Hz and the carrier modulator ratio is set to 1:2, the modulator would be set to 880 Hz. Octave relationships like this work well in FM synthesis and are the basis for many of the patches on the original DX7. On Native Instruments FM8, this ratio relationship can be easily broken or taken to an extreme.

One example of a Skrillex-style sound would involve three operators— one carrier and two modulators—as illustrated in Figure 4.6 (in FM8, the six operators are labeled A–F). Operator F is being sent to the output so it takes the role of a carrier, while operators D and E are both modulators. In this scenario, E is modulating F, and D is modulating E. The arrowhead direction helps define this relationship. The ratio for the three operators is set to 32:1:1, as D is thirty-two times the frequency of E and F. An extremely high ratio of this type produces upper harmonics in the spectrum that when modulated over time can produce a human vowel-like quality. Another critical aspect of this sound design approach is that the three operators are not set to standard sine waves. As the

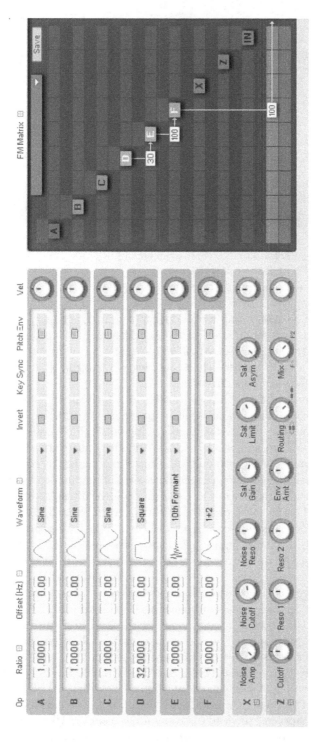

Figure 4.6 FM algorithm using three operators: one carrier and two modulators

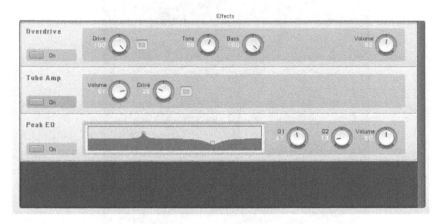

Figure 4.7 Effects section on Native Instruments FM8

diagram illustrates, all three operators are set to different waveforms. To create change over time, the amplitude envelopes of operators E and D are shaped to have a long attack and a long decay. This is one of the underlying concepts guiding Skrillex's sound design. This movement over time is critical to establish a vowel-like quality; automation within the DAW is also used to change these parameters constantly and produce variations in the sound spectrum.

Skrillex's bass timbre in "Scary Monsters and Nice Sprites" sounds more like a lion's growl than human speech. To transform these vowel sounds into a monstrous growl, the effects processing within FM8 come into play. One of the most common effects used throughout dubstep music is distortion. Distortion of a waveform will result in a buzzy and gritty sound with a loss of definition and an increased compression of amplitude. A controlled distortion of the entire harmonic spectrum will result in additional harmonics related to the ones present. In Native Instruments FM8, there are two effects processors that can be used to create the distortion effect: the Overdrive and Tube Amp. Figure 4.7 illustrates the use of the Overdrive and Tube Amp effects to distort the signal; a Peak Equalizer is also used to bring out certain harmonics in the spectrum while suppressing others.

While the aggressive quality of Skrillex's bass sounds takes center stage in most of his music, the sweeter timbres of his lead instruments create a pleasant contrast. The contrasting character of the lead instrument in "Scary Monsters and Nice Sprites" seems almost inseparable from the growling monstrosity of the bass. The lead instrument's sound is created using a technique similar to FM synthesis that is based on vibrato. Typically, vibrato is produced by making a sine-wave low-frequency oscillator (LFO) set to the rate of 6–7 Hz modulate the audible oscillator. In the case of "Scary Monsters and Nice Sprites," the lead instrument has a similar vibrato effect, but the LFO is set to approximately 100 Hz. This rate sets the LFO into audio range, yet the main difference between this technique and FM synthesis is that the operators maintain their frequency ratio, regardless of what note is played in a true FM synth engine. For example, in a simple FM synthesizer with one carrier and one modulator, if the ratio is set to 1:1, when A = 440 Hz is played, the modulator is also 440 Hz. When A = 880 Hz is played, the modulator is now 880 Hz as well. In the previous case, in which the LFO is set to 100 Hz, there is no fixed mathematical relationship between the modulator and the carrier. Instead, the mathematical relationship constantly changes for each note played. When A = 440 Hz is played, the LFO is at 100 Hz; when A = 880 Hz is played, the LFO is still at 100 Hz. This inconsistency in pitch relationship produces a unique distortion in the overall timbre yet maintains some aspects of the original timbre. For the lead instrument in "Scary Monsters and Nice Sprites," Skrillex uses a sawtooth wave as the carrier and a sine wave as the modulator. The sawtooth timbre is audible, but the fast vibrato effect creates distortion that provides an effective contrast with the more aggressive bass sound.

Sampling

Appropriation of audio material from a variety of sources has a long history in EDM. Its genesis can be attributed to hip-hop music and the 1980 track "Freedom," in which Grandmaster Flash sampled "Get Up and Dance" by Freedom.[16] The track is one of the earliest examples of hip-hop music to sample a portion of a published song. In the 1990s, sampling became more common and accessible due to hardware devices such as the Akai MPC-60 and MPC-3000 (popular hardware sampling workstations developed in the late 1980s to the early 1990s). One of the pioneers in the practice is James Dewitt Yancey, better known as J Dilla, who was a highly sought-after producer known for his unique style of sampling.[17] Fast forward to 2010 and the era of high bandwidth internet and access to YouTube, and EDM producers now had a wealth of new material to sample, from classic songs that had achieved mainstream success to unknown B sides that would be unrecognizable if disguised well in the production. In "Scary Monsters and Nice Sprites," Skrillex samples a spoken word phrase from a video posted on YouTube by Rachael Nedrow, an amateur speed cup stacker who uploaded her personal cup stacking records. In one of the videos in which she beat a personal record, she exclaims, "Oh my gosh!" This is the phrase we hear at the beginning of the *Bass* sections at 0:39 and 1:59. Skrillex's initial use of this sampled phrase builds anticipation for the *Bass* section that is about to be heard for the first time in the track, almost preempting the listener's reaction to this highly unusual section. This form of preempting or anticipating a heavy bass section became very common in dubstep music that followed the release of "Scary Monsters and Nice Sprites." Knife Party, another dubstep group, took a similar approach in their track "Resistance" (2014), which samples dialogue from The Simpsons TV series in which a character says "This is a knife." The sample is placed right before the main bass section of the track and again near the end of the track. This technique of emphasizing a section with sampled speech right before a heavy bass section has appeared in varied forms in other subgenres of EDM and is now associated with a section known as "The Drop."

The last production element of "Scary Monsters and Nice Sprites" I want to expand upon is the vocals. Prior to starting his EDM career, Sonny Moore (Skrillex) was a vocalist in the hardcore band From First to Last. Skills developed in his years with the band helped him with penning lyrics as well as performing vocals. Listening to the vocals on "Scary Monsters and Nice Sprites," it is obvious that the recording has some form of digital manipulation, with the result that the lyrics are unintelligible. Skrillex is approaching vocal production from a sampling point of view: unlike a vocalist in a contemporary pop song who records specific parts to a fixed arrangement, here Skrillex samples his vocals to be manipulated later and conformed to the arrangement using a technique called "slicing."[18] J Dilla was a master at slicing tracks using his MPC-3000 for the hip-hop tracks he produced, but here Skrillex is working within a DAW that simplifies the process, as the waveform of the recording is visible, unlike with the MPC-3000. Slicing is a process in which a prerecorded audio sample is chopped up into smaller parts based on a musical grid. For example, a one-measure musical phrase can be sliced into eight eight-note slices. These slices are then mapped onto a software sampler instrument, which will allow the playback of any of the slices with a MIDI input device like a keyboard. This is a popular technique used to shuffle an existing musical idea to discover new ideas. The DAW can produce new permutations and combinations of the original, or the composer can manually input new patterns. In "Scary Monsters and Nice Sprites," Skrillex first reversed the recorded vocals and then created the slices. We can hear the original (unsliced) vocals in the *Outro* section at 3:19. This compositional technique has similarities to theme and variation form, except, in this case, we hear the variations first, in the form of the gibberish-like reverse-sliced vocals, and only at the end do we hear the original recording in which we can identify the lyrics.

Empirical Account

I have been teaching EDM in university courses in one form or another for the past ten years. Since my primary curricular focus has been production techniques relating to EDM, I have not encountered barriers to incorporating the genre in my teaching. Having experience with producing EDM has markedly informed my teaching in these courses. One of the pedagogical techniques I use is imitation analysis. I require students to pick a track they find interesting and recreate it from scratch. The process involves importing the original audio recording into the DAW, finding the tempo of the track, and setting the DAW to match that. Then I encourage students to start recreating the drum patterns they hear in the original track, eventually working their way up to the harmonic accompaniment and main melody. The focus here is not timbral imitation but song structure. Through this process, the student develops a deeper insight into the compositional structure of the track. Another technique I employ is sound dictation. This method is designed for the more advanced student who has completed fundamental sound design courses. In this exercise, students pick a pool of EDM tracks with unique sounds and, through the course of a semester, they recreate the collection of bass, lead, harmony, and drum sounds from a variety of EDM tracks using a digital synthesizer in the DAW. They can use subtractive synthesis, FM synthesis, or even sampling techniques to recreate these sounds. In this course, the focus is solely on sound design and not so much on composition.

With the introduction of the EDI at the Berklee College of Music as one of the many principal instruments a student can declare, I have also been implementing EDM performance techniques in ensembles and performance labs.[19] Briefly, an EDI constitutes a computing device running a user-configured software being controlled by performance controllers, and the EDI program is designed for musicians who perform EDM with digital instruments. In the EDI ensemble, I work with a group of five to six students, each using a unique EDI. Each student is assigned as a music director for at least one EDM song that will be performed by the group. Their role as music director is to create lead sheets for the track as well as to develop a collection of sound patches in Ableton Live for each performer in the group. The music director then allocates various musical roles to individuals in the group in order to perform the song live using the sound patches developed in Ableton Live. With songs that have extensive arrangements, some performers take up multiple roles, and sometimes the arrangement is altered to accommodate any limitations due to the size of the group. Through this process, each student gets a deeper understating of the instrumentation and arrangement of a typical EDM song while also developing skills to perform these songs in an ensemble.

Assuming the students have a strong core set of musical skills, the technology-mediated performance courses become an enriching experience for them as they find new and innovative ways to perform electronic music. Students develop ways to apply knowledge gained from production courses toward the live performance ensembles. Having a strong foundation in sound design principles, the performer can contextualize core production concepts with aural awareness and translate this awareness and knowledge into a digital performance.

My experience with teaching electronic dance music and EDI performance has proven to a lot of critics and skeptics of the program that this is not a passing fad. There is a lot of value in stepping outside the canon of classical or art music and exploring commercial electronic dance music. We do not have to wait another ten years before someone like Skrillex makes use of prevalent technology and resources to innovate for the future. The future is today.

Notes

1. Ed Komenda,"EDC 2019 by the Numbers: What Ingredients Go into Entertaining 450,000 People?," *Reno Gazette Journal*, May 16, 2019, accessed February 25, 2020, www.rgj.com/story/news/2019/05/16/electric-daisy-carnival-2019-las-vegas-numbers-edc/3668105002/.
2. Burial, "Burial: Unedited Transcript," interview by Mark Fisher, *The Wire*, December 2012, accessed February 25, 2020, www.thewire.co.uk/in-writing/interviews/burial_unedited-transcript.
3. "What's That Sound? The Rhythm That Ruled 2011," *NPR*, December 30, 2011, accessed February 25, 2020, www.npr.org/2011/12/31/144482049/whats-that-sound-the-rhythm-that-ruled-2011.
4. D. J. Pangburn, "4 Trends in 2018 Pop Production," *iZotope*, August 3, 2018, accessed February 25, 2020, www.izotope.com/en/learn/4-trends-in-2018-pop-production.html.
5. Rob McCallum, "Skrillex Reportedly Working on Rihanna's New Album," *DJMag*, July 20, 2018, accessed February 25, 2020, https://djmag.com/content/skrillex-reportedly-working-rihanna-new-album.
6. Laura Bradley, "Decoding Dubstep: A Rhetorical Investigation of Dubstep's Development from the Late 1990s to the Early 2010s" (Undergraduate thesis, Florida State University, 2013), 9–10.
7. As a foil to Skrillex's innovations with "Scary Monsters and Nice Sprites," students may explore the following tracks, which had helped to define the genre before 2010: "The Judgement" (Skream & Benga), "Midnight Request Line" (Skream), and "Nine Samurai" (Kode9 & The Spaceape).
8. Mark J. Butler, *Unlocking the Groove: Rhythm, Meter, and Musical Design in Electronic Dance Music* (Bloomington, IN: Indiana University Press, 2006), 7–8.
9. John Chowning, "The Synthesis of Complex Audio Spectra by Means of Frequency Modulation," *Journal of the Audio Engineering Society* 21, no. 7 (1973): 526–7.
10. Megan Lavengood, "What Makes It Sound '80s?: The Yamaha DX7 Electric Piano Sound," *Journal of Popular Music Studies* 31, no. 3 (2019): 73–94.
11. Bob Doerschuk and Ted Greenwald, "Q: Are We Not Progressive? A: We Are Marillion!," *Keyboard*, July 1986, 19.
12. Debbie Poyser and Derek Johnson, "Native Instruments FM7," *Sound on Sound*, July 2002, accessed February 25, 2020, www.soundonsound.com/reviews/native-instruments-fm7.
13. Students might compare, for instance, the timbral qualities of the Verse/Bass in "Never Gonna Give You Up" (Rick Astley) to the bass part in "Scary Monsters and Nice Sprites."
14. Native Instruments was not the first to introduce additional waveforms in the FM engine. In 1987 Yamaha released the TX81Z, which was a rack-mountable FM synthesizer with additional waveforms aside from the sine wave. Unfortunately, this was also difficult to program, just like the original DX7.
15. Skrillex, "Interview: Skrillex on Ableton Live, Plug-Ins, Production and More," *Music Radar*, November 3, 2011, accessed February 25, 2020, www.musicradar.com/news/tech/interview-skrillex-on-ableton-live-plug-ins-production-and-more-510973.
16. Norman Abjorensen, *Historical Dictionary of Popular Music* (Lanham, MD: Rowman & Littlefield, 2017), 447–8.
17. Rob Fitzpatrick, "J Dilla: The Mozart of Hip-Hop," *The Guardian*, January 27, 2011, accessed February 25, 2020, www.theguardian.com/music/2011/jan/27/j-dilla-suite-ma-dukes.
18. Skrillex,"Interview: Skrillex Talks Production, Plug-Ins and Power Edits,"*Music Radar*,May 25,2012,accessed February 25,2020,www.musicradar.com/news/tech/interview-skrillex-talks-production-plug-ins-and-power-edits-545529.

19. "Principal Instruments Electronic Digital Instrument," *Program Description, Berklee College of Music*, accessed February 25, 2020, www.berklee.edu/electronic-digital-instrument-principal.

Selected Bibliography

Abjorensen, Norman. *Historical Dictionary of Popular Music*. Lanham, MD: Rowman & Littlefield, 2017.

Berklee College of Music. "Principal Instruments Electronic Digital Instrument." Program Description. Accessed February 25, 2020. www.berklee.edu/electronic-digital-instrument-principal.

Bradley, Laura. "Decoding Dubstep: A Rhetorical Investigation of Dubstep's Development from the Late 1990s to the Early 2010s." Undergraduate thesis, Florida State University, 2013.

Burial. "Burial: Unedited Transcript." Interview by Mark Fisher. *The Wire*, December 2012. Accessed February 25, 2020. www.thewire.co.uk/in-writing/interviews/burial_unedited-transcript.

Butler, Mark J. *Unlocking the Groove: Rhythm, Meter, and Musical Design in Electronic Dance Music*. Bloomington, IN: Indiana University Press, 2006.

Chowning, John. "The Synthesis of Complex Audio Spectra by Means of Frequency Modulation." *Journal of the Audio Engineering Society* 21, no. 7 (1973): 526–7.

DJ Pangburn. "4 Trends in 2018 Pop Production." *iZotope*, August 3, 2018. Accessed February 25, 2020. www.izotope.com/en/learn/4-trends-in-2018-pop-production.html.

Doerschuk, Bob, and Ted Greenwald. "Q: Are We Not Progressive? A: We Are Marillion!" *Keyboard* (July 1986): 19.

Fitzpatrick, Rob. "J Dilla: The Mozart of Hip-Hop." *The Guardian*, January 27, 2011. Accessed February 25, 2020. www.theguardian.com/music/2011/jan/27/j-dilla-suite-ma-dukes.

Komenda, Ed. "EDC 2019 by the Numbers: What Ingredients Go Into Entertaining 450,000 People?" *Reno Gazette Journal*, May 16, 2019. Accessed February 25, 2020. www.rgj.com/story/news/2019/05/16/electric-daisy-carnival-2019-las-vegas-numbers-edc/3668105002/.

Lavengood, Megan. "What Makes It Sound '80s?: The Yamaha DX7 Electric Piano Sound." *Journal of Popular Music Studies* 31, no. 3 (2019): 73–94.

McCallum, Rob. "Skrillex Reportedly Working on Rihanna's New Album." *DJMag*, July 20, 2018. Accessed February 25, 2020. https://djmag.com/content/skrillex-reportedly-working-rihanna-new-album.

NPR. "What's That Sound? The Rhythm That Ruled 2011." December 30, 2011. Accessed February 25, 2020. www.npr.org/2011/12/31/144482049/whats-that-sound-the-rhythm-that-ruled-2011.

Poyser, Debbie, and Derek Johnson. "Native Instruments FM7." *Sound on Sound*, July 2002. Accessed February 25, 2020. www.soundonsound.com/reviews/native-instruments-fm7.

Skrillex. "Interview: Skrillex on Ableton Live, Plug-Ins, Production and More." *Music Radar*, November 3, 2011. Accessed February 25, 2020. www.musicradar.com/news/tech/interview-skrillex-on-ableton-live-plug-ins-production-and-more-510973.

Skrillex. "Interview: Skrillex Talks Production, Plug-Ins and Power Edits." *Music Radar*, May 25, 2012. Accessed February 25, 2020. www.musicradar.com/news/tech/interview-skrillex-talks-production-plug-ins-and-power-edits-545529.

5 Teaching Principles of Interactive Sound

A Practice-Based Approach

Lucy Ann Harrison

This chapter proposes a set of principles and practical approaches to interactive sound and music that can be applied to the teaching, analysis, and description of interactive audio. These principles have been developed from theoretical and practice-based models building on existing literature and experiences through composition and sound design practices. While the examples used are primarily drawn from a video games environment, it is intended that the general principles can be applied across virtual and real-world settings, due to the formal similarities between immersive theatre and video games, which both give a large amount of exploratory and narrative control to the audience member or player. Interactive audio presents structural and musical challenges to composers and sound designers, given that they must adapt audio to the behaviors and expectations of audiences while guiding them through narrative structures. This unique characteristic of interactive audio also presents a particular challenge to analysis and interpretation, and this chapter argues that understanding principles underlying sound design practices in these environments will provide useful insight for critical analysis.

The curriculum and teaching techniques presented in this chapter have been developed through two university modules taught between 2017 and 2020. The first module focused on sound design for an interactive games environment, with students being assessed on their ability to implement realistic and appropriate sound effects and environmental sound. The second module had a sound-tracking focus, with students being assessed on their ability to create appropriate interactive music for a game. Both modules were taught to Level 5 students (second-year equivalent) within the UK university system. These practical approaches have been informed by industry practice in composition and sound design across a range of interactive media, including games and immersive theatre.

For use as an analytical framework, this chapter aligns theories of interactive sound with a composer and sound designer's perspective. Practical examples are given throughout, providing insight into creative and pragmatic solutions used by composers and designers working within interactive audio. While analytical approaches such as those developed by Karen Collins and Tim Summers analyze the music from a player's perspective, as this is a key occasion in which the player has creative control over audio and musical structures, the approach presented in this chapter is intended to complement their work by providing insights from a practice-based perspective.[1]

A software agnostic approach has been taken throughout, instead focusing on theories of applied sound. While it is important that students are versed in game engines and middleware (additional software that is used as a bridge between audio development and game engines), the risk with being too reliant on one piece of software, rather than the underlying techniques, is that students will connect the techniques to the software and believe that this is what is needed to achieve a particular sound—for example, that they cannot create a convincing reverb zone without using WWise. In addition, students may find themselves working with collaborators who use different software, or current software may become obsolete.

By taking a software agnostic approach, students learn the reasons why they are accessing different settings within software—for instance, if they need a sound that changes based on the material in the scene, they can apply this knowledge across a range of different software. In terms of analysis, this chapter provides an overview of techniques that have not been closely aligned with only one school of software users, thus allowing for wider application.

This chapter is divided into two sections. The first section outlines formal and theoretical differences between fixed-media composition and interactive audio, including information on audience motivations, heuristic frameworks, and aesthetic challenges. The second section offers practice-based solutions that allow students to use and test applied interactive audio techniques while developing their own creative instincts. These experiences provide insights into compositional approaches and priorities when creating interactive audio that can also be used as a framework for analysis.

Compositional Challenges in Interactive Audio

Applied Sound and Guiding Audiences

Within interactive media, sound has a very practical function; it is intended, in places, to guide the audience and influence audience behaviors. There are multiple considerations for composers and sound designers working with interactive audio. First, the audio needs to build a cohesive sound world that supports the artwork and world being developed, including building a sense of space through atmospheric sounds and creating the inner audio logic of the scene—for example, the sounds that all creatures or machinery make within a world. This world building is essential for creating an immersive audio experience. Second, the composer needs to build a score that, again, matches the visual style of the scene and supports any emotional components of the narrative. When creating the score, the composer also needs to consider how the music will adapt to player actions and how it will influence player behavior—for example, a higher tempo score will push a player to move through a level at a faster pace while taking more risks. Finally, the audio designer needs to consider how the sound guides the player through the game and any semiotic implications of the sound. For example, if a strongly directional high-frequency sound is placed near a doorway, a player will be guided toward the door and consider it a clue or a guidance point, or if an object is radiating a dissonant sound, then a player may believe that they should not touch the object, as it will cause them damage.

Michel Chion's three modes of listening provide a framework for understanding the practical use and audience interpretation of sound and music.[2] "Causal listening" refers to listening to a sound to determine the source—for example, listening to the location of a car alarm on the street to determine whether your vehicle has been broken into or not. "Semantic listening" occurs when a person listens for detailed information from an audio source, such as listening to the tone of a person's voice in addition to the words they are saying. "Reduced listening"—a term and concept Chion directly draws from the work of Pierre Schaeffer—is a more abstract form of listening, in which a listener pays attention to the qualities of the audio rather than its content and source. This type of listening focuses on timbre and the musical features of abstract audio sources. Chion emphasizes that reduced listening relies on a sound being captured in a recording so that the sound is always standardized and able to be analyzed.

Karen Collins has drawn upon Chion's work to describe the functions of audio within games, ascribing the modes of causal listening, listening for the source of the sound, and semantic listening (listening for the meaning of clues) to game environments.[3] For example, in *Batman: Arkham Asylum*, when The Joker speaks, the player can listen to where the sound is located (e.g., at the top of the tower) and then listen for further clues about what he might be doing to characters he has kidnapped. Collins also uses David Huron's extension of Chion's work to include "signal listening," to refer to listening for cues for action, "sing-along listening," for when a person physically or mentally sings along with a track, and "retentive listening," for when a person tries to remember musical cues or patterns.[4] Considering applied interactive audio skills, the most relevant of these forms of listening is signal listening, in which a player listens in anticipation of a sound cue that functions as a guidance object in the game—for example, listening to the beat in a level to know when to jump.

Jacob Nielsen's usability heuristics for "User Interface Design" offer an additional model for sound applications.[5] When selectively applied to a game environment, in which the whole game world is considered an extension of the interface, these heuristics require audio to support the following areas:

- **Visibility of system status:** In a game environment, audio can be key to informing players how well they are playing without them having to look at a performance bar. For example, as a player is losing life, dynamic high-cut filtering can be used to remove detail from the sound in the scene to indicate the system status.
- **Match between system and the real world:** Sound created within a game either needs to follow real-world examples and standards or maintain its own internal logic of how sound works. For example, *Call of Duty: Modern Warfare* is known for its realistic sound effects and panning. In *Yoshi's Woolly World*, sound effects have a musical sound or an equivalent effect to match the knitted woolen style of the artwork in the game environment.
- **Consistency and standards:** Sound within an interactive environment must be consistent in order to support gameplay. The extent to which consistency is needed is genre dependent. For example, in a platformer environment such as the *Super Mario* series, consistency is vital to reflecting the genre. When Mario jumps, you hear a jump sound, and when he smashes a block, you hear the smash sound, etc. In other games, consistency is expected with real-world variation. In *Call of Duty: Modern Warfare*, for instance, small changes to the sounds of individual bullets add realism to a scene.
- **Error prevention:** Audio can provide a key tool for error prevention. For example, a character can call you over to a space if you are walking in the wrong direction, and the panning of the audio can support this indication.
- **Aesthetic and minimalist design:** All sound within the game must serve the immersion within the game or provide a practical function for the work.
- **Help users recognize, diagnose, and recover from errors:** Error message sounds must be consistent and fit within the inner world of the game.

Students need to be aware of how the meaning of sound changes within a game based on particular types of listening and how these functions should shape their creative process. For example, students cannot create a main musical theme for their work that includes a Morse code-style pattern, as a player looking for deeper meaning (listening in a "semantic" or "semiotic" manner) will expect this sound to be a game clue. The student should also be aware of how practical functions of sound can add to the player's understanding of a game—for example, where they should be walking and how they should interact with the world. Additionally, musicologists and theorists analyzing interactive media must always keep in mind the practical and guiding approaches being used by composers and sound designers. Any analysis of interactive audio should take into account the intended modes of listening and how the audio designer guides the player through the gameplay.

Designing for a Three-Dimensional Environment

In video game development, a proxy is needed for the listener so that panned sounds can react based on player location. To facilitate this, an audio listener object is placed within the game, normally on the camera object, so the sound will be heard from the perspective of the player's view, not necessarily the character's view. Mixing from the camera perspective is similar to sound mixing in film and television, which is relative to the camera showing the audience's viewpoint.

When working in an interactive and immersive environment, height and panning information supports the player's immersion in the game, particularly in open world and exploratory games in which sound is needed to fill all of the spaces within a world to add to the inner logic of the environment. Collins refers to this feature as "sonic envelopment," which she defines as "the sensation of being surround by sound or the feeling of being inside a physical space (enveloped by that sound)."[6] She observes that enveloping sounds typically have a prominent amount of bass so that they can be felt by a player; such sounds will not contain panning information but will fill all audio spaces.

Three-dimensional (3D) sound information can also guide players within a space by showing them where they should be aiming or moving toward. In order to achieve this effect, highly directional sounds are needed that can be panned easily and located with accuracy in an immersive environment. These need to be mono sounds with higher frequency information and little bass.

Ordinarily students are asked to consider sound within a stereo environment or using surround sound setups. While this layout does include sound movement in a 360-degree context, it does not consider the additional challenge of designing within a 3D interactive space and how students can represent 3D spaces through the use of sound. Furthermore, traditional approaches to production analysis need to be adapted to take into account a dynamic 3D context. Sound is not fixed within a mix, and any panning automation will be player dependent and, therefore, not always developed through fixed automation.

Audience Unpredictability and Expectations

For a work to be truly interactive, the audience member or player needs to have some agency within the work, and conversely, the composer and sound designer must give up some of their control over the work, essentially making the player a collaborator in the audio output.[7] Tim Summers has elaborated on this type of interaction in a recent conference paper that examined "playful listening," in which the audience becomes a part of the musical creation through their ludic actions.[8] This notion of play suggests that engaging with game audio is a form of "musicking," a term and concept introduced by Christopher Small that includes the engagement of audience members with musical artifacts either by ritualized behavior (e.g., in a concert setting) or through activity that adds to the music being played.[9] While a designer can set up a work or narrative to suggest that users follow a specific route, compliance cannot be guaranteed within an interactive work, as routes are highly dependent on audience motivations and how users choose to engage with the game and the audio within it.

How a player approaches an interactive environment provides a particular challenge to composers and sound designers, as they need to build music and audio that is effective, regardless of how a user approaches an environment. To be wholly successful, composition must have the same impact for all players, whether they are skilled in a game and capable of moving through a narrative at speed or if they are newer to interactive environments and move through scenes at a slow place. In addition, players may find enjoyment from games in different ways; they are motivated to play by different features within a game, and sound and music must account for these differing approaches. The user research company *Quantic Foundry* has grouped potential player motivations into six categories.[10] This information is distinct from other demographic information about a player such as age and gender, and it instead analyzes the type of games they choose to play and how they approach gameplay. A player can have motivations from more than one category. The categories are as follows:

- **Action:** these players look for fast-paced and action games such as *Grand Theft Auto*.
- **Social:** players enjoy team and social games—for example, couch co-op games like *Overcooked* or games with a co-op function like *Fortnite*.
- **Mastery:** players will look for high-difficulty games that require strategic thinking—for example, a puzzle game such as *Portal*.
- **Achievement:** these players approach a game looking to complete it as fully as possible, including finding all collectibles and earning all trophies.
- **Immersion:** players are motivated by complex characters and storylines.
- **Creativity:** creative players will approach and interact with the game inspired by the question "what if . . ."; this type of player will appreciate character customization and take an explorative approach to challenges within the game.

How each of these players approaches a game will have an impact on interactive audio. For example, players within the "achievement" category may look for additional interaction within a scene to ensure that they have found all collectables and will want the audio to guide them to any potential objects to collect, whereas players motivated by creativity may not take a linear approach to a scene. They may move around a space in a different order or attempt to interact with objects in an unexpected way to see if there is a changed outcome.

In *Untitled Goose Game*, in which the player is a goose who terrorizes a village, the player motivated by achievement will work through the task list methodically and try different doors and objects to check if they unlock additional to-do list items. A player motivated by creativity may think "what happens if I honk into this milk bottle or these pipes," showing that they are looking for additional interaction and responses within a scene. The sound designer Em Halberstadt has accounted for players testing the world in *Untitled Goose Game* and has designed the sound to adapt accordingly. If a player chooses to honk into a milk bottle, the goose sound adapts and is filtered to sound like it is being heard through a milk bottle, acting as an additional reward for creative players.

Interactive music within a game needs to be written in a nonlinear format, which supports audio cohesion based on how a player explores a virtual environment. If a player is motivated by immersion, they may spend a long time exploring a scene to find all narrative pieces, meaning that they will need extended audio cues. A player motivated by achievement may choose to attempt a speed-run through the level, exploiting shortcuts to jump between worlds, and they may never hear full audio cues. Music composed to take speed-runs into account requires a loop and layer-based approach to adaptive sound that recognizes player locations, adding and removing complexity as needed based on the location in the game. In addition, the composer needs to be able to create cohesion across different worlds or levels within a game so that the sound can change between different musical cues without too jarring an effect.

For students, this requires a new structural understanding of music that is not written in a linear format but is instead written as changeable blocks of sound. Analysts will also need to take this structure into account. A traditional, linear approach to structure, of the type used to analyze film composition, does not allow for considering the changing use of loops and layers. To fit interactive sound and music within this traditional analytical approach, the musicologist would need to create one definitive version of the music within the game by recording one playthrough, yet preserving only one version of the structure would not represent the unique nature of interactive audio or the player's experience of audio through gameplay. Interactive music must, therefore, be analyzed in its dynamic form, which reflects the interactive nature of the work.

Whether analyzing interactive audio or assessing student work, it is important to test the interactive elements of the sound as well as the creative success of the audio and its semiotic roles within a scene. In order to assess key areas of the audio, a similar approach can be taken to play testing for games used in the Quality Assurance stage of game development and used on smaller scales by composers and sound designers to test the effectiveness of their audio as it is added into the game. As ambient audio and music in a scene are built on loops, it is important to stay in scenes long enough to hear the end of an audio loop. This allows any analysis to consider what structures the composer was working with: for example, was there an internal extended structure to the sound, or was the composer working in short four-bar loops? The tester must then move between different areas in the game, in places repeating sections or moving backward through scenes. This will show when new music cues are triggered or when additional layers are added to the music. By repeating sections or moving backward in a scene, the tester can determine whether audio is used only once or if it is triggered every time a player moves past an object.

This analysis can help identify whether the audio is there to guide the player in the scene (music that occurs every time an object is passed to highlight the object) or to guide the emotional development of the scene (an additional piece of music that is triggered once). In addition, although counterintuitive when playing games, it is useful in any analysis for the assessor to die multiple times in scenes, as this allows the player to hear what dynamic filtering has been applied to sound and music in a scene, how musical cues change in the death state, and whether additional audio clues are given after a certain number of death states. As the ludomusicologist becomes more familiar with a game through analysis and testing, approaches can be taken to simulate different player motivations by playing in modes that are different from one's usual playing style. For example, a player can take additional time to search for trophies and hidden boxes, looking for how the sound guides them to these objects, or through a speed-run they can assess how quickly the sound adapts to their actions and whether any glitches in the audio occur, with cues and loops being triggered differently from the initial play-through.[11]

Practical Skills and Approaches

In response to the challenges raised in this chapter, I have created a practical approach to teaching interactive audio. This approach includes an introduction to interactive music theories and aesthetics contrasted with practical sessions in which students create sounds for physical and interactive spaces. For use in analysis, the interventions aligned in the subsequent section provide a framework for understanding the decisions and considerations taken by composers and sound designers, illustrating how practical approaches intersect with creative decisions.

For each technique, unless stated otherwise, students worked within a game engine and used audio middleware, with all audio being created within lecture and workshop time. This achieved two aims: to get students used to implementing sound in games ready for their assessment and to help them learn how to work at speed when needed, preparing them for quick turnaround times that are common within an industry that still relies in places on a crunch culture to ensure that games are released to advertised deadlines.[12]

Two Roles of Sound: To Immerse and to Inform

To address approaches to teaching interactive audio, and to provide a structure for audio and music analysis, sound can be categorized into two roles that address modes of listening and heuristics. These roles are to *immerse* and to *inform*: to immerse the player in the game or scene and to inform them how to play the game or interact with the scene. This categorization of audio reflects the question that composers and sound designers need to consider when creating interactive work: "What is this telling the player?"

Immersive sound and music are used to further draw the audience into the game or scene, addressing Nielsen's heuristic of creating a match between the system and the real world. Sound that immerses is intended to support the inner logic of the game and any emotional development within the game. This role includes semiotic information about the setting and implications from the music about the tone of the scene. For example, immersive sound in the "Bogano" planet levels of *Star Wars Jedi: Fallen Order* includes the atmospheric sound of creatures and weather alongside the emotional components of the score.

The role of sound and music to inform includes heuristic information and semiotic implications reliant on signal listening that suggest how the player must act within a scene. Again, in the "Bogano" level in *Star Wars Jedi: Fallen Order*, this function includes the panning of creature sounds that are about to attack, so that the player can locate the risk, and beeping sounds from *BD-1* when the player is walking in the wrong direction.

The role of sound to inform may be divided into the following categories:

- Directing the player
- Inviting them to interact with objects
- Telling them how to interact
- Telling them if they have played the game correctly

From this list of functions, students are introduced to the semiotics of sound and music and how they can be used to influence player behavior. Parameters include intervallic information such as rising fifths for a heroic character action and the power of a positive *ding* sound indicating that the character has picked up a collectable. For example, when Mario hits a block, the sound is the same every time. Negative actions will always provide the same negative sound, and positive actions will give a positive sound, usually a bell or a ding, to encourage the player to repeat the action. As Collins observes,

> Repeatability establishes an expectation that we will hear the same sound as a reaction to the same action. This helps players learn the sound's meaning, increasing efficiency for the players, who can rely on the feedback to help them play the game.[13]

According to Nielsen's heuristics, repeatability relates to consistency and standards, error prevention, and helping users to recognize and recover from errors.

For game designers, these repeatable sounds need to be chosen carefully in order to be the most effective sources of instructions for games. A balance needs to be struck so that a distinctive sound that may be heard hundreds of times within a game to inform the player of how they are playing is not so distinctive that it becomes irritating.

Some sounds may fit within both categories, immersing the player in the game logic as well as informing them how to play the game. For example, the Castle Rock level of the platformer *Rayman Legends* is soundtracked by a re-scored version of the song "Black Betty" sung by Livingstones and Frankys (the goblin-like villains for the level). The sound is immersive, as it draws the player further into the inner logic of the game, while players using signal listening can listen to rhythmic changes in the music to predict when they need to jump or kick, helping them to complete the level.

Before creating any sound for an interactive environment, students are given these two categories of sound and asked to analyze a range of cross-genre game clips and answer the questions "What is the sound doing here?" and "How is it doing it?" To reinforce student understanding of the roles of audio to immerse and to inform within interactive sound, they are then set a research task to test a game and categorize the use of sound into these two functions.[14] The categorization of sound into "immerse" and "inform" helps students to think about how their sound will influence audience behaviors and expectations. All heuristic and semiotic understanding is shaped in reference to these categories.

Conclusion

Interactive audio design poses unique challenges for students, as it requires composers and sound designers to work in nonlinear forms that contrast with traditional modes of sound design and composition. Students must consider how the applied elements of their sound may influence audience behaviors and expectations within a level or a scene. They need to be aware of how player motivations will impact their approach to the game, and following Nielsen's heuristics standards, students need to consider different levels of listening, among them the tendency of players to look for hidden meaning within a scene's sound design.

By providing a range of applied activities, including activities that ask students to fully consider how sound acts within 3D spaces and how audiences react to and are guided by sound, students develop their own instincts for how to create immersive and consistent sound worlds that make use of the full virtual space within a game as well as considering semiotic implications of the audio they create.

By taking an approach to teaching that focuses on the aesthetic and structural challenges of interactive audio, in place of focusing on a software-centered approach, students are able to develop instincts for interactive sound that can be applied to any software they learn to use in the future. Through this approach, students develop audio projects that can support the inner logic of the game, the match between the system and the real world, and audio signals that can effectively guide a player through games across multiple genres. This objective is reinforced throughout by the categorization of audio that is intended to immerse and to inform the player. Student understanding of these roles, along with modes of listening, semiotics, and heuristics, can guide practical decisions and approaches in sound design as well as serve as a framework for analysis.

Notes

1. Karen Collins, *Playing with Sound: A Theory of Interacting with Sound and Music in Video Games* (Cambridge, MA: The MIT Press, 2013) and Tim Summers, *Understanding Video Game Music* (Cambridge and New York: Cambridge University Press, 2016).
2. Michel Chion, *Audio-Vision: Sound on Screen*, trans. Claudia Gorbman, 2nd ed. (New York: Columbia University Press, 1994), 25–34.
3. Collins, *Playing with Sound*, 4–5.
4. David Huron, "Listening Styles and Listening Strategies," paper presented at the *Society for Music Theory 2002 Conference*, Columbus, OH, 2002.
5. Jakob Nielsen, "10 Heuristics for User Interface Design," *Nielsen Norman Group*, 1994, www.nngroup.com/articles/ten-usability-heuristics/.
6. Collins, *Playing with Sound*, 54.
7. I have written in further detail about audience roles in interactive work in Lucy Ann Harrison, "Control, Collaboration and Audience Engagement in Interactive Sound Installations" (PhD diss., Royal Holloway, University of London, 2018), https://pure.royalholloway.ac.uk/portal/en/publications/control-collaboration-and-audience-engagement-in-interactive-sound-installations (438d4040-1b31-46aa-ac6f-d33766772b2e).html.
8. Tim Summers, "Playful Listening and Video Games," paper presented at *Ludo2020: Ninth European Conference on Video Game Music and Sound*, Malta, April 24–25, 2020.

9. Christopher Small, *Musicking: The Meanings of Performing and Listening* (Middletown, CT: Wesleyan University Press, 1998).
10. Nick Yee, "Gaming Motivations Group into 3 High-Level Clusters," *Quantic Foundry*, 2015, accessed February 1, 2020, https://quanticfoundry.com/2015/12/21/map-of-gaming-motivations/.
11. Tim Summers has created a standardized approach to investigating video game music structures that include variations of layers and loops; see Summers, *Understanding Video Game Music*, 27.
12. Alana Semuel, "'Every Game You Like Is Built on the Backs of Workers': Video Game Creators Are Burned Out and Desperate for Change," *Time*, 2019, accessed September 4, 2020, https://time.com/5603329/e3-video-game-creators-union/.
13. Collins, *Playing with Sound*, 33.
14. A range of free-to-play indie games that use HTML5 protocols and are suitable for this project are available on itch.io Itch.io, "Download the Latest Indie Games: Itch.Io," accessed February 1, 2020, https://itch.io/.

Selected Bibliography

Chion, Michel. *Audio-Vision: Sound on Screen*. Translated by Claudia Gorbman. 2nd ed. New York: Columbia University Press, 1990.

Collins, Karen. *Playing with Sound: A Theory of Interacting with Sound and Music in Video Games*. Cambridge, MA: The MIT Press, 2013.

Harrison, Lucy Ann. "Control, Collaboration and Audience Engagement in Interactive Sound Installations." PhD diss., Royal Holloway, University of London, 2018. https://pure.royalholloway.ac.uk/portal/en/publications/control-collaboration-and-audience-engagement-in-interactive-sound-installations(438d4040-1b31-46aa-ac6f-d33766772b2e).html.

Horowitz, Steve, and Scott Looney. *The Essential Guide to Game Audio: The Theory and Practice of Sound for Games*. Burlington, MA: Focal Press, 2014.

Huron, David. "Listening Styles and Listening Strategies." Paper presented at the *Society for Music Theory 2002 Conference*, Columbus, Ohio, 2002.

Itch.io. "Download the Latest Indie Games: Itch.Io." Accessed February 1, 2020. https://itch.io/.

Jensenius, Alexander Refsum. "An Action-Sound Approach to Teaching Interactive Music." *Organised Sound* 18, no. 2 (2013): 178–89.

Kamp, Michiel. "Four Ways of Hearing Video Game Music." PhD diss., Cambridge University, 2015.

Laurel, Brenda. *Computers as Theater*. 2nd ed. Upper Saddle River, NJ: Addison-Wesley, 2000.

Nielsen, Jakob. "10 Heuristics for User Interface Design: Article by Jakob Nielsen." *Nielsen Norman Group*, 1994. Accessed February 1, 2020. www.nngroup.com/articles/ten-usability-heuristics/.

Ryan, Marie-Laure. "Beyond Ludus: Narrative, Videogames and the Split Condition of Digital Textuality." In *Videogame, Player, Text*, edited by Barry Atkins and Tanya Krzywinska, 8–28. Manchester: Manchester University Press, 2007.

Semuel, Alana. "'Every Game You Like Is Built on the Backs of Workers': Video Game Creators Are Burned Out and Desperate for Change." *Time*, 2019. Accessed February 1, 2020. https://time.com/5603329/e3-video-game-creators-union/.

Small, Christopher. *Musicking: The Meanings of Performing and Listening*. Middletown, CT: Wesleyan University Press, 1998.

Summers, Tim. "Playful Listening and Video Games." Paper presented at *Ludo2020: Ninth European Conference on Video Game Music and Sound*, Malta, April 24–25, 2020.

Summers, Tim. *Understanding Video Game Music*. Cambridge and New York: Cambridge University Press, 2016.

Yee, Nick. "Gaming Motivations Group Into 3 High-Level Clusters." *Quantic Foundry*, 2015. Accessed February 1, 2020. https://quanticfoundry.com/2015/12/21/map-of-gaming-motivations/.

Multimedia Examples

Activision Blizzard Int'l BV. "Call of Duty: Modern Warfare." Activision, 2019.

Electronic Arts. "Star Wars." 2014. www.ea.com/games/starwars.

Electronic Arts. "Star Wars Jedi: Fallen Order." 2019. www.ea.com/games/starwars/jedi-fallen-order.

Epic Games. "Fortnite." 2017. www.epicgames.com/fortnite/en-US/home.

Ghost Town Games Ltd. "Overcooked." *Team17 Digital Ltd*, 2016. www.team17.com/games/overcooked/.

House. "Untitled Goose Game." 2019. https://goose.game/.

Nintendo. "Super Mario Bros." 1985. www.nintendo.co.uk/Games/Nintendo-Characters-Hub/Super-Mario-Hub/Super-Mario-Bros-Hub-Mario-Games-627604.html.

Nintendo. "Yoshi's Woolly World." 2015. https://store.nintendo.co.uk/nintendo-wii-u-games/yoshi-s-woolly-world/11110615.html.

Rockstar Games. "Grand Theft Auto." 1997. www.rockstargames.com/grandtheft auto/.

Rocksteady Studos. "Batman: Arkham Asylum." Warner Bros. Interactive Entertainment, 2010. https://rocksteadyltd.com/#arkham-asylum.

Ubisoft Montpellier. "Rayman Legends." 2013. www.ubisoft.com/en-us/game/rayman-legends/.

Valve. "Portal." 2007. http://orange.half-life2.com/portal.html.

6 Algorithmic Composition

Implementations in Western Tonal Art Music, Video Games, and Other Music Technologies

V. J. Manzo

To some, the phrase "algorithmic composition" may evoke images of computers, wires, and speakers strewn across a stage, while snarky hipsters sit backstage with a computer in one hand and artisanal coffee in the other. Perhaps the phrase even conjures up the *bleeping-blooping* sounds one might hear in classic "mad laboratory" scenes from science fiction films of the 1950s. Algorithmic compositions, in fact, *can* sound electronic and avant-garde or not like that at all. Put simply, an *algorithm* is a process, and *algorithmic composition* is the use of one or more processes that result in the creation of a musical piece.

While many, if not most, of the algorithmic compositions one might encounter today are created with the use of computers or, generally speaking, "digital technology," the notion of using clearly defined "processes" in composition is not a new idea and is entirely a human invention. Unsurprisingly, the composition of many pieces of music may be initiated with or created entirely by the use of prescribed "rules"; in some instances, the rules are much less restrictive, but anytime you have ever decided to "sing the next verse as a round," written a *cantus firmus*, or gone back to fix those parallel fifths, you have composed with "algorithms."

The aforementioned musical techniques are, again, uniquely human, yet the use of computers in facilitating compositional ideas or exploring new ones generally makes things easier if you have some expertise with the technology you are using. One of the earliest known compositional algorithms comes from Guido of Arezzo, a music educator and Benedictine monk who lived in the Italian region of Arezzo in the eleventh century. Those familiar with medieval music history will recall that Guido developed many unique processes to help others compose and learn about music (the so-called "Guidonian Hand," for example). To summarize one such method by Guido, which one might consider "algorithmic," a composer maps the vowels a-e-i-o-u onto the letters of the scale laid out in a horizontal sequence.[1] To follow this algorithm, a composer needed only to look up a passage of scripture and, while reading the text, apply pitches to individual syllables in the passage. Figure 6.1 represents how this algorithm might work using a seven-note scale notated on staff lines:

a   e   i   o   u   a   e   i   o   u   a   e   i   o   u

Figure 6.1 Notes on a staff with vowels marked beneath each note

As an example, each syllable in the phrase *Kyrie eleison* would corre-spond to a vowel beneath the plotted notes and, as a result, each syllable of the text would have a corresponding pitch that could be sung (see Figure 6.2).

Such a process can be used rigidly to prescribe an entire composition or to merely generate a few starting compositional ideas that could be judiciously refined by a composer.

Guido's approach to algorithmic composition is just one of many examples of nondigital algorithmic compositions: wind chimes, music boxes, and other devices are all algorithmic approaches that predate the use of computers. Another early technique of algorithmic composition, often credited to Mozart, involved the use of a page of "starting phrases" and "ending phrases." The starting phrases might be such that they all end on a half cadence, and, in application, all ending phrases are com-posed in such a manner that, harmonically, they resolve to the tonic and, when preceded by *any* starting phrase, sound cohesive (see Figure 6.3).

The "algorithm" in this case is that, from this set of composed phrases, the order in which the phrases occur is determined by some pseudo-ran-dom events; that is, starting phrases will be paired with ending phrases according to some chance operation. For example, students walking into a classroom might draw a slip of paper from one of two bags: one labeled "A phrases," and another labeled "B phrases." The instructor notes the order in which students arrive and the selected phrase associated with each student. Once all of the students have arrived, the original page of phrases is re-ordered according to the order in which the phrases were selected (by student arrival) and a new composition (from previ-ously composed ideas) is generated. The instructor might then have the new piece performed for the students; after all, they played a role in its creation.

Similar mechanisms are known for determining the random elements of these types of algorithmic compositions; a *Musikalisches Würfelspiel* ("musical dice game") version of this algorithmic composition might use dice rolling instead of the selection of paper slips from two bags.[2] As we begin to look at the role of digital technology in algorithmic composition, we can note that the process of preparing a page of "starting and end-ing phrases" can be understood analogously to the similar "tool-making"

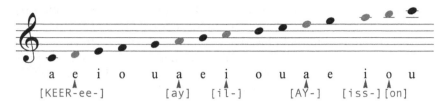

aei o u a e i o u a e i o u

[KEER-ee-]   [ay] [il-]   [AY-] [iss-] [on]

Figure 6.2 Phonetic syllables in text corresponding to specific vowels/pitches

Figure 6.3 A composed example of interchangeable "starting phrases" (marked 1A and 2A) and "ending phrases" (marked 1B and 2B)

process by which some contemporary musicians record vast "loop libraries" (ostinatos) of short, digitally recorded musical phrases that are then ordered in novel ways within Digital Audio Workstations (DAWs) such as GarageBand, Ableton Live, Logic Pro, FL Studio, and Pro Tools.

Valuable pedagogical applications can be obtained from an examination of algorithmic compositions and the processes that facilitated these compositions. In this chapter, we explore algorithmic approaches to composing Western tonal music, electroacoustic music, algorithms used in video games, and other use cases. Each approach can generate student-led and teacher-facilitated discussion about such techniques as well as potentially inspire further inquiry by students to begin creating their own music.

Terminology

Before we examine several different types of algorithmic compositions, it is worth noting that, colloquially, the phrase "algorithmic composition" as a descriptor for certain technology-facilitated compositions is distinct from referring to all music made by a DAW as "algorithmic composition," despite the fact that DAWs do employ algorithms in order to facilitate a user's compositional objectives. For example, if a pitch-correction plugin is used to alter an unintentionally chromatic performance into one of just a few notes, that resulting composition is generally not regarded as a form of algorithmic composition, although a case could be made that it is.

Commonly, and in the examples discussed later, the phrase "algorithmic composition" is used to denote some aspects of "artificial intelligence" (AI) or "machine learning" as part of a compositional process. If those two phrases seem unfamiliar, just consider the feature in most notation software that warns you when you have composed something out of range or with parallel voices and that suggests a few alternatives. These features are examples of "AI," and the degree of "intelligence" in the software has less to do with the "composers of algorithms" who wrote it in some programming language and more to do with the behaviors, knowledge, and general understanding that those algorithms are trying to represent in some musical context.

There are many different approaches to algorithmic composition, and classifying them into "methods" or "schools of thought" can be difficult for a variety of reasons. Among these difficulties is that a single composition may employ a variety of "approaches" to implementing algorithms. It is useful, however, to speak about some of the overarching approaches one might pursue. In *Interactive Music Systems*, for example, Robert Rowe describes three methods of algorithmic composition:

1. **Generative** methods use sets of rules to produce complete musical output from the stored fundamental material.
2. **Sequenced** techniques use prerecorded musical fragments in response to some real-time input. Some aspects of these fragments may be varied in performance, such as tempo playback, dynamic shape, and slight rhythmic details.
3. **Transformative** methods take some existing musical material and apply transformation to it to produce variants. According to the technique(s) used, these variants may or may not be recognizably related to the original. For transformative algorithms, the source material is complete musical input.[3]

As noted, there are certainly mixed-methods and other approaches to algorithmic composition that, within one piece, blur the lines between the three Rowe gives us here. Much of the way we describe these approaches is determined by the body of work by composers that already exists and by new compositions.

Computers in Algorithmic Composition

No discussion of algorithmic composition would be complete without some mention of the work of American composer David Cope (b. 1941), whose work in algorithmic music is so important. Cope was a pioneer in the use of AI in music composition, and an overview of his approaches to exploring algorithmic composition through "data-driven" and "rule-based" methods introduces a few of the important approaches to algorithmic composition that are still used today.

Cope is best known for his work developing algorithmic composition and the numerous books and articles he has written on this subject and AI in music. Of note, and perhaps surprisingly, despite his use of methods that rely heavily on software that he writes himself, Cope's compositions are predominantly works that are conventionally notated and intended to be performed by acoustic instruments. Prior to his work writing compositional algorithms, Cope composed chamber music, piano sonatas, and, in 1959, his first symphony.

In 1981, Cope was commissioned to write an opera, and, as one might expect from a seasoned composer, Cope did many of the same things any composer might do when undertaking the composition of an opera: he analyzed well-known and highly regarded operas from the standard repertoire. Even after immersing himself in Verdi, Wagner, and others, however, Cope found himself struggling to compose anything of his own that he felt had substance. As he explained in a lecture, had his writing process continued in this manner, he would have likely abandoned composition altogether.[4]

In his first book, *Computers and Musical Style* (1991), Cope describes his exploration into personal computers as a means of gaining further insight into extant operas through objective data-derived means—that is, through an analysis of patterns, trends, and other phenomena that exist in the compositions themselves (as data) as opposed to an analysis by way of traditional Western tonal music theory. For example, a computer looking at a composition might recognize that, hypothetically, every twenty-seventh note in the violin I part is a G♯, which is always followed, eleven notes later, by an F♯. The relevance of such information to a composer may or may not be significant, yet it may be to the point for a data-derived analysis. This type of observation might not be part of what music theory students are looking for when they begin putting Roman numerals beneath a score, but it is something that a computer is, in principle, quite good at pointing out.

In the 1980s, computers seemed to present potentially limitless opportunities for a variety of tasks. Cope paused his compositional efforts in opera and focused on exploring what could be done with personal computers to assist his compositional process. With no prior computer programming experience, Cope began studying how to write software that could aid in the analysis and creation of music, and he soon identified two approaches to composition that he employed in his early experiments: *rule-based algorithmic composition* and *data-driven algorithmic composition*.

Rule-Based Algorithmic Composition

As the name suggests, rule-based algorithmic composition is an approach in which an understanding of compositional practices such as voice leading, tertian harmony, and other techniques is coded into software. When the composer defines these rules in the software, the information can be used in a variety of compositional processes, including the generation of new music based on these rules and the analysis of existing works to identify violations of the coded rules. Cope's program *Gradus* is an example of rule-based algorithmic composition; when supplied with a *cantus firmus*, the software will generate a second voice according to an understanding of species counterpoint coded into the software.[5]

Data-Driven Algorithmic Composition

Data-driven algorithmic composition is the approach that Cope eventually used to complete his opera, and, in many regards, this approach is the one for which he is best known. Using one of the earliest-developed programming languages, *LISP* (derivative of "LISt Processing"), Cope constructed a software database of 300+ Bach chorales in such a way that he could have the computer recall, for example, "Voice 2, Measure 15, Beat 3," or "All voices, Measure 1, Beat 1" for one or more of the chorales, and have the software return a note or chord value for that specific beat. The ability to recall this information with computer commands is a key aspect of data-driven algorithmic composition; another key aspect is an understanding of the context of this data (the notes) within the larger set (body of work).

Cope's program utilized Markov chains, a well-known concept in computer science that helps define how a computer will make decisions. A Markov chain is, in short, a means by which software can make contextual choices based on previous choices. As an example of how a Markov chain is useful to a composer, in Cope's *LISP* program, coding a Markov chain into the software allowed him to ask the computer the following types of prompts:

> '*Of all the Bach chorales in this database, randomly choose one and give me the chord as it is voiced on beat 1.*' The computer then returns an A minor chord voiced in some way as chosen from one of Bach's chorales. This random selection from the available options of

starting chords is what is known as a 0th-order Markov chain; there is not yet an established context by which the software has made and can make decisions.

'*Of all the Bach chorales that start on an A minor chord voiced in this way, look at all of the chords that occur on beat 2 and choose one of those.*' The computer returns a B diminished chord voiced in some way as it occurs in one of Bach's chorales. This manner of 'selection based on a previous choice' is what is known as a 1st-order Markov chain; the decision is made with consideration of the preceding decision. Depending on what type of program is written, an *nth* order Markov chain can be developed that considers all previous choices in the decision.

For Cope's program, tasked with the objective of generating a new chorale, the software could continue making decisions for successive chords based on the organized data (the Bach chorales) in his database. Inevitably, at some point in the process of generating music in this manner, the software will select chords that begin a cadential section, and, ultimately, a few beats later, the software will select the chords to end the piece. Oddly, the resulting composition is a newly composed piece of music that is made entirely of material by Bach, yet while it sounds like a Bach chorale, it is not a work composed by Bach. Cope's website hosts 5,000 generated chorales for free download, none of which was composed by Bach but all of which sound very much like his chorales, because in a way, they *are* Bach chorales.

The Data

In Cope's view, building a database of Bach chorales is a good starting point for data-driven algorithmic composition, even if you are hoping to compose music for an opera: there are at least 335 Bach chorales, which is a fairly robust sample size for drawing an analysis of chorale-style works, and of course, Bach's chorales are worth being analyzed by both humans *and* computers.[6] Instead of relying on his own understanding of theory and his own analysis of extant works (arias or otherwise), Cope's data-driven software was able to construct new pieces through this recombinatory approach; the structural and harmonic "rules" and other phenomena were derived from the analysis of the data itself, and these "rules" were effectively built into the generated pieces.

This software, which Cope named *Emmy* for Experiments in Music Intelligence (EMI), propelled his career in a very different trajectory from when he first set out to write his opera. Eight years later, the opera Cope was commissioned to compose, *Falling Cradle*, was completed in just two days in 1989 with the assistance of the tools he developed. Since that time, Cope has adapted *Emmy* to produce "new" Bach inventions, Beethoven piano sonatas, and Chopin nocturnes, all described in his book *Computers and Musical Style*.[7]

Composers of Algorithms and Composers Who Use Algorithms

In his book *The Algorithmic Composer* (2000), Cope distinguishes between composers who use algorithmic processes in their music and those, like him, who first compose algorithms and then compose with those algorithms. A third classification can be made: composers of algorithms who do not use those same algorithms to compose at all (e.g., software developers). Related to these classifications are questions of authorship, originality, and even ownership: did Cope "compose" those 5,000 Bach chorales? Did Bach compose them? Is "compose" the appropriate term here? Surely, some new composition was "made," albeit "generated"; is this not composition?

Cope argues that as the author of the algorithmic processes by which those pieces were made, all works produced with those algorithms are *his* work since they are *his* techniques. For the matter of printed scores, Cope docs prominently include the note "in the style of Bach" for these pieces, much in the same way that Bach, for example, arranged some works in the style of Vivaldi and indicated "after Vivaldi" in the score.

Algorithmic Composition in Arvo Pärt's *Cantus in Memoriam Benjamin Britten*

Returning to the tripartite distinction of algorithmic composition introduced by Rowe with regard to the work of Cope, we have been discussing what Rowe describes as *generative* methods of algorithmic composition. As noted with the prior example of Guido's work, algorithmic compositions do not need to leverage digital technology, although, in Cope's case, it is clear that his particular approach to composing in this vein was facilitated by the use of new digital technology in a way that made his efforts more efficient than if he had followed the same approach "by hand."

Estonian composer Arvo Pärt's *Cantus in Memoriam Benjamin Britten* (1977) is an example of a composition composed algorithmically without the use of generative methods in the "digital technology" sense. Many of Pärt's works employ a compositional process that he calls tintinnabuli, or "tintinnabuli style"; fundamental to this process, one instrumental voice arpeggiates the tonic triad, while another voice moves diatonically in mainly stepwise motion.[8] In *Cantus in Memoriam Benjamin Britten*, a work for string orchestra and bell, Pärt employs the tintinnabuli process with a descending note pattern of the A minor scale, which is played in different rhythms by the ensemble.

As shown in Figure 6.4, the divisi voices (except for the viola) play one of two roles: one voice plays the descending pattern, while the other arpeggiates the tonic triad in the same register. In the violin I part, for example, two notes from the descending A minor scale are played, then three, then four, and so on, as shown in Figure 6.5. Each divided instrumental group plays one of the two roles beginning with different notes in different registers.

Each instrumental group continues descending in the process described until ultimately arriving at one of the notes from the A minor triad in the lowest register of its instrument. The groups then continue to sustain that note until all of the remaining instrumental groups have also finished descending.

Casual listeners might note the minimalist style of this piece but be unaware of the particular compositional process Pärt has used; that is to say, the piece may not sound "algorithmic," yet again, the composer used a clearly defined algorithm as a central part of the compositional process. If Pärt had written software, like Cope does, he may have been able to write and realize this piece more efficiently, but regardless of which tool Pärt used to facilitate his concept, it would have resulted in the same piece.

Google Magenta and Coconet

The database and related software that Cope created to generate "new" Bach chorales is an example of what is known as a "neural network." Just like the biological neural networks that humans have in their brains, an artificial neural network can be used by researchers to get a sense of a phenomenon (in Cope's case, the structure of Bach's chorales) and use that information to solve problems (such as making new "Bach" chorales based on some understanding of the ways in which Bach structured his chorales). The notion that one can *teach* a computer something is an ideal that researchers have been exploring since the early days of AI. This area of "machine learning" focuses on understanding and refining the ways in which software can identify some phenomenon and make sense of what is being observed, often through the development of vast neural networks of information.

Google's Magenta project, for example, is an effort to explore the role of machine learning in artistic and musical efforts.[10] There are several ways in which these efforts have been realized by this research team in musical capacities.

One such suite of tools is Magenta Studio, a series of stand-alone applications of plugins for DAWs; for most tools in Magenta Studio, the

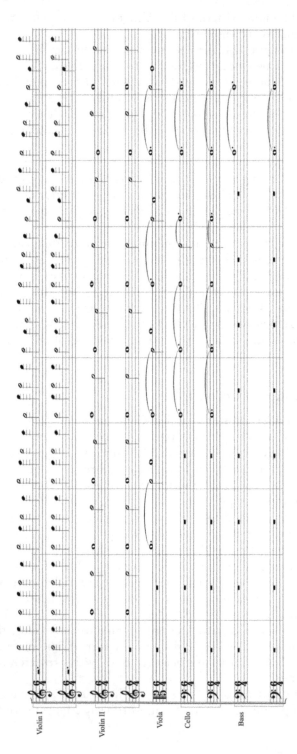

Figure 6.4 String orchestra entrance in Arvo Pärt, *Cantus in Memoriam Benjamin Britten*[9]

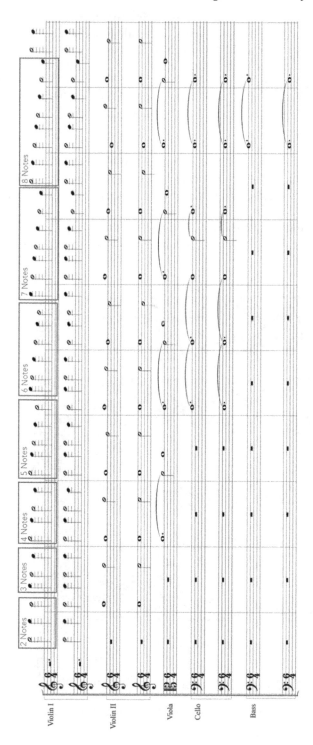

Figure 6.5 Descending pattern algorithm highlighted in violin I

user supplies some musical source material and then uses the controls in the software to vary this source material in some way. In the app *Drumify*, for example, a MIDI drum pattern is supplied, and the user can select a slider to control some aspects of how the pattern will be varied (see Figure 6.6). When the user clicks "Generate," a new MIDI file is written that is a variation of the original pattern. This is an example of what Rowe describes as a *transformative* method of algorithmic composition.

Magenta Studio has many other tools, all of which are free to download, that have similar abilities to create variations based on existing musical source materials or even to generate new musical ideas without user-supplied data (based on some information resident within the software).

The underlying machine learning model behind some of the Magenta applications is called *Coconet*.[11] Of note, just like the neural network

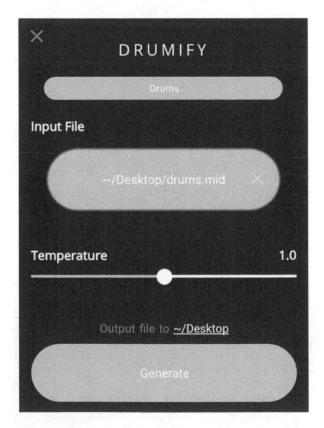

Figure 6.6 Drumify, from Google's Magenta Studio suite of algorithmic composition tools

Cope built in the 1980s, Google researchers used Bach's chorales as the source material from which they "trained" their network in 2016.

The primary implementation of algorithmic composition described thus far has been in the tradition of tertian harmony in a Western tonal context, but algorithmic approaches can and are used to create new works that focus on novel timbres. Google's NSynth project, also part of Magenta, is one such example of this implementation. In NSynth, the neural network is not made of carefully organized Bach chorales but of the characterization of timbres. Instead of combining waveforms together in ways to achieve synthesis, using this type of neural network can create new timbres that have the timbral properties of one or more instruments, or any combination of sounds, such as a sitar-flute.

Procedural Music

Given its potential for limitless variation within a specified style or genre, algorithmic compositional processes have been implemented in video game design and other multimedia environments. The terms "procedural music," "adaptive music," and "procedural generation" are often used to describe scenarios in which new musical compositions are played in response to gameplay or some other activity a user initiates or experiences in a game. In the 1985 video game Super Mario Bros., a single composition was used during each level of gameplay. Japanese composer Koji Kondo wrote a number of short pieces designed to loop back to the beginning on beat throughout the player's gameplay experience; unlike games that employ procedural music techniques, the music in each level of Super Mario Bros. continues to play regardless of what the player is doing or whether the player is winning or losing, with the exception of a few moments in which the music is, in fact, adaptive to gameplay: for example, when the game timer is running out, the musical piece suddenly stops, a shorter transitional piece is played, and the original piece then plays again at a much faster tempo.

In principle, video game developers can program their games so that different music files play in response to anything the player does or experiences during gameplay. The use of procedural music in a game is a variant of this notion: instead of a composer writing new pieces for a variety of experiences in the game, such as when the player's health is running low or when the player is in a "bonus stage," the composer can develop algorithms that describe the kinds of musical ideas that could play in response to something that happens in the game. For example, in the video game *Mini Metro* by Dino Polo Club, players develop a transit system for growing cities by building stations and connecting lines between those stations at peak times to address congestion (see Figure 6.7).

American composer Rich Vreeland used algorithms in *Mini Metro* to map the phenomena happening in the game world to specific

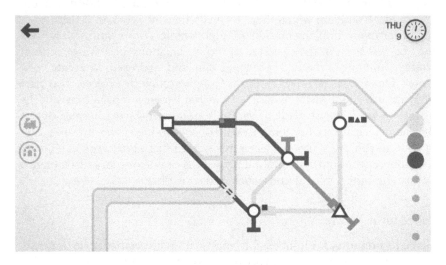

Figure 6.7 Basic layout of *Mini Metro* while beginning to construct a transit system

compositional ideas. In an interview, Vreeland describes how the music for *Mini Metro* is generated in real time using algorithms he developed:

> Each city/level has an inherent set of musical qualities; access to certain rhythms, harmonic choices, and train engine sounds among other things. Which of those are played at any given time is somewhat controlled by the player through their decisions around the size and shape of their subway system. Each level contains strings of notes that represent the harmonic structure and the voice leading of the music. Each subway line has a rhythm and a note tied to it at any given time. Altering the subway line least recently altered replaces the oldest note in the harmonic structure with the next one in line. The rhythms work in a similar way. Altering a line alters the rhythm by shifting it to the next available rhythm in a list of possible rhythms. Sometimes the harmonic structure of the music will change depending on which week of gameplay you are currently in.[12]

Electroacoustic Music

DAWs like Pro Tools, Ableton Live, Logic Pro, and GarageBand allow users to edit and alter recorded audio and MIDI files. Mash-ups, remixes, and loop-based compositions blur the lines among the three approaches to algorithmic composition described by Rowe. DAWs and many software-based music systems allow for music to be generated through the use of plugins similar to and including Magenta; DAWs allow for sequences of prerecorded music to be triggered and played back in novel ways, and they also facilitate all sorts of transformative methods of altering data.

Electroacoustic music is in many ways distinct from the type of algorithmic compositions that have been examined thus far; however, the use of algorithms toward facilitating a musical objective does warrant some discussion of this style. Argentine-American composer Mario Davidovsky (1934–2019), for example, composed a series of pieces entitled *Synchronisms* in which one or more acoustic instrumentalists perform with "tape"—that is, they perform live with a prerecorded audio recording of sounds that have been prepared in a recording studio or similar environment.

Synchronisms No. 10 (1992), for example, first performed by David Starobin, is a roughly 9½-minute work for solo classical guitar and tape; the piece begins with solo guitar and, at roughly 4½ minutes into the piece, a recording of classical guitar sounds edited by Davidovsky begins to play with the live performer. In this regard, the tape, which could very well be any recording playback system such as a laptop computer, contributes to the performance something novel that, indeed, no human performer could create with an acoustic instrument.

Synchronisms No. 10 presents a unique and special combination of a live performer doing what a human being does exceptionally well and technology doing what it does exceptionally well in following an algorithmic process. Both the creative expression and the implementation of algorithmic processes are fundamentally different from the expression and implementation of algorithms explored by Cope. Common to both of these approaches and, indeed, to all of the aforementioned approaches, is that composition begins with a novel concept, and the algorithms help facilitate and realize those concepts.

In a classroom, discussing algorithmic composition as an alternative to "traditional" composition is sure to appeal to a certain type of student seeking to abolish the dominant musical paradigms of yesteryear. The use of algorithms in composition, as discussed, is just part of the overall terrain of composition. As educators, discussing "algorithmic composition" does present a unique opportunity to ask students to think conceptually and specifically about one or more aspects of composing music. In some regard, this approach can be a great starting point for non-composers to begin setting some parameters that will refine their compositions. For example, an algorithmic thought process might take the following form: "I want to compose something for guitar" leads to "I want to compose something for open-string tuning on a guitar," which leads to "I want to compose something for open-string tuning on a guitar where diatonic pitches are played pseudo-randomly," which finally leads to ". . . where diatonic pitches are played pseudo-randomly by me and my friends tossing guitar picks at the guitar from across the room." There are no laws that forbid algorithmic compositions like this from being refined further, and, as educators, we can prepare algorithmic composition exercises as a starting point toward facilitating discussions about creative and theoretical concepts, not unlike, we can assume, Guido did with his algorithmic compositions. A good idea for a composition is a good idea for a composition, and a conversation about the mechanics of realizing these ideas through algorithms can be interesting and enriching. Such conversations can consider computers centrally in the process or not at all.

Notes

1. Gareth Loy, "Composing with Computers: A Survey of Some Compositional Formalisms and Music Programming Languages," in *Current Directions in Computer Music Research*, ed. Max V. Mathews and John R. Pierce (Cambridge, MA and London: The MIT Press, 1989), 297–9.
2. "Musikalisches Würfelspiel, K.516f (Mozart, Wolfgang . . .: IMSLP)," accessed February 25, 2020, https://imslp.org/wiki/Musikalisches_W%C3% BCrfelspiel,_K.516f_(Mozart,_Wolfgang_Amadeus).
3. Robert Rowe, *Interactive Music Systems: Machine Listening and Composing* (Cambridge, MA: The MIT Press, 1993), 2–3.
4. David Cope, "Workshop in Algorithmic Composition," *Experiments in Music Intelligence* (class lecture, University of Santa Cruz, Santa Cruz, CA, July 1, 2008).
5. "Software," accessed February 25, 2020, http://artsites.ucsc.edu/faculty/ cope/software.htm.
6. Malcolm Boyd, *Bach*, 3rd ed. (Oxford: Oxford University Press, 2006), 6.
7. David Cope, *Computers and Musical Style: The Computer Music and Digital Audio Series*, 6th ed. (Madison, WI: A-R Editions, 1991).
8. For a detailed discussion of Pärt's "tintinnabuli" style and the *Cantus* in particular, consult Paul Hillier, *Arvo Pärt* (Oxford and New York: Oxford University Press, 1997), 86–97 and 102–3.
9. Arvo Pärt, "Cantus in Memory of Benjamin Britten," accessed February 27, 2020, www.universaledition.com/arvo-part-534/works/cantus-in-memory-of-benjamin-britten-1465.
10. "Magenta," accessed February 25, 2020, https://magenta.tensorflow.org/.
11. See Cheng-Zhi Anna Huang et al., "Counterpoint By Convolution," *Arxiv. org*, 2019 (full URL listed in bibliography).
12. Richard Gould, "The Programmed Music of 'Mini Metro': Interview with Rich Vreeland (Disasterpeace)," *Designingsound.org*, 2016 (full URL listed in bibliography).

Selected Bibliography

Boyd, Malcolm. *Bach*. 3rd ed. Oxford: Oxford University Press, 2006.
Cope, David. *The Algorithmic Composer*. 16th ed. Madison, WI: A-R Editions, 2000.
Cope, David. *Computers and Musical Style: The Computer Music and Digital Audio Series*. 6th ed. Madison, WI: A-R Editions, 1991.
Cope, David. "Workshop in Algorithmic Composition." *Experiments in Music Intelligence*. Class lecture at University of Santa Cruz, Santa Cruz, CA, July 1, 2008.

Dinosaur Polo Club. *Basic Layout of Mini Metro While Beginning to Construct a Transit System*, 2016. Image. Accessed August 23, 2020. https://dinopoloclub.com/games/mini-metro/.

Gould, Richard. "The Programmed Music of 'Mini Metro': Interview with Rich Vreeland (Disasterpeace)." *Designingsound.org*, 2016. Accessed August 23, 2020. http://designingsound.org/2016/02/18/the-programmed-music-of-mini-metro-interview-with-rich-vreeland-disasterpeace/?fbclid=IwAR1O6wodBN ZvG-qgjsE2vBX9zvfNz8yYvAuPT1-SrFXZnXEzZwgWrzRA3Bo.

Hawthorne. "Coconet: The ML Model behind Today's Bach Doodle." *Magenta*, 2019. Accessed August 23, 2020. https://magenta.tensorflow.org/coconet.

Hillier, Paul. *Arvo Pärt*. Oxford and New York: Oxford University Press, 1997.

Huang, Cheng-Zhi Anna, Tim Cooijmans, Adam Roberts, Aaron Courville, and Douglas Eck. "Counterpoint by Convolution." *Proceedings of the 18th International Society for Music Information Retrieval Conference*, ISMIR 2017, 2019. *Arxiv.org*. Accessed August 23, 2020. https://arxiv.org/abs/1903.07227.

Loy, Gareth. "Composing with Computers: A Survey of Some Compositional Formalisms and Music Programming Languages." In *Current Directions in Computer Music Research*, edited by Max V. Mathews and John R. Pierce, 291–396. Cambridge, MA and London: The MIT Press, 1989.

Magenta Studio. *Drumify Creates Grooves Based on the Rhythm of Any Input*, 2020. Image. Accessed August 23, 2020. https://magenta.tensorflow.org/studio.

Mozart, Wolfgang Amadeus. *Musikalisches Würfelspiel*, K.516F [1787]. *Imslp.org*. Accessed August 23, 2020. https://imslp.org/wiki/Musikalisches_W%C3%BCrfelspiel,_K.516f_(Mozart,_Wolfgang_Amadeus).

Nierhaus, Gerhard. *Algorithmic Composition: Paradigms of Automated Music Generation*. Vienna: Springer, 2009.

Pärt, Arvo. *Cantus in Memory of Benjamin Britten for String Orchestra and Bell* [1980]. Vienna, Austria: Universal Edition, 1996.

Rowe, Robert. *Interactive Music Systems: Machine Listening and Composing*. Cambridge, MA: The MIT Press, 1993.

Zaslaw, Neal. "Mozart's Modular Minuet Machine." In *Essays in Honor of László Somfai on His 70th Birthday: Studies in the Sources and the Interpretation of Music*, edited by László Vikárius and Vera Lampert, 219–35. Lanham, MD: Scarecrow Press, 2005.

Part II
Unifying the Curriculum

7 It's Not (Just) About History and, by the Way, Which History?

Leigh Landy

Higher education institutions have the funny habit of teaching music history, theory, and performance in isolation. Some offer history programs over the length of an undergraduate program and only arrive at current trends in an advanced year, meaning that students interested in today's music start studying composition well before they learn the relevant history. Furthermore, in Europe until the so-called Bologna agreement, universities tended to focus on theory and conservatories on practice. Although Anglophone teaching does combine both, the silo mentality of separating musical subjects in terms of curriculum lives on.

This chapter offers the view that the teaching of electroacoustic (or sound-based) music, which possesses its own paradigm, should ideally be presented holistically by introducing relevant aspects of theory and practice with regard to any given subject simultaneously. It further supports the view that creating electroacoustic music without a broad knowledge of its various disciplines, its technologies, techniques, and histories indicates a pedagogical flaw, as does the notion of undertaking analytical and other musicological studies of electroacoustic composition without hands-on experience of sonic creativity. This chapter suggests that collaborative musicking, as it is relevant to both sampling and do-it-yourself electronics (hacking) cultures, should be integrated into any twenty-first–century electroacoustic curriculum, as should socio-cultural awareness regarding the place of sonic creativity in today's and tomorrow's world. Finally, the scope of making music with sounds is very broad these days. Histories tend to be selective. Holism is a means of avoiding that.

The following discussion is not a scholarly survey; instead, it is intended to present this educational vision based on the author's experience as a composer, scholar, and pedagogue, offering a vision of curriculum design for electroacoustic music studies at the tertiary education level and thus including the subject's musicological components. Its premise is that the more holistically presented a given curriculum, molded to local circumstances, the better informed and more adaptable (e.g., to employment, future opportunities) the students involved will be. To this end, the notions of the "thinking musician" and "practicing musicologist" will be introduced.

Getting Started: Does a Curriculum for Electroacoustic Music Exist?

Let's commence by inspecting what might be called three generic examples of higher education curricula, all of which this author has encountered:

- The first example considers a music major curriculum with a music history strand that takes over two years before students are introduced to twentieth- and twenty-first–century art music. In such cases, how do those wanting to focus on new music performance and/or composition find a way to engage knowledgably with their specialty well before this introduction is offered?
- The second example represents one of the many variants of electroacoustic music modules being presented within the auspices of a music technology program. In this case, the term "theory" may have more to do with learning to use MAX/MSP or SuperCollider than with what most music departments consider to be theory. Such courses will also normally include a survey of electroacoustic music history, but who and which types of music will be presented and which omitted, and how much aesthetic and analytical knowledge will be included in this curriculum?[1]
- The third example concerns introducing electroacoustic music as an optional subject for someone majoring in music. Inevitably, the amount of electroacoustic music modules offered will be limited, as is most likely the case in the first example within a general music course, meaning the inevitable reduction of subjects covered. Does this lead to catastrophe or are there intelligent ways of covering a wide variety of aspects of electroacoustic music within limited time?

The abovementioned examples have been consciously presented rhetorically to enable the author to present an alternative basis for any of the three. To cut to the quick, recycling one of the author's titles, one needs to know whether a given electroacoustic music curriculum is focused on music Technology, Music technology, or Music Technology, and, regardless of the focus, how to ensure that those aspects seen to be of lesser importance can be integrated into any given curriculum.[2]

Putting this another way, it is proposed that what might be called the "silo approach" to an electroacoustic music curriculum, separating history from music theory, various forms of technology, performance, production, and composition, and so on, is not an ideal way of presenting a subject that is, by definition, an interdiscipline (with a wink of an eye to Pierre Schaeffer).[3] Instead, finding means to present knowledge holistically, ideally in the form of intensive projects (which are not always feasible given various institutions' timetable constraints), offers an alternative to engage both sides of the brain as it were simultaneously, where creative endeavor can be triangulated by way of scholarly and technological knowledge and vice versa.[4] In short, the arts (creative endeavor)/ humanities (musicology)/technology (science) triangle need not be seen as three phases of study but instead as three aspects of knowledge that are best presented holistically with regard to the subject of the day. With this in mind, it is suggested that any curriculum should produce both "thinking musicians" and "practicing musicologists" as an ideal. These two notions, which we shall return to later in the chapter, stand in dire contrast to traditional European teaching, where universities primarily develop scholars and academies musicians. It is suggested that in the twenty-first century, this distinction should be reconsidered. Furthermore, although somewhat outside the scope of this chapter, similar curricula should be considered for pre-tertiary education, as exemplified subsequently.[5]

Prior to continuing on to the core of this chapter, a remark linked to both unorthodox and progressive pedagogical thinking deserves mention. A large percentage of electroacoustic music courses are embedded within traditional music departments or institutions. Of these internationally, many are either requesting that students complete traditional music modules such as keyboard harmony and counterpoint alongside the specialist program, or they are assessing traditional musical knowledge through their entrance examinations, or both. The question arises as to what extent such knowledge and skills are relevant to the student of electroacoustic music or even necessary. In the United Kingdom and a few other countries, some institutions offer admission to candidates demonstrating both knowledge of and experience in electroacoustic music who may not even possess musical literacy. As someone involved in this field on a daily basis, this author has found that for many students, it is a rarity that the five-line staff is needed, and although musical knowledge such as that gained from traditional theory courses is never wasted, there are so many other things that could be offered to the student of sonic creativity. In short, traditional entrance requirements deserve to be *mises en question* in any state-of-the-art course that sees electroacoustic music as a more sound- than note-based idiom.

On Electroacoustic Music Studies and Education[6]

In this central section of the chapter, the author retraces the steps that led him to some of his writings, projects, and pedagogical decisions; after this, we arrive at a section in which the holistic approach introduced earlier is exemplified in greater detail. It includes some suggestions that readers may find slightly unexpected, such as teaching students involved in sonic creativity to work collaboratively.

How the Author's Writings/Scholarship Fit in

During much of the author's career, his research has focused on the combination of issues related to better understanding the area called electroacoustic music studies alongside the desire to make this corpus of music accessible to a public larger than its active community. If there is one publication that covers this entire scope, it is *Understanding the Art of Sound Organization*, in which an attempt was made to categorize the key areas of the field, reflecting previous work on the ElectroAcoustic Resource Site (EARS, www.ears.dmu.ac.uk) and bringing together all major theoretical approaches that had been presented by that time within the Musicology of Electroacoustic Music (MEM) index category on the EARS site.[7]

Beyond these objectives, the 2007 publication focused on the urgency for all involved in the field of scholarship and electroacoustic music practice to take access into account, thus making the subject more relevant to nonspecialists while seeking means to develop new communities of interest and of practice. The volume discussed access-focused research and presented access tools. Issues related to terminology, the original focus of the EARS site in the mid-2000s, were presented—for example, that what Europeans and most of the world calls "electroacoustic music," the United States largely continues to call "electronic music," which has the significance elsewhere of being a subset of electroacoustic music, namely, music based on generated sonic materials. There exists a host of dynamic, still unresolved terminological issues that are worthy of inclusion in today's electroacoustic music studies courses.

This terminological discussion in the book led the author to avoid utilizing any of the various terms for electroacoustic music, as none was unambiguous in covering the full area; instead he chose to propose a new term: sound-based music.[8] This decision led the author to create the notion of the *sound-based music paradigm* in the same volume, suggesting that there exists a body of knowledge related to sound-based music, as there is one for note-based varieties, that covers knowledge related to practice, theory, and reception. It is the discovery of this paradigm that helped lead to the proposed approach to teaching electroacoustic music studies holistically. Before discussing the approach in some detail, one subarea of the field deserves special attention.

A Brief Word on the Importance of Socio-Cultural Awareness and Its Relevance to Electroacoustic Music Studies

In the 1990s, prior to commencing the EARS project, it appeared that there were some subareas within the field of electroacoustic music studies that were underrepresented. At the top of the list would be what one might call the ethnomusicology of electroacoustic music, in the sense of the study of the music as a cultural phenomenon. Some twenty years later, this remains, relatively speaking, a "hole in the market." This seems odd, as there are forms of this body of music that relate to disparate communities.

Take the examples of acousmatic composition and noise. Although both practices exist within the sound-based music paradigm, their performance venues are largely different; their communities of interest are largely different; their means of presentation and reception are different, and, frankly, it is the latter that has caused more resonance (no pun intended) than the one more frequently discussed in higher education that evolved from *musique concrète*. Although both are an acquired taste in a sense, history has made one more of a people's (or folk) music, while the other has remained one more associated with elite culture. However, based on the data gathered in the intention/reception project, this elitist position does not need to remain the case.

Neither practice neatly fits within the category of art music or commercial (or popular) music. As discussed in the subsequent section regarding collaboration, both are in fact open to anyone. As noise is not everyone's cup of tea, one might suggest that music based on recording any sound could theoretically become more ubiquitous than noise performance. Why do specialists not investigate such subjects, and consequently, why do educators normally not engage with societal impact when teaching this music? For example, for those involved in teaching electroacoustic music production, why not ask students to consider for whom their pieces are being made as opposed to perpetuating the more arrogant (and vague) notion of "for anyone"?

This is but one of many examples that could be cited investigating this music as a cultural phenomenon. Knowing from the intention/reception project that the majority of participants in case studies, now spanning over one and a half decades, would like to know more about and hear more electroacoustic music after they have been introduced to it, it is the role of both musicians and educators (often the same people) to ensure that these types of introductions are facilitated. Educating students to be aware of relevant cultural opportunities and challenges such as making their music accessible should be embedded into any curriculum.

This Chapter's Proposal

The three scenarios proposed as "generic" in this chapter's introduction all suggest that local circumstances and traditions, alongside the people involved with teaching modules, determine the type of curriculum, time offered, means of teaching, facilities, and so much more. As someone who also studied mathematics, the author often thinks in terms of "optimizing within given constraints," and that is what is being suggested here. For example, demanding that a very traditional conservatory drop its entrance examination for electroacoustic music candidates may be a step too far. Still, constantly accepting something that is superannuated, in particular for this field, is not right either.

We are living in a time in which most students are so-called digital natives. Many used software like GarageBand or similar when they were young. Although one can have many qualms with such packages (where you cannot really make a mistake), the ability for people to organize sounds, first intuitively, then with skills obtained on the way, can be astonishing.

Similarly, these students' knowledge regarding today's sampling and do-it-yourself cultures may be greater than their knowledge of renaissance or baroque music. Frankly, the former is of greater relevance to electroacoustic music than the latter, although knowledge of both is even better. Still, one has limited time to teach in this field. It all depends on those circumstances.

Let's return to that art/humanities/technology triangle and contemplate the silos or distinct subject areas within them. Regardless of the thrust of a given course, it would be unfair to the student to skip any of the three within this interdiscipline. Yet no undergraduate course can ever do justice to all areas. Why not combine modules that "span the space" of a given area—musicology, for example—and then treat subareas of each simultaneously, allowing concepts to be put into practice, practice to be backed up by knowledge, and relevant context supported by appropriate scientific and technological knowledge and tools?[9]

The next step is to apply the above within potential curricula focusing on electroacoustic music or offering the subject as a supplementary study. To achieve this, the goal of creating thinking musicians and practicing musicologists is a fundamental point of departure. Therefore, we shall first tease out this notion a bit and then exemplify it for diverse educational circumstances.

In today's world, no one would dispute that the composer, performer, and musicologist each represents a specific vocation. Thus, one might conclude that training should lead to one of these. What is being proposed here, in particular in the case of this young and very dynamic art form, is that training these specialties in isolation is erroneous.

Prior to investigating specific examples, let's pursue this point. People involved in the production of electroacoustic music may call themselves composers; however, most of them also present, and thus perform, their work, write about their compositions, and are highly involved in the dissemination of their work. The *métier* of composer is thus dependent on an understanding of—if not direct involvement in—the areas of performance/presentation, contextualization of a work, and the organization of dissemination.

Given the somewhat marginal position of much electroacoustic music in today's society, it is logical that the musician is aware of and takes into account the listener's point of view, not as an abstract notion, but more specifically as one based on the diversity of potential listeners. For new listeners, this author has suggested that musicians offer them "something to hold on to" in order to provide them with navigation tools to avoid confusion and lack of connection with their work.[10] This is related, therefore, to the "for whom" aspect of musical production.

In order to achieve the goals sketched earlier, anyone involved in sonic creativity must have sufficient musical, technical, and musicological knowledge to be aware of where their work sits with respect to today's extremely diverse musical as well as new media landscapes. The musician should be aware of where innovation is taking place, assuming that this is relevant, and how a given work links with previous works. Similarly, the musician should be aware of both the conceptual and more formal means of production, as should any trained musician; this goes hand in hand with knowledge related to the listening experience. In other words, aspects traditionally related to reception and analysis are equally pertinent for the musician with respect to production. Taking all of this into account, the notion of the thinking musician seems self-evident.

For those who are more interested in the scholarly study of this music— and, to be honest, the vast majority of these currently are also practicing musicians—experience in musical production is not only useful but also fundamental to understanding the music under investigation. To achieve this, one need not reach the same level of expertise as the electroacoustic musician, but one must nonetheless have some experience regarding the ins and outs of the relevant means of production.

To this end, there have been initiatives to support engagement with the production process beyond introductory modules in most curricula. To choose one outstanding example, Michael Clarke and his colleagues have developed tools for interactive analysis over many years.[11] They have created a number of analyses where the user engages with compositional situations and decisions similar to the composer of a given work. In this way, several aspects of a given composition are presented to a user, who not only can learn the conceptual knowledge related to the work but also can listen to sound examples concerning whatever is being discussed and then explore the sonic materials and their means of generation and/ or manipulation in a user-friendly environment in circumstances not dissimilar from those of the original creator of a work. The goal is not to remix but instead to participate in a simulation of the creative experience while learning about both production and analytical techniques.

Remaining with the subject of analysis for a moment, Simon Emmerson and the author made a number of strategic decisions when editing a recent book on electroacoustic music analysis.[12] We not only suggested a template to those submitting to the book, offering a framework for discussion, but also presented a four-part question to situate their analyses: For which users? For which works/genres? With what intentions? With which tools and approaches? Although this publication does not involve active practice as does the interactive analysis initiative, the editors consciously opted for a very eclectic selection of works to be investigated, demonstrating the breadth of electroacoustic music from soundscape to sound art to acousmatic to IDM to aural computer games and to mixed performance, as well as demonstrating both universal issues and issues related to specific genres and categories. In the author's contribution discussing a text-sound work, the analysis was created for school teachers to introduce to young children, illustrating how analysis combined with visual representation presented with a work can aid the introduction to and understanding of this type of music among new audiences. The choice of content in this book supports the arguments suggesting introducing the full breadth of sonic creativity as well as addressing different user groups (as reflected in diverse curricula).

Both of the previous examples, as should a creative work, involve a project dramaturgy; let's call it the "why" of the initiative. In the case of the book, the "for which users" part of the four-part question supports the opportunity to take the notion of for whom an analysis is primarily intended into account. The question "for which work/genre" offers the editors the opportunity to cover an extremely diverse repertoire of works. In the case of the interactive analysis tools, the in-built didactic element, which holistically combines theory with practice, strongly supports this chapter's premise.

Hopefully, the scene is set to tie a number of remarks together in terms of creating an up-to-date module or curriculum for electroacoustic music studies for a given group at a given level of experience, based on the available facilities over a particular period of time and covering a given number of hours per week. The previous sentence is rather long, as it suggests that a module is not a module (in the sense of being standardized or fixed) due to the diverse local circumstances that exist where electroacoustic music is taught.

A Specific Example Applied to Diverse Curricula

Let's take a subject, namely, the gesture as a compositional tool, and apply it using the proposed holistic approach in a number of circumstances: a general music curriculum, a specialist curriculum, a one-off elective module, and lessons and workshops for pre–higher education students or people in the community interested in extending their education. The gesture might be seen to be a compositional building block and should normally be integrated into a composition or performance curriculum. It equally is an object of analysis both from the poietic point of view and the esthesic. For more experienced learners, it would be unthinkable to introduce this concept without moving up from the sound object-based theory of Schaeffer as presented in the *Traité des objets musicaux* to the spectromorphological theory of Denis Smalley, which works at the gestural level.[13] For more advanced curricula, Smalley's development regarding gestures in space can also be introduced, whereas for less experienced audiences, the concept itself may be sufficient.[14]

In the author's *Making Music with Sounds*, chapter 4 is entirely devoted to gesture, which not surprisingly is placed between the level of choosing sounds and developing larger scale structures.[15] This book is intended for teachers and for amateurs of all ages, but the logic behind the inclusion of gesture is relevant to anyone studying this music. It is introduced as a concept on the EARS 2 site within the project "Manipulated Sounds Intermediate."

How might one, then, place this subject into a holistic curriculum? Let's look at all four educational situations one at a time:

General music curriculum: In the general music curriculum where it is not assumed that students will specialize in this area, a class or series of classes could commence by focusing on the traditional music gesture and subsequently investigate where what we call gesture in electroacoustic music is synonymous or not. Clearly, part of this discussion would deal with the fact that a sonic gesture without human live effort is different in terms of perception from other forms of music in which gesture is also linked with the physical (i.e., where the term originated). The fact that most music today is consumed by way of media does not take away the fact that listeners can envision what the physical gesture is in any note-based composition. In electroacoustic music, by contrast, gesture is often a more conceptual notion.

Therefore, the course (or sessions therein) would evolve from note- to sound-based gestures and could introduce the basics of Smalley's theory. Illustrating the theory with carefully chosen examples from the repertoire supports appreciation, listening, and analytical knowledge. Choices can be made historically and across genres and categories, indicating that in some cases, gestures do not appear in certain (types of) works at all. However, learning about this without applying it is only half the story. Assuming that this general curriculum is not solely theoretical (at which point this chapter is entirely irrelevant), students should be offered the opportunity to create various electroacoustic gestures out of context and, time permitting, within a greater musical context.

In this way, the electroacoustic musical gesture is introduced holistically, relating it to the traditional musical gesture, to a relevant theory within electroacoustic music, to repertoire-based sound examples, and applied creatively to understand better the means of construction and the placement of gestures into a larger context.

This exemplifies the proposed approach. How many such subjects would appear in a module is dependent on the total time available. The point here is to link it to scholarship and practice while applying relevant available technologies.

Specialist curriculum: One can only assume that, in a specialist curriculum, there is more time for a subject such as gesture. In this case, one might be able to come to grips with both Schaefferian and Smalley's theories in greater detail. Students could create gestures using dissimilar platforms (e.g., a sequencer-based software, a real-time platform, and/or postdigital instruments), and they could analyze works focusing on gestural development within larger musical structures. Again, this is dependent on time allocation, previous experience, facilities, and so on. It is fairly unthinkable that this subject would not appear in a specialist curriculum and equally unthinkable that it would only be taught with respect to either practice or just theory.

An elective curriculum: Clearly, students gaining an introduction to electroacoustic music in an elective curriculum will have less time than others. Therefore, the question is: why introduce this subject at all? As gesture is a fundamental concept in electroacoustic music, and as it exists in traditional music as well, it is an ideal subject for identifying similarities and differences with respect to note-based genres.

Given limited time, a well-designed creative exercise would be needed where potential material, means of combining that material, and potential musical gesture types would need to be restricted. Again, elements from Smalley's theory can be used to determine any of the abovementioned considerations. Listening to relevant note- and sound-based examples would ensure understanding of how the notion of gesture is often essential to both types of music. Gaining an elementary level of knowledge of how gestures can work as building blocks of a work's evolution (or structural framework) is feasible at this level. Therefore, the subject is easily integrated into an elective curriculum, even with very little time available in class by using those creative and listening examples outside the classroom.

A curriculum for schools or extended education: For this situation, it is clear that listening and making will deserve a higher priority than theory, which will primarily be of value in terms of basic concepts, given the practical interests of young people and amateurs (for lack of a better word; the potential interest in this music is well built into this term). As stated, both in *Making Music with Sounds* and on the EARS 2 site, gestures are introduced.[16] Using Compose with Sounds that, like EARS 2, is free to all users, the creation of musical gestures with pre- or self-chosen sonic materials and basic gesture types is easy to facilitate. Again, introducing the gesture without allowing students to hear various examples is not ideal. Thus, as in the other examples, an appropriate technology (an eLearning platform or a textbook plus creative software for beginners) is directly linked with the introduction of knowledge, both general and by way of listening and creative application. How much is achieved is directly based on the time available and the level of the group in question. Experience demonstrates that at the pre–middle school level, the number of concepts should be well constrained. From middle school (age 11–14) onward, everything in the book and on EARS 2 can be of relevance. The eLearning site works at three levels and could thus be introduced over three years, with a finite number of music sessions annually.

Clearly gesture is not the sole focus in any module. It would normally be embedded within a modular curriculum focusing on compositional building blocks, again a subject that can be approached holistically as easily as gesture is above.

It is not possible to detail how to work this out further within the constraints of this chapter. Gesture might form a single or multiple sessions within a higher education module or a subject within a single session in schools, reflecting the fact that a specialist curriculum will normally last three to four years, a module in a general music curriculum one academic year, an elective one semester, and a school- or community-based introduction a matter of hours, often ranging from three to six (per year).

Taking this one step further, what might be the foci of an entire course or that year- or semester-long module? The answer is that this is the art of creative curriculum development. What one can achieve is a reflection of the intake of the module, the time and resources available, and so on. The educator or teaching team should attempt to define the essential aspects of what they believe needs to be delivered and ideally package this in a manner that offers the widest number of genres and categories within sonic creativity, a good overview of current technologies, repertoire, and scholarly underpinnings.

A course is, at best, a *capita selecta*, which optimally delivers a number of basic aspects of knowledge and skills as well as, in our case, creative developmental opportunities. As long as these are met and the skills and knowledge for future work opportunities are satisfied (not in the sense of a liberal arts graduate's ability to work anywhere, but instead within the field itself), a curriculum founded on holism is an efficient and educationally rich means of becoming acquainted with and increasing interest and skills in any area within electroacoustic music and its cognate field of studies.

A Word About Collaborative Endeavor: Toward Electroacoustic Musicking

Before coming to this chapter's conclusion, a final section focused on collaboration deserves attention. Traditionally performers and composers, at least within the realm of art music, the traditional focus of musical study, were taught primarily to work individually. In the case of performance, working in ensembles forms an essential part of learning as well, but note that these ensembles are generally directed. Collective creativity is not usually part of a music program unless jazz and other forms of collective endeavor are being taught.

Ironically, the vocational approaches of "the electroacoustic composer" and (to a lesser extent) "the electroacoustic performer" live on, continuing a tradition rooted in the craft of art music production. The reality is nonetheless different. As mentioned previously, today's electroacoustic musician is often involved in every aspect of production, performance, and dissemination. Still, this can and often remains an individual endeavor.

It is strongly suggested that, within today's and tomorrow's electroacoustic music curricula, collaborative endeavor should be integrated and encouraged.

Let's take two examples, namely, sonic sampling and do-it-yourself music making, both of which are means of electroacoustic music production and both of which exist within music as well as many other areas within today's society, whether related to the arts or elsewhere. These examples are chosen in part because they both rather defy the art music tradition in which electroacoustic music's early years resided, thus again pointing to the socio-cultural dimension of the subject area.

Either or both could form an extremely holistic theme for a curriculum as described earlier. Although an individual can be involved with each of these areas, their main traditions involve working collaboratively. In the case of do-it-yourself production, one can speak of the co-creation of instruments and performance based on the hacked instruments; in the case of sampling, this involves either the creation of a sample-based work that can be sequentially recomposed by others (and often includes feedback from those involved) or the simultaneous use of samples in a live context.

In particular, in the case of sampling, one might speak of the reverse of the norm where innovative concepts from high art are applied in commercial art. Here, collaborative protocols from popular culture are applied within innovative sonic artistic creation.

As stated, sampling and hacking cultures permeate society, although one can make the case that at least sampling occurred in music first. Their collectivist nature, their counter-cultural *raison d'être*, and the fact that both are *not,* by definition, elitist, suggest that such innovative art forms may be of direct relevance to a larger sector of the population than is currently the case. "Do It Together" and sampling cultures, the latter sometimes involving pseudonyms due to ongoing legality issues, often combine innovative trends with collaborative making and, at times, a political dramaturgy, thus linking art to society in a more direct manner than high art normally involves.[17]

The teaching of electroacoustic music in traditional music departments might make such scenarios challenging, but as a dynamic art form that is very much a reflection of today's highly technological society, such subcultures form an integral part of the whole. With this in mind, investigating collaborative making and relating it to the act of musicking is an element well worth integrating into an electroacoustic music curriculum, whether for young children, who love to work together, or for the specialist postgraduate student and beyond, or students in between.

Looking Forward

The author has often wondered why, in a research-driven environment such as a university, so many aspects of music education are based on celebrating the known. Art is about challenging society, it is said, or at least, challenging the norm. If this is so, why do so many popular music courses, for example, avoid originality? Even electroacoustic music courses run the risk of simply perpetuating the successful means of production developed over decades of acousmatic music production, which in a positive sense led to a critical mass of musicians but in a negative sense created a less dynamic subfield of electroacoustic music than many others.

The field is still evolving quickly, is highly innovative, and continues to grow both in terms of its breadth and depth. If there is one part of the field that is less dynamic, it is its (ethno)musicological areas, and this should change. Higher education, at least in terms of developing interest and tomorrow's specialists, should reflect these needs for innovation and cultural understanding. What this means is not only celebrating the past and better understanding the present but also helping to predict and build the future. Electroacoustic musicology needs to take its interdiscipline into account and deal with its unique aspects, borrowing from traditional musicology where applicable as well as exploring other areas of new media art, its home in today's art world. As stated earlier, the inclusion of musicology—or of electroacoustic music studies—within a curriculum is a requirement. Integrating this with relevant studies in science and technology and, of course, in artistic production is a formula to create tomorrow's thinking musicians and practicing musicologists. Such holistic approaches take the sound-based paradigm into account, applying it to local circumstances within the wide diversity of forms and contexts of today's as well as tomorrow's music and music education.

Notes

1. This subject is of great interest to the author, who went to a university that favored a particular aesthetic that was not his own and where some staff members spoke of certain experimental composers with disdain, reflecting the diversity of 20th-century history books of the time that favored specific composers above others, ranging from the more neo-classically oriented to the more radical. In our postmodern society, perhaps presenting the broadest possible spectrum of repertoire is the best way to help students discover their own interests.
2. Leigh Landy, "music Technology, Music technology or Music Technology," *Contemporary Music Review* 32, no. 5 (2013): 459–71.
3. Schaeffer's most important text, the *Traité des objets musicaux* (1966), included the subtitle "essai interdisciplines."

4. The Music Department at the University of York (UK) introduced the project system in its curriculum in the latter decades of the last century. This inspired the author to do the same at Bretton Hall (UK) during his years as Head of Music. Here he developed an innovative curriculum for the BA (Hons) Contemporary Musics course in which two-thirds of the program was project-based and taught in intensive blocks.

5. As part of the outreach aspect of his research, the author has spent a great deal of time investigating potential interest in electroacoustic music among people of all ages (e.g., the Intention/Reception project, documented in Weale 2006 and Landy 2006), as well as generating data supporting its introduction into pre-tertiary education and developing access tools, both pedagogical and creative (e.g., Landy 2012, the EARS 2 eLearning site, ears2.dmu.ac.uk, and its associated creative software, Compose with Sounds, ears2.dmu.ac.uk/cws, all aimed at middle school age but open to users from late primary age to older adults). We shall return to the latter tools in our holistic curriculum examples.

6. In 2003, when the Electroacoustic Studies Network (www.ems-network.org) was established, the founding directors, including the author, felt that using the word "musicology" could limit the number of people who might want to attend their events, which are focused on musical knowledge related to electroacoustic musical practices (as opposed to the more technical knowledge that is the focus of many other organizations' events). As the term "electroacoustic music studies" has subsequently been adopted internationally, it will be used here.

7. Leigh Landy, *Understanding the Art of Sound Organization* (Cambridge, MA: The MIT Press, 2007).

8. It is true that some works of sound-based music involve no plugged-in technology, but its signification was the least ambiguous.

9. The EARS site may be helpful in this regard in terms of thematic areas. Readers can view the subject index and focus on the section "Musicology of Electroacoustic Music," including all bibliographical citations related to each entry.

10. Leigh Landy, "The 'Something to Hold on to Factor' in Timbral Composition," *Contemporary Music Review* 10, no. 2 (1994): 49–60.

11. See, for example, the website "Technology and Creativity in Electroacoustic Music (TaCEM)" (full web address given in the bibliography) and Michael Clarke, Frédéric Dufeu, and Peter Manning, *Inside Computer Music* (New York: Oxford University Press, 2020).

12. Simon Emmerson and Leigh Landy, eds., *Expanding the Horizon of Electroacoustic Music Analysis* (Cambridge: Cambridge University Press, 2016).

13. See, for example, Denis Smalley, "Spectro-Morphology and Structuring Processes," in *The Language of Electroacoustic Music*, ed. Simon Emmerson (Basingstoke: Macmillan, 1986), 61–93, and idem, "Spectromorphology: Explaining Sound Shapes," *Organised Sound* 2, no. 2 (1997): 107–26.

14. Denis Smalley, "Space-Form and the Acousmatic Image," *Organised Sound* 12, no. 1 (2007): 35–58.

15. Leigh Landy, *Making Music with Sounds* (New York: Routledge, 2012), 95–126.

16. In fact, on EARS 2, all "projects" (one or more lessons with a given theme at a given level) involve aspects related to the general categories: learn, listen, and create, reflecting this chapter's vision.

17. Another example of note regarding collaborative sonic musicking would be telematic multi-location performance, which is obviously relevant to both practices.

Selected Bibliography

Clarke, Michael, Frédéric Dufeu, and Peter Manning. *Inside Computer Music.* New York: Oxford University Press, 2020.

Compose with Sounds (software). ears2.dmu.ac.uk/cws.

EARS (the ElectroAcoustic Resource Site). www.ears.dmu.ac.uk.

EARS 2 (the EARS 2 pedagogical project). ears2.dmu.ac.uk.

Emmerson, Simon, and Leigh Landy, eds. *Expanding the Horizon of Electroacoustic Music Analysis.* Cambridge: Cambridge University Press, 2016.

Landy, Leigh. "The Intention/Reception Project." In *Analytical Methods of Electroacoustic Music*, edited by Mary Simoni, 29–53 + appendix on DVD. New York: Routledge, 2006.

Landy, Leigh. *Making Music with Sounds.* New York: Routledge, 2012.

Landy, Leigh. "music Technology, Music technology or Music Technology." *Contemporary Music Review* 32, no. 5 (2013): 459–71.

Landy, Leigh. "The 'Something to Hold on to Factor' in Timbral Composition." *Contemporary Music Review* 10, no. 2 (1994): 49–60.

Landy, Leigh. *Understanding the Art of Sound Organization.* Cambridge, MA: The MIT Press, 2007.

Schaeffer, Pierre. *Traité des objets musicaux: essai interdisciplines.* Paris: Éditions du Seuil, 1966.

Smalley, Denis. "Space Form and the Acousmatic Image." *Organised Sound* 12, no. 1 (2007): 35–58.

Smalley, Denis. "Spectro-Morphology and Structuring Processes." In *The Language of Electroacoustic Music*, edited by Simon Emmerson, 61–93. Basingstoke: Macmillan, 1986.

Smalley, Denis. "Spectromorphology: Explaining Sound Shapes." *Organised Sound* 2, no. 2 (1997): 107–26.

Technology and Creativity in Electroacoustic Music (TaCEM) (project and software). https://research.hud.ac.uk/institutes-centres/tacem/.

Weale, Rob. "Discovering How Accessible Electroacoustic Music Can Be: The Intention/Reception Project." *Organised Sound* 11, no. 2 (2006): 189–200.

Part III

Critical Interventions and Methods

8 Posthuman Sound Design
Describing Hybridity, Distributed Cognition, and Mutation

Patti Kilroy

The modern performer's sound is increasingly mediated by electronics. A dazzling variety of electroacoustic works feature electronic parts with a range of musical roles, as computers, amplification, and effects processing are more versatile and portable than ever.[1] This trend is coupled with a broad expansion of electronic music across genres. Electronic elements may include the playback of a prerecorded track, mixing and equalization of amplified sound, live processing effects such as reverberation and a variety of timbral and delay effects, and generative computer parts resembling a human performer's actions. These categories, the contents of which are also extremely varied, might appear on their own or in combination with others in an electroacoustic work.

Amplification and effects processing are also increasingly found in music initially meant to be unamplified, as classical instrumentalists adapt to spaces outside the traditional concert hall. Amplified concerts in Central Park by the New York Philharmonic enable the softest orchestral textures to be heard across Central Park's 55-acre Great Lawn. Bar venues like Le Poisson Rouge in New York City project classical programs above the din of table seating and drink orders. Acoustic instrumentation is amplified for weddings and corporate events; the noise and spaces used pose unique challenges in sound design for engineers and performers. Instrumentalists playing these events—often a lucrative source of income—are frequently asked to provide a microphone or pickup and navigate amplified settings of various complexity, ranging from projection via a single speaker to performing within a complex multichannel context managed by an engineer.

The many ways in which electronic mediation is currently transforming musical performance, composition, and reception present significant challenges and opportunities for music studies. In this chapter, I argue that the concepts of distributed cognition, hybridity, and mutation—all subsumed under the broader category of "posthumanism"—can help students to understand these transformations in musical practice. These concepts may meaningfully shape student work in performance, musical analysis, and cultural interpretation. I focus on two pieces for solo performer and live electronics as case studies for exploring these issues. In *Industry* (1992), a work for solo cello and distortion effects by the American composer Michael Gordon (b. 1956), electronic effects cause the cello timbre to sound "dirtier" and "noisier"; these effects highlight difference tones created from sustained intervals of a third that sound as distinct pitches in higher registers. In *NoaNoa* (1992) for flute and electronics by the Finnish composer Kaija Saariaho (b. 1952), live processing effects such as infinite reverberation and harmonizers are used alongside playback of prerecorded sound files. The reverberation extends the resonance of pitches, spoken syllables, and noisier extended techniques in the flute. Harmonizers and sampled flute and speech thicken the texture and change the room's perceived acoustic. These two works use electronic elements with very different roles and require sharply contrasting types of coordination from the soloist. They thus serve as effective case studies for students to examine the range of issues I associate here with the concept of the "posthuman," issues that are increasingly prominent features of the musical practices students will face as professionals.

Posthumanism in Music

Electroacoustic musical contexts are "posthuman" in the sense I will apply the term when they are created with electronics and are impossible to replicate via exclusively human means.[2] Accounts of electroacoustic performance practice have frequently relied on parallels with contexts containing only human performers and have often regarded electronic parts as a type of accompanist or chamber music partner.[3] This approach may work for music in which the electronic part creates musical material that can be notated, but when used to describe contexts with live processing that modifies timbre or spatial perception (such as distortion or reverberation), the comparison becomes tenuous: the output is not comparable to that of a human performer, although it may be integral to a work's identity. The scholarly literature has prioritized describing interactive relationships with electronics, in which an "active–reactive reciprocal relationship" occurs, comparable to chamber music with only human performers and more dialogue-oriented styles of music-making.[4] Instead, a performer might *coexist* with electronic sound—that is, perform alongside or have their sound mediated through electronics that are transformative rather than generative, and perform without consciously regarding the electronic material as they interpret performance instructions. While playing within a space made to sound more resonant through the use of reverberation, a performer may not actively change their articulations but still understand that their chosen articulations are heard differently by a listener. "Posthumanism" provides a conceptual model through which unprecedented relationships like coexistence—in contrast to reciprocal interaction—may be analyzed.

Posthumanism is a broad, interdisciplinary field concerned with the impact of modern technology on human experience, and it offers several concepts that are useful in describing electroacoustic contexts and musical processes not adequately described by models privileging interactivity. The larger body of literature is concerned with a variety of topics within the arts and sciences, ranging from how technology impacts the creation and consumption of art, to the psychological, physiological, and cultural impacts of technologies and tools including computers and the internet. Definitions of terminology, including the term "posthumanism" itself, are in flux, as are the technological developments that inspired the field. Peter Mahon characterizes studies of the posthuman as "the exploration of scientific research on current, cutting-edge and future tools and technologies and how they affect, and will continue to affect, humans."[5] J. Thomas Brett describes posthumanism as a "category of life that involves the construction of a particular technological-human subjectivity in which humans are defined as hybrid material-informational entities with porous boundaries."[6] For the literary critic N. Katherine Hayles, posthumanism is a point of view that privileges information patterns over physical embodiment, deprioritizes consciousness as a relatively new phenomenon in human history, considers the body as a tool to manipulate and extend via prostheses, and believes it possible to seamlessly integrate humankind with intelligent machines.[7]

Hayles unpacks the origins and implications of these assumptions through examination of discourse surrounding cybernetics in the sciences as presented in the Macy Conferences and the parallel developments of these concepts in literature, particularly science fiction literature, including Bernard Wolfe's *Limbo* and the collected works of Philip K. Dick, as well as in works incorporating new technologically oriented writing techniques like the "cut-up" technique used by William S. Burroughs. Through narrative description in both contexts, Hayles pushes back on the separation of information from the body, establishing that information is necessarily based in material embodiment:

> Information, like humanity, cannot exist apart from the embodiment that brings it into being as a material entity in the world; and embodiment is always instantiated, local, and specific. Embodiment can be destroyed, but it cannot be replicated. . . . As we rush to explore the new vistas that cyberspace has made available for colonization, let us remember the fragility of a material world that cannot be replaced.[8]

Hayles proposes a framework that regards embodied experience and technological innovation as complementary rather than at odds with one another. Technology may provide new ways for humans to think and act, but embodiment continues to have a deep evolutionary precedent in how humans navigate the world around them.

Another key feature of posthumanism is "distributed cognition": through tools and technology, humans belong to larger systems of objects and other individuals, impacting attention span, memory, reasoning, comprehension, and problem-solving abilities.[9] The smartphone is a common means of distributed cognition that augments communication, memory, and problem-solving abilities.[10]

A collection of terms broadly applicable to electroacoustic music can be gleaned from the wider literature on posthumanism, including control, transcendence, communication, disembodiment, encoding, cyborg, hybridity, infection, mutation, programming, regeneration, simulation, trauma, and virtuality.[11] These terms have been applied to a variety of contexts within Brett's work and in my own work documenting performance practices. I will suggest ways in which instructors can draw upon concepts from posthumanist studies to describe phenomena particular to electroacoustic music, beginning with three fundamental terms: distributed cognition, hybridity, and mutation.

Distributed Cognition

The term *distributed cognition* originates from anthropologist Edwin Hutchins' book *Cognition in the Wild*, based on his ethnographic study of navigation processes on a US Navy ship.[12] The concept is discussed at length by Hayles and Mahon as a fundamental aspect of the posthuman condition, in which cognitive processes are aided by nonbiological means. For Mahon, distributed cognition means that consciousness

> is understood as not being confined to the interior—the mind, brain, or body—of an individual human being, but [is instead] carried out by a system in which a human interacts with objects, artefacts, tools and other humans. In such a system, all sorts of nonbiological materials become part of the process of carrying out particular tasks.[13]

Distributed cognition is present in amplified musical contexts, as performers exist as part of a larger network of electronics and other individuals such as an engineer. The performer's actions may be mediated by one or more elements within a network. Considering distributed cognition within posthuman musical contexts allows for increased nuance in discussion of electroacoustic contexts, particularly regarding cases in which performers coexist rather than directly interact with electronics. A performer may need to interact with other elements within the network, which might include parameter controls found on equipment as well as an engineer or another performer on stage. Multiple rehearsals may be needed to arrive at an appropriate configuration of actions and roles for each element within a posthuman context. This implementation might significantly impact what is heard and, therefore, have broad implications for analysis.

For more common contexts, there are already conventions in place. Touring rock bands, particularly groups with smaller touring budgets, work with a different engineer at each venue and, therefore, have to state their preferences regarding house mix and monitor levels to the house engineer clearly and concisely. As training and practices among engineers vary widely, performers typically manage the level of detail of their requests to the engineer so as not to micromanage them but to create a workable context for performances.

In contemporary classical music, conventions vary due to the greater range of instrumentation, musical material, and technology used. The pianist Xenia Pestova, in her work on "models of interaction," uses distributed networks to articulate points at which a performer may interact with electronic elements.[14] By also including options for indirect agency such as interactions with equipment and engineers, this framework can articulate the complex network of actions by human and machine elements, such as those in *Industry* and *NoaNoa* in which traditional interactivity does not necessarily occur.

The distortion in *Industry* can be created and controlled through a variety of means, with possible models found in performances by cellists Ashley Bathgate, Maya Beiser, and Zhu Mu. These performances collectively create a goal that a performer new to configuring electronics might aspire to. *NoaNoa*'s electronics are implemented entirely within software designed specifically for that work. Although options exist for microphones, speakers, and other equipment, most parameters for live processing in the work are predetermined and not adjustable. There is some range possible regarding mix, as Saariaho gives a general directive for a "rich, 'close' sound." In both *NoaNoa* and *Industry*, an engineer is necessary for mixing the acoustic and electronic sound, as it is nearly impossible for the performer to determine appropriate levels while on stage. The engineer controls the distortion and the performance's overall volume in *Industry*, and in *NoaNoa*, the engineer manages the levels of amplification, effects, and the prerecorded track.

Even the simplest contexts pose options for a performer's agency. In a "simple context" incorporating a microphone and single amplifier, a performer might exercise agency over their dynamic level, timbre, or tone quality at multiple points, including adjustments to their playing as they would do in an acoustic context, changing microphone position and altering controls over volume or tone quality found on the microphone or amplifier (see Figure 8.1). Adjusting dynamics on the instrument as one might within an acoustic context is the most "natural" approach, but specific practices might differ with amplification. A second option is to adjust microphone placement and parameters such as volume and tone quality; this makes new dynamic levels possible that were previously not an option in (usually loud) dynamic contexts. George Crumb's *Black Angels*, for example, utilizes this technique; when amplified, softer sounds such as the *col legno tratto* in "Sounds of Bones and Flutes" and the bowing on the "wrong" side of the left hand in "Sarabanda de la muerte oscura" are audible in a chamber context, regardless of hall size.[15] Amplification, however, may alter the tone quality of the instrument beyond what is naturally perceived in an unamplified context, therefore making it necessary that a performer decide how "natural" they would like to sound. Although they theoretically have full agency in this context, performers on stage need a second person to gauge the loudness or tone quality of amplified sound.

Live processing and an engineer introduce further points at which sound may be modified. In *Industry*, the cellist is processed by a distortion pedal (Gordon suggests a vintage Ibanez Tube Screamer), and an engineer manages pedal settings and levels (see Figure 8.2a).[16] To exercise agency over the sound, the soloist might adjust their playing technique or ask the engineer to adjust the levels. In performance, the cellist has less direct agency and is processed through an independently controlled distortion effect, which adds extra forcefulness to the cellist's playing. Considered as a distributed context, a performance of *Industry* is collaborative, despite its identity as a solo work. The cellist's interactions with the engineer, integral to the performance of the piece, are not comparable to that of a fellow chamber musician on stage, as the engineer performs a mediating role, something without precedent in acoustic contexts. It is occasionally necessary to perform the work without an engineer; this type of performance would change the distribution of agency, although the performer, as in the previous example of "simple" amplification, may still not be able to gauge their loudness as well as an engineer would (see Figure 8.2b).

The engineer's influence is felt more acutely in large ensemble contexts, in which multiple performers and potentially electronic elements are amplified, mixed, and processed before reaching an audience. Chamber

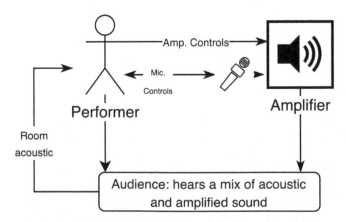

Figure 8.1 Distributed cognition diagram: performing with simple amplification

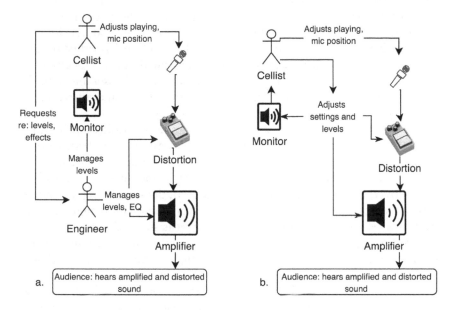

Figure 8.2 Distributed cognition diagrams for *Industry*, with and without engineer

orchestras such as Alarm Will Sound and International Contemporary Ensemble have member engineers who actively take part in rehearsal and are primarily responsible for the ensemble's sound design. The ensemble's ability to hear and be heard depends on the engineer, particularly for string players and vocalists who would otherwise be covered by louder woodwinds, brass, and percussion instruments. Engineers also navigate doubling and electronics within these large contexts. The expectations of composers and listeners regarding instrumental roles and combinations are consequently transformed, resulting in greater diversity in timbral combinations and instrumentation.

Hybrid Environments and Performers

Hybridity occurs when the output of machines is integrated with human action; given that humans use computers of all shapes and sizes to aid in scheduling, self-care, transport, entertainment, and communication, hybrids are everywhere. In music, hybridity is created through the commingling of electronic and acoustic sounds and interfaces; every electroacoustic context, therefore, is a hybrid. Interacting with prerecorded elements has been discussed extensively, particularly by pianist Shiau-uen Ding, who examines ways in which a performer might coordinate with fixed media, depending on its role.[17] The means by which hybridity occurs and its impact on performers and listeners vary widely;

beyond discussion of the electronics creating it, hybridity may be quali-fied through discussion of its impact on performers, how it is perceived by the audience, and the new choices it may enable. Timbral hybridity is distinguished from ensemble hybridity in that timbral hybridity results from the blend of acoustic and electronic sounds without specifically sug-gesting an additional performer or instrument, whereas ensemble hybrid-ity suggests the presence of a separate performer or distinct instrument. Other types of hybridity may emerge as technology develops.

NoaNoa presents many instances of ensemble hybridity, as the flut-ist coordinates with prerecorded flute samples and spoken text. In one instance, the flutist triggers a prerecorded flute sample in measure 37 and follows this with similar pitch material in measure 38. Consider-ing the overlap of pitch and rhythmic material, the soloist might explore how the sampled flute's timbres, articulations, and intonation might inform their own performance. The flutist's solo part is situated within a larger texture through the use of infinite reverberation, which sustains reverb indefinitely for the duration the effect is on, and through the playback of prerecorded samples. While it is usually not suitable to equate the electronic part to a chamber music partner, the presence of other musi-cal material may still encourage the flutist to perform their notated part as if it were less exposed than a typical solo. In a scenario that is nei-ther chamber music nor purely a solo context, performers have a novel opportunity to base their decisions in practices from either category as they decide whether to exaggerate or underplay dynamic and timbral gestures, choose timbres, and identify contextual information to use for intonation. In the case of dynamic gestures, both approaches are valid. Exaggerating a dynamic gesture, for instance, could be justified in mea-sures 37–38 of *NoaNoa* by the performer playing soloistically, in con-trast with the unshaped, "robotic" sampled flute melody in the electronic track. Conversely, a decision to underplay the dynamic gesture could be justified by a performer's desire to match and support the electronic part, as if in a chamber music context. The decision would depend on how the performer wishes to frame their relationship with the electronics for the listener.

Performers may also act as hybrids themselves when managing ampli-fication and effects processing to create musical gestures. Vocalists, for example, might alter their proximity to the microphone depending on their vocal register and dynamic level, or choose microphones that boost or cut selected frequencies of their singing. Microphone choice and place-ment creates a substantial range in timbre and presence separately from physical technique. Control surfaces let performers operate electronics; in *NoaNoa* and other works for live instrumentalists and electronics by Saariaho, the soloist triggers different configurations of processing and samples using a foot pedal. *Industry*, also a hybrid context, differs from *NoaNoa* in that the cellist does not control the electronics, and the acoustic cello sound is covered by distortion rather than blended. The cellist instead listens to the distortion to gauge their loudness at the level of the instrument. Cellist Ashley Bathgate describes how hearing the distortion effect helps her pace her performance of *Industry*:

> Psychologically, it helps to have that huge sound of the effect to heighten one's own intensity and performance. . . . If I don't hear myself loud enough I will almost always force and overplay to compensate, which tends to tire me out before I get to the end.[18]

Hybridity and Perception

Hybridity may be perceived by the audience differently from how it is felt by the performer. The extent to which performers interact or coexist with electronics, how electronics redistribute performer agency, and the visual appearance of electronics may impact how audiences perceive hybridity. The prominence of electronics within a hybrid context varies depending on the musical content and setting, the presence of physical signs such as control devices and conspicuous speakers, and how prominently electronic sound is mixed in a work.

Both pieces discussed have a minimal visual footprint: in *Industry*, there are no visual signs that the cellist is amplified aside from a microphone or pickup, and all hybridity is perceived aurally, as the cello sound gradually becomes distorted in performance. Hybridity in *NoaNoa* is also perceived mostly aurally by the listener, as the flutist only needs to step on a single foot pedal. This approach contrasts with more complicated setups, such as those described by flutist Elizabeth McNutt in her discussion of "prosthetics" involving continuous controller pedals, complex foot controllers such as those utilized by violinist Todd Reynolds, and conspicuous armband controllers such as the MYO armband used by violist Trevor New.[19] Other performers may seek to downplay the presence of electronic interfaces in performance; violinist Mari Kimura, for example, designs her electroacoustic works so that there are few visual cues for the electronics.[20]

Mutating Sound and Performance Practices

Mutation, described by R. L. Rutsky as "an ongoing, autonomous process of change," refers to any type of change resulting from the application of technology, at least somewhat independently of human activity.[21] A now-ubiquitous example of mutation outside music is self-portrait filters on social media platforms such as Snapchat and Instagram, which move with the user and alter facial features. Widely available, filters have effected changes in beauty standards, as users seek filter-achieved looks in real life. In music, mutation occurs as sound is manipulated by electronics to the point that it is rendered distinct from the original. Examples include the resultant effects of any sort of timbral live processing, such as distortion and modulation effects. Reverberation, which simulates the process of sound reflected or absorbed by materials within a space, mutates a space's acoustic. Sampling practices mutate source material (ranging from "found sounds" to excerpts from produced tracks) into new musical material.

While hybridity is a feature created through coexisting elements, mutation is a process applied to acoustic sound or recorded source material. Describing mutation focuses more on the process of change and less on features of the environment in which change occurs. Two hybrid contexts with similar electronic and acoustic elements—for example, an acoustic cello with distortion as in *Industry*—might possess different mutation processes, depending on how the distortion is utilized. Mutation may be discussed in terms of the means by which it is achieved, how mutation changes the source acoustic material, the extent to which the mutated material differs from its source, and how much agency and awareness the performer possesses over the process of mutation.

In *Industry*, the mutation process is the gradual introduction and adjustment of distortion by the engineer. The cello sound becomes gritty and fuzzy, as if the cellist were gradually changing their instrumental technique. Feedback and grit become an expressive device, as distortion and amplification highlight harmonic richness not normally perceptible in an acoustic setting. Difference tones are highlighted through the distortion and equalization of the cello signal, and the cello's natural resonance is extended in the middle of the work as feedback caused by the unmuffled open strings after a loud high-register double-stop section concludes a phrase.[22] The result is an aural depiction of Gordon's vision of "a 100-foot cello made out of steel suspended from the sky, a cello the size of a football field, and, in the piece, the cello becomes a hugely distorted sound."[23]

In *NoaNoa*, infinite reverberation mutates the perceived acoustic; a more reverberant space thickens the texture surrounding solo flute gestures, particularly during passages with glissandi and noisier techniques such as flutter-tongue and air sounds. The sampled flute and vocal sounds triggered throughout the work are segmented, layered, or processed to an extent that renders them distinct from both their source material and the live flutist's sound. Sampled flute gestures sound "stitched" together from sampled individual notes, and they sound less human due to the lack of dynamic variation and abrupt changes between pitches.[24] The flutist often performs gestures with similar pitch and rhythmic material after the electronic gesture, further accentuating the differences between live and electronic elements.

Musical mutation has on occasion been genre-defining: distortion and fuzz effects began as an incidental feature of overdriven speakers and are now widespread in rock music.²⁵ The overdriven effect was emulated by stand-alone pedals, and further diversity resulted as the effect was adapted to suit other genres. Whether incidental or intentional, mutation processes are a defining feature of posthuman musical contexts and are as varied as the sounds created through them.

Aspects of Performance Practice: Research and Documentation

As the previous exploration of posthumanist concepts has demonstrated, the presence of electroacoustic elements significantly impacts performance practice. A performer may need to maintain an awareness of amplification, blend with novel sounds, or envision their instrument's sound transformed beyond that of an unamplified, unprocessed instrument. They must consider the impact of electronic elements, their role in operating the electronics and tasks entailed, and the impact of other individuals. Both *NoaNoa* and *Industry* have a rich performance history with multiple recorded examples that a performer might follow.

In newer works without such a rich history, practices might be inspired by prior experience with other works, through emulation of the approaches of peers, or through consultation of online resources. As a violinist working with electronics, many of my practices were developed through modeling musicians based in New York City, online research on platforms like YouTube, and polling via social media. Composers face new variables and options to consider with regard to orchestration, and listeners experience unprecedented ensemble configurations and timbres made possible by new trends in mixing techniques and live processing. Wider documentation of practices and contexts may help demystify practices within electroacoustic settings and facilitate the learning process for new and experienced practitioners alike.

Documentation of electronic contexts involves describing the electronic sound, the technology used to create it, how that technology is operated, and how the presence of electronics impacts the work. The impact can be described with nuance through the use of posthuman terms and concepts, and it can be addressed from several viewpoints. Discussing performance practice involves noting the actions and awareness necessary to perform effectively in a given setting, and it varies depending on the musical material and electronics used. In contexts with simple amplification as represented in Figure 8.1, a key topic for students to explore is how performers exercise agency over tone quality and dynamic level in conjunction with the musical material. Electronics also influence a listener's experience, particularly in works with a pronounced spatial component such as Pierre Boulez's *Répons* (1981–84), in which the 4X digital processor transforms and plays back the sound of performers on stage at different locations in the hall. Arguably, the most potential for discussion might lie in the possibilities electronics have opened up for composition, as new means for motivic development are created, new sounds are introduced, and new interfaces create novel ways to manipulate musical material.

Many of the aforementioned ideas may be investigated and analyzed through qualitative approaches with data collection through interviews, documentary analysis of scores and recordings, and the review and synthesis of existing discourse on the topic. However, more ephemeral features such as the process of refinement and acclimation over rehearsals and successive performances in electroacoustic settings are often overlooked. By employing a grounded theory approach in which data is methodically collected, analyzed, and used to inform further inquiry, themes that emerge may create a more nuanced representation of practices often missed.[26] Data collection, particularly for practice-oriented fields such as performance and composition, can be as simple as noting our observations as a practitioner, listener, or composer in the form of memos, and analysis would then involve coding those notes for themes to investigate during later data collection.

In my own work investigating amplified popular music, I have explored the differences between the perceived balance and timbres on stage and what is heard by the audience during a seven-show tour. I made reflective memos while listening to recordings of each show, focusing on how the sound in the hall confirmed or contrasted with my perception on stage, and these reflections influenced my later actions as a performer as well as the details I focused on as an observer. Recording in this way created a partial record of the approaches I employed to determine appropriate practices to hear and be heard, as well as appropriate settings for the electronics I used on stage. This type of documentation may act as a resource for those determining their own amplified setups.

Research projects that document posthuman musical contexts and the impact of electronics are key in building a robust body of concepts and terminology that reflect current practice. Projects incorporating the discourse of performers through interviews or self-study are underrepresented in the literature, yet they are invaluable in describing the immediate impact of electronic sound. Investigations that describe technology's impact on compositional process, and how electronic sound impacts the perception or creation of musical structure and meaning, would also be useful, particularly if many small studies systematically investigate a body of work sharing something in common, such as a composer, genre, or technology. For example, electronics used in works by Kaija Saariaho warrant further study, as they typically feature a similar one-pedal interface for performers yet result in a very different experience for the performer depending on the function of the electronics and the material for acoustic instruments. The impact of Digital Audio Workstations such as Ableton Live on music performance and composition would also be worthy of investigation. A collection of case studies of posthuman contexts such as those introduced earlier would act as a repository of practices that save interested practitioners time and help build nuance into how posthuman tropes are defined. With a large enough body of work, broader trends and predominant practices may emerge.

Conclusion: Posthumanism and Electroacoustic Music

Contemporary practices in performance, composition, and music production are in flux; the field is vast, varied, and often preserved in audio and video recording. The range of technology creating posthuman musical contexts compounds this variety in practice. Though complete representation of electroacoustic contexts seems unlikely, even partial documentation via interviews, performance and rehearsal footage, and descriptions of equipment is valuable as a source of insight not only to performers, but also to musicologists and theorists interested in how musical meaning and the perception of musical structure are impacted in electroacoustic contexts.

Student researchers of all levels can contribute meaningfully to this field through outreach to performers and composers working with electronics, who are often happy to speak about their process. Rather than isolating "right" or "wrong" practices within a context, documentation today serves practitioners by recommending equipment and interfaces and by determining practices that ensure comfort and efficiency as they work. Articulating distributed networks acknowledges the many actors and processes at play in a typical performance scenario.

Concepts such as distributed cognition, hybridity, and mutation allow for precise articulation of the variety of practices created in light of new environments and processes. Conceptual and terminological clarity is especially imperative when new technologies are introduced regularly. While today's practices may seem intuitive to practitioners, undocumented practices may be forgotten as new devices are introduced. Descriptive terminology, therefore, is key to ensuring that the complexities of today's electroacoustic contexts are not missed by future researchers.

Music incorporating electronics is increasingly common today, as the financial and logistical barriers to access continue to shrink. Free or low-cost education in music production over platforms like YouTube has also influenced how music is consumed and made. Mutation and hybridity within these more accessible settings might differ from the works discussed here and, therefore, merit further study. While access has improved, the work and experiences of women, nonbinary individuals, and people of color have been traditionally underrepresented in repertoire and discourse in electroacoustic music.[27] It is imperative that researchers incorporate the perspective of these underrepresented groups as posthuman vocabulary is applied and built further, so that the concepts and terms remain inclusive and able to describe a broad range of artists, processes, and points of view. If built inclusively, posthuman frameworks will help preserve practices and perspectives frequently overlooked in current musicological discourse.

Notes

1. I use the term "electroacoustic" to refer to any setting that blends electronic sound with acoustic sound, as it is used in Joel Chadabe, *Electric Sound: The Past and Promise of Electronic Music* (Upper Saddle River, NJ: Prentice Hall, 1997), x.
2. For a more thorough introduction to posthumanism that summarizes the concepts most fundamental here, consult Peter Mahon, *Posthumanism: A Guide for the Perplexed* (London and New York: Bloomsbury Academic, 2017), 1–24 ("Introduction: Posthumanism—A Dialogue of Sorts").
3. Elizabeth McNutt, "Performing Electroacoustic Music: A Wider View of Interactivity," *Organised Sound* 8, no. 3 (2003): 297–304; Julieanne Klein, "Live and Interactive Electronic Vocal Compositions: Trends and Techniques for the Art of Performance" (DMus thesis, McGill University, 2007).
4. Klein, "Live and Interactive Electronic Vocal Compositions," 27.
5. Mahon, *Posthumanism*, 25.
6. J. Thomas Brett, "Minds and Machines: Creativity, Technology, and the Posthuman in Electronic Musical Idioms" (PhD diss., New York University, 2006), 16.
7. N. Katherine Hayles, *How We Became Posthuman: Virtual Bodies in Cybernetics, Literature, and Informatics* (Chicago and London: University of Chicago Press, 1999), 2.
8. Hayles, *How We Became Posthuman*, 48.
9. Mahon, *Posthumanism*, 4.
10. Mahon, *Posthumanism*, 7.
11. Brett, "Minds and Machines," 16.
12. Edwin Hutchins, *Cognition in the Wild* (Cambridge, MA: The MIT Press, 1995).
13. Mahon, *Posthumanism*, 4.
14. Xenia Pestova, "Models of Interaction: Performance Strategies in Works for Piano and Live Electronics," *Journal of Music, Technology and Education* 2, nos. 2–3 (2009): 113–26.
15. George Crumb, *Black Angels: Electric String Quartet* (New York and London: C.F. Peters, 1971).
16. Ashley Bathgate, email correspondence with author, January 12, 2020.
17. Shiau-uen Ding, "Developing a Rhythmic Performance Practice in Music for Piano and Tape," *Organised Sound* 11, no. 3 (2006): 255–72.
18. Ashley Bathgate, email correspondence with author, January 12, 2020.
19. McNutt, "Performing Electroacoustic Music," 299; "Todd Reynolds playing Michael Lowenstern's Crossroads at the Stone," YouTube video, 6:15, May 26, 2011, www.youtube.com/watch?v=get3bZGICfg; Trevor New, "MYO armband – controlling sound through movement," YouTube video, 22:14, February 5, 2019, https://www.youtube.com/watch?v=PXuIaFit5K0.
20. Mari Kimura, "Creative Process and Performance Practice of Interactive Computer Music: A Performer's Tale," *Organised Sound* 8, no. 3 (2003): 289.
21. R. L. Rutsky, "Mutation, History, and Fantasy in the Posthuman," *Subject Matters: A Journal of Communication and the Self* 3, no. 2/4, no. 1 (2007): 103.
22. "Ashley Bathgate plays 'Industry' – by Michael Gordon," YouTube video, 11:58, January 7, 2015, www.youtube.com/watch?v=Tf2FcKlgQH4, 9:00–9:12.

23. "Industry," on Michael Gordon's official website, accessed January 10, 2020, https://michaelgordonmusic.com/music/industry.
24. "Kaija Saariaho: Noanoa (1992)," performed by Camilla Hoitenga, flute, YouTube video, 8:53, February 7, 2015, www.youtube.com/watch?v=0b9l-7Cwsj0, 1:24 (m. 33), 1:34 (m. 37), 1:59 (m. 45).
25. J. J. Anselmi, "Ride the Feedback: A Brief History of Guitar Distortion," *Noisey*, February 23 2017, https://noisey.vice.com/en_us/article/wn7ja9/ride-the-feedback-a-brief-history-of-guitar-distortion.
26. For an introduction to grounded theory, consult Anthony Bryant and Kathy Charmaz, *The SAGE Handbook of Grounded Theory* (London: SAGE Publications, 2007).
27. Tara Rodgers, *Pink Noises: Women on Electronic Music and Sound* (Durham, NC and London: Duke University Press, 2010), is a foundational text on women in electroacoustic music.

Selected Bibliography

Anselmi, J. J. "Ride the Feedback: A Brief History of Guitar Distortion." *Noisey*. Published February 23, 2017. https://noisey.vice.com/en_us/article/wn7ja9/ride-the-feedback-a-brief-history-of-guitar-distortion.
Auner, Joseph. "Sing It for Me: Posthuman Ventriloquism in Recent Popular Music." *Journal of the Royal Music Association* 128, no. 1 (2003): 98–122.
Auslander, Philip. *Liveness: Performance in a Mediatized Culture*. New York: Routledge, 2008.
Badmington, Neil, ed. *Posthumanism*. Houndmills, Basingstoke, Hampshire, and London: Palgrave, 2000.
Brett, J. Thomas. "Minds and Machines: Creativity, Technology, and the Posthuman in Electronic Musical Idioms." PhD diss., New York University, 2006.
Brinkmann, Svend. "Unstructured and Semi-Structured Interviewing." In *The Oxford Handbook of Qualitative Research*, edited by Patricia Leavy, 277–99. New York: Oxford University Press, 2014.
Bullock, Jamie, et al. "Live Electronics in Practice: Approaches to Training Professional Performers." *Organised Sound* 18, no. 2 (2013): 170–7.
Chadabe, Joel. *Electric Sound: The Past and Promise of Electronic Music*. Upper Saddle River, NJ: Prentice Hall, 1997.
Crumb, George. *Black Angels: Electric String Quartet*. New York and London: C.F. Peters, 1971.
Ding, Shiau-uen. "Developing a Rhythmic Performance Practice in Music for Piano and Tape." *Organised Sound* 11, no. 3 (2006): 255–72.
Gordon, Michael. "Industry." *Michael Gordon Music*. Accessed January 10, 2020. https://michaelgordonmusic.com/music/industry.
Hayles, N. Katherine. *How We Became Posthuman: Virtual Bodies in Cybernetics, Literature, and Informatics*. Chicago and London: University of Chicago Press, 1999.
Hutchins, Edwin. *Cognition in the Wild*. Cambridge, MA: The MIT Press, 1995.
Kilroy, Patti. "Posthuman Musical Contexts: Live Processing's Impact on Performance Practice in Electroacoustic Music." PhD diss., New York University, 2019.
Kimura, Mari. "Creative Process and Performance Practice of Interactive Computer Music: A Performer's Tale." *Organised Sound* 8, no. 3 (2003): 289–96.

Kimura, Mari. "Performance Practice in Computer Music." *Computer Music Journal* 19, no. 1 (1995): 64–75.

Klein, Julieanne. "Live and Interactive Electronic Vocal Compositions: Trends and Techniques for the Art of Performance." DMus thesis, McGill University, 2007.

Mahon, Peter. *Posthumanism: A Guide for the Perplexed*. London and New York: Bloomsbury Academic, 2017.

McNutt, Elizabeth. "Performing Electroacoustic Music: A Wider View of Interactivity." *Organised Sound* 8, no. 3 (2003): 297–304.

McNutt, Elizabeth. "*Pipe wrench*: A Recording of Music for Flute and Computer." DMA diss., University of California, San Diego, 2000.

Pestova, Xenia. "Models of Interaction in Works for Piano and Live Electronics." DMA diss., McGill University, 2008.

Pestova, Xenia. "Models of Interaction: Performance Strategies in Works for Piano and Live Electronics." *Journal of Music, Technology and Education* 2, nos. 2–3 (2009): 113–26.

Riikonen, Taina. "Shaken or Stirred: Virtual Reverberation Spaces and Transformative Gender Identities in Kaija Saariaho's *NoaNoa* (1992) for Flute and Electronics." *Organised Sound* 8, no. 1 (2003): 109–15.

Rodgers, Tara. *Pink Noises: Women on Electronic Music and Sound*. Durham, NC and London: Duke University Press, 2010.

Rutsky, R. L. "Mutation, History, and Fantasy in the Posthuman." *Subject Matters: A Journal of Communication and the Self* 3, no. 2/4, no. 1 (2007): 99–112.

Saariaho, Kaija. "NoaNoa." *Saariaho.org*. Accessed January 20, 2020. https://saariaho.org/works/noanoa/.

Sanden, Paul. *Liveness in Modern Music: Musicians, Technology, and the Perception of Performance*. New York: Routledge, 2013.

Yoder, Rachel. "Performance Practice of Interactive Music for Clarinet and Computer with an Examination of Five Works by American Composers." DMA diss., University of North Texas, 2010.

Additional Performances Available Online

Ensemble Intercontemporain, ensemble. "Pierre Boulez, Répons – Ensemble intercontemporain – Matthias Pintscher." YouTube video, 46:34. December 18, 2015. www.youtube.com/watch?v=OQE5TYnD58k.

Zhu Mu, cellist. "Michael Gordon: Industry (1992) – Zhu Mu | Hong Kong New Music Ensemble." YouTube video, 8:54. September 20, 2016. www.youtube.com/watch?v=PodrHUMac8w.

9 Composing by Hacking

Technology Appropriation as a Pedagogical Tool for Electronic Music

Raul Masu and Fabio Morreale

Throughout history, the development of new technologies has continually supported the creation of new instruments and music. The relationship between technological advancements and new music predates the electronic and digital ages, a prominent example being *Das Wohltemperierte Klavier* (1722) by Johann Sebastian Bach, which became possible with the invention of new temperaments. In the early twentieth century, this relationship underpinned the emergence of electronic music, the development of which was often led by composers and inventors with a need to develop new ways of realizing their musical or artistic visions. The creative act of *composing* new music indeed started coinciding—to an ever-increasing extent—with the act of *making* new technologies. In addition to unlocking access to their vision for new musical territories, some composers of the previous century regarded technology as a means of questioning the status quo by *appropriating* (i.e., improvising and adapting around technology) and *hacking* (exploring of the limits of what is possible) technologies as means for artistic innovation and as tools for user emancipation.

The origin of the do-it-yourself (DIY) movement in the late twentieth century constituted an important milestone in the development and spread of technology hacking and appropriation. DIY enthusiasts convened in *communities of makers* to disassemble, modify, repurpose, and appropriate existing technologies to understand the underlying mechanisms of these technologies and to create new art pieces and objects of design. These communities are based on open hardware and/or free software, the ethos of which follows that of the hacker movement of the 1960s, which endorsed open and hackable solutions that provided support for creative "playfulness, cleverness, and exploration."[1]

The technical and ideological continuum between early electronic music composers and the maker movement resulted in the latter rapidly penetrating the music domain and reinforcing the symbiotic relationship between the acts of composing and hacking. On the one side, open hardware and free software proved useful for musicians to create their own tools for creating music. On the other side, musicians' direct involvement in inventing new musical tools allowed them to "give back" by offering new application scenarios and setting new challenges that encouraged technology to develop further. Additionally, open-source computing offered the sociotechnical infrastructure to encourage peer-to-peer knowledge sharing among musicians, which resulted in a composer's work being easily shared and contributing to the technical and aesthetic growth of a broader community.

While this symbiotic relationship between music and technology evolved in the hacker and (some) academic communities, its expansion in mainstream contexts encountered some resistance. Many tertiary and pre-tertiary institutions indeed solely recognized electronic music as the use of proprietary music software and hardware (e.g., Logic Pro, Ableton, Max). While these products tend to be reliable and offer direct support, their qualities of being "paid for" and "closed" have a number of drawbacks. For what concerns their commercial cost, their use reinforces a socially inequitable model that grants access to creative tools on a classist basis. The consequences of these systems being closed are less obvious but equally important. First, the functionalities of these products are finite, predefined, and mostly invariable. As a consequence, the range of what is creatively possible is limited by the list of available functionalities, which end up shaping the creative process and standardizing musical outcomes. Second, these tools are impenetrable, monolithic black boxes that can be either accepted or rejected for what they are; they prevent students and musicians from looking under the hood of their technological implementations and learning about them.

We argue that an uncritical adoption of closed music technologies in the classroom has strong political and pedagogical implications. Whereas proprietary solutions carry neoliberal ideologies based on individualism and acceptance of the technological status quo, open-source solutions are focused on collective growth and knowledge sharing and embody a vision for developing critical citizens that question techno-solutionism and techno-inevitability ideals. By highlighting the benefits of *open-source solutions* and *technology hacking*, in this chapter, we propose an alternative model for electronic music teaching that is centered on user-modifiable open technologies rather than closed, proprietary solutions.

This chapter is organized in four parts. First, we present a brief overview of the development of hacker and maker cultures. Second, we analyze some early electronic music and computer music practices using the lens of appropriation and hacking. Third, we describe the case of Bela, an open-source maker platform specifically designed for musicians, detailing its emergence from the academic community and its development into a tool for electronic music teaching. In the fourth and last part, we combine discussion from the previous sections to pinpoint the pedagogical benefits of technology hacking and appropriation, and we provide guidance for electronic music instructors who may wish to develop courses aimed at stimulating students to be creators of tools and instruments rather than operating within technological environments created by others. Notably, this discussion not only is relevant for electronic music teachers but can also be of interest for musicologists, historians, theorists, and sociologists seeking to understand how DIY, hacking, and making cultures have the potential to transform contemporary and future music.

Hacker and Maker Cultures

In the late 1940s, a group of MIT students founded the Tech Model Railroad Club (TMRC), a club that was initially focused on electronic engineering but that soon turned its attention to computing.[2] When describing their activities, they used the term "hack" to describe a project that was undertaken "not solely to fulfill some constructive goal, but with some wild pleasure taken in mere involvement."[3] Central aspects of their practice were peer-to-peer learning and the free circulation of code. The term "hacking" was later extended from the computing domain to describe any creative explorations, including music. For example, Richard Stallman, the founder of the Free Software Foundation (FSF), argued that "the controversial 1950s 'musical piece' by John Cage, 4'33'', is more of a hack than a musical composition."[4]

With the advent of personal computers, the FSF collected and standardized the hacker culture with the goal of promoting personal freedom in the use of computers.[5] The movement set the basis for the further development of a *hacker culture*. In parallel, the reduction in cost and dimensions of computer hardware allowed the ideologies and objectives of this rising culture to spread from software to hardware in the so-called *maker culture*—a term that indicates a community engaged with repurposing or modifying existing materials and technologies to produce something new.[6]

Aligned with the goals of hacker culture, the political commitments of the maker culture are centered on collaboration, peer production, and the design of technologies that are open and user modifiable. Central to the success of maker communities are the diverse backgrounds and skill sets of their members, a variety that offers a fertile ground for the development of interdisciplinary skills.[7]

These ideological foundations of hacker and maker cultures underpin a desire to be involved in collaborative practices that might result in the formation of communities of practice whose members share similar interests and passions and support each other.[8] Following an intrinsic motivation to collaborate on developing common values and ideals through joint effort, people started contributing to these communities for social and political reasons (e.g., defying economies of scale, refusing the necessity of mass production, and rejecting proprietary software and private property copyrights) as well as to develop personal abilities or shared knowledge.[9] In a few cases, some communities clustered around specific open-source hardware or software platforms, the most successful examples being that of Arduino. In the musical domain, several communities emerged around free programming languages (e.g., Csound, SuperCollider, Pure Data) and open maker platforms like Bela, which is analyzed in detail in a subsequent section.

Hacking in Music

As Helen Leigh extensively described in a recent talk given at the Chaos Computer Club (CCC), the largest European association of hackers, a hacking approach to music creation can be found in many stages of electronic music history.[10] In the following paragraphs, we present an overview of historical developments of electronic music through the lens of appropriation and hacking/making. By doing so, our aim is not to provide a comprehensive account of the link between the evolution of music technology and electronic music; rather, we aim to show instances of this link to exemplify how a hacking/making approach to music technology has already successfully accompanied musical creativity and innovation for many decades. We define a first stage of development consisting of various forms of hacking, appropriation, and making that emerged in an early, predigital period. In this stage, composers worked with electric and electronic physical devices such as tape recorders, audio oscillators, noise generators, and audio filters. The end of this stage roughly coincides with the end of the past century, when building digital hardware ceased being the prerogative of large companies thanks to reductions in the cost of manufacturing and components. This shift resulted in a second stage of development, marked by the exponential growth of relatively inexpensive hardware components, which, in turn, resulted in composers and musicians building their own Digital Musical Instruments (DMIs).

Stage 1: Electronic (Twentieth Century)

In this section, we consider some milestones in the development and use of technologies for composition, which we have selected as representative of specific types of hacking or appropriation. In doing so, we highlight a distinction between technology as a compositional *tool* and as compositional *material*. In the former case, a technological invention is used to introduce new compositional techniques or sonic possibilities; in the latter case, the technological invention itself coincides with the composition.

Steve Reich's early experiments with tape recorders mostly involved the use of voice. In these early experiments, Reich developed the "phase" technique, in which two (or more) lines play the same part at a slightly different speed and whose overlapping results in a continuous and slow separation of the various voices. Reich discovered this technique by accident while working on his composition *It's Gonna Rain* (1965). The composer reported that he was playing with two different tapes when he unexpectedly obtained the phasing effect.[11] The very act of experimenting with technology (an audio recorder) in an unconventional way resulted in the development of a new compositional technique. This experimentation, which was also applied in the compositional process of *Come Out* (1966), underpinned an ontological shift for the tape recorder: from an audio recorder to a compositional tool.

A different compositional tool was created by Karlheinz Stockhausen for his piece *Kontakte* (1958–60), in which he aimed to create a spinning effect to be spatialized over four speakers. In order to obtain this effect, Stockhausen mounted a loudspeaker on a rotating platform and arranged four microphones around it, each recording a different track. By rotating the platform while the loudspeaker was reproducing the sound to be spatialized, the composer could thus record four different tracks. When playing back these tracks on four spatially distinct speakers, this configuration reproduces the original sound with a spatialized spinning effect around the audience.[12] This practice allowed Stockhausen to achieve a sonic and musical objective (the spatial spinning of sound) by appropriating—or hacking—the technological artifacts at his disposal: he combined them in a new way and changed their functionalities to create a new compositional tool.

In some cases, the relationship between hacking a technological apparatus and composing a new piece was possibly even more substantial. While Reich and Stockhausen invented techniques that were adopted in a composition, other electronic music pioneers used electronic systems as compositional material to create new instruments, the characteristics of which shaped the aesthetics of the entire piece. Emblematic of this approach is the Sonic Arts Union, a collective of musicians, performers, composers, and technologists that created new technological artifacts, whose affordances they explored in a semi-improvised context in live performance.

I Am Sitting in a Room (1969) by Alvin Lucier, a member of the Sonic Arts Union, exemplifies this approach. The composition starts with a short paragraph recorded on a tape. The recorded audio is then played back in the same room and recorded again using the same microphone. This process is repeated many times; at each new iteration, the environmental reverberation is enhanced. The resulting effect is that words are gradually transfigured into nonverbal sounds. *I Am Sitting in a Room* is representative of a process of technology appropriation that corresponds to the entire process of composition and, to a certain extent, to the piece itself. Another example from the Sonic Art Union is Gordon Mumma's *Hornpipe* (1967). When performing this piece, Mumma played a French horn and a "cybersonic console" embedded in a belt. The electronic console, which Mumma designed and developed himself, included a microphone and eight variable resonance circuits.[13] This piece blurs the edges between composition and hacking and between music and performance art. The hacking of the horn, which resulted in an "augmented" horn, using terminology typical of the NIME (New Interfaces for Musical Expression) community, corresponds with the compositional material itself.[14]

Lucier explained that in their pieces "there were no scores to follow; the scores were inherent in the circuitry."[15] The score was embedded in the instrument, which was the piece itself. This relationship between a musical piece and a technological artifact has been influential in the next stage of development with the design of novel DMIs.[16]

Stage 2: Digital (Twenty-First Century)

The interconnection between DIY and instrument design has drastically strengthened in the twenty-first century. Factors that contributed to this interconnection are not limited to advances in technology but also include the increased appreciation for hacking, subverting, and repurposing technology for sonic explorations[17] as well as the formation, at the turn of the century, of new academic and artistic communities and hubs centered on designing new musical instruments like NIME. At the first NIME conference in 2001, Perry Cook set one of the principles for designing new instruments: "Make a piece, not an instrument or controller."[18] Cook also described the process of making music and designing an instrument and developing its code as an iterative process: "new algorithms suggest new controllers [and] new controllers suggest new algorithms."[19] In a subsequent NIME volume, Norbert Schnell and Marc Battier proposed another form of instrument–composition relationship: a "composed instrument," which is a musical tool that embeds characteristics of an instrument (it can be played), a computational system (it can be programmed), and a representation (it can be written as a score and defined events).[20]

These two early NIME papers set the stage for understanding the evolving relationship among composition, performance, and digital luthiery (i.e., the design of new musical controllers and the development of their interactive behavior via software). The relationship among these three creative acts became evident in the ever-increasing overlapping of the roles of composer, performer, and designer: two recent anthologies of new musical interfaces describe several artists (Michel Waisvisz, Marije Baalman, and Jeff Snyder) for whom these roles have overlapped.[21]

This trend quickly evolved and consolidated among many NIME practitioners: a recent survey showed that four of five performers self-developed the instrument that they play.[22] On the one hand, the three roles and the actions that they represent are considered inseparable. In describing his *Auditorium*, a piece for small percussion instruments whose sound is captured by binaural microphones and then processed, Rui Penha has observed: "It was an instrument/composition. I will not use it for any other composition nor could I do the composition with a different instrument."[23] On the other hand, composers may need to develop new instruments to make their artistic vision possible. This was the case, for instance, with Nicole Carroll, who has stated that her instrument "addresses a need that no other mass-produced instrument/controller does," a need that Mercedes Blasco has described as being driven by a "frustration derived from commercially available hardware."[24]

These comments speak to the centrality of instrument design, craft, and hacking for a new generation of electronic musicians and music students. When describing the importance of making DMIs, Joe Cantrell identified the very act of making as being a means to its own end: "the result of the project is less important than the act of doing it."[25] This act is one that the psychologist Mihaly Csikszentmihalyi would define as an "autotelic" experience.[26] The focus of artistic practice for DMI composers/designers, in other words, is creation, exploration, and experimentation itself. As discussed by Cantrell, the success of a hacked DMI should not be measured in terms of audience experience or techno-scientific advancements; instead, the more or less tacit goal of instrument hacking is "to promote and explore a communal egalitarian embrace of trial and error and an embodied focus on technical and artistic learning."[27]

Given the NIME community's stance of self-designing the instrument that one will compose for—and/or perform with—it is not surprising that the main efforts to promote a maker attitude among musicians come from members of the NIME community, who have developed a number of open-source platforms for creating musical instruments—the most notable examples being Satellite CCRMA[28] and Bela. In the remainder of the chapter, we introduce Bela and discuss the advantages of using open hardware and free software in electronic music pedagogy.

Open Hardware in the Classroom

Bela is a custom cape (expansion board) for the single-board computer BeagleBone Black.[29] Both Bela's hardware and software are open source. It was initially developed in 2014 by Zappi and McPherson for the D-Box, a self-contained instrument designed to be hacked by the performer using techniques borrowed from circuit bending.[30] Zappi and McPherson needed a self-contained platform (i.e., one that does not need to be connected to a laptop) for ultra-low-latency audio and sensor processing.[31] Soon after, the platform started being adopted for teaching signal processing courses at Queen Mary University of London. The platform was then promoted at several hackathons, and the number of users exponentially grew in 2016 following a successful Kickstarter campaign in which the platform was made available to the general public.[32] Since then, the adoption of Bela has been steadily growing among artists and musicians, who have been developing dozens of new self-contained musical instruments and installations.

In parallel, Bela has continued to serve as a teaching support tool. It is currently used in several universities and tertiary institutions around the world. Given its highly customizable features, the board is used as a teaching support tool to deliver a variety of courses to students in music, computer science, new media, and digital signal processing. We interviewed Robert Jack, one of the founding members of Bela, who has considerable experience in delivering Bela workshops to students from different backgrounds. In the past two years, Jack has been teaching Bela at Aalto University (Helsinki, Finland) as part of the Masters course "Physical Interaction Design" run by Koray Tahiroğlu. The course is normally attended by students from different pathways, but mostly from the "Sound and New Media" and "Game Design" programs. The course is project based and aimed at preparing students to build their own instruments or installations, with a focus on learning how to design and program the interaction between people and digital devices.

As part of this course, the students are also taught how to build their own sensors. For instance, by using cheap and widely available materials like card and velostat, they are able to create a simple circuit that works like a pressure sensor. This craft exercise allows students to create a pressure sensor of any shape and material (e.g., big sensors, sensors that wrap around simple or complex surfaces). In a similar way, students can also create their own buttons by means of simply opening/closing connections or, by using Trill Craft—a newly developed thirty-channel breakout board—they can build their own touch interfaces out of anything conductive. The possibility offered to students to build their own sensors is particularly important for the topic of this chapter insofar as it enables an extra level of technological understanding and control. Following a direction opposite to that of closed software and hardware products, this solution thus moves the technology closer to the learner. As elaborated by Jack, Bela's computational power is the equivalent of what was available in commercial smartphones only a few years ago. The difference is that these computing resources are dedicated to the purpose of building our own creations: as Jack has argued, "It's about taking back control of the technology which surrounds us."

Although the students in his course are not exclusively music students, Jack suggests that the benefits he describes can be applied to a class of electronic music students. The potential of Bela to be used by music students is currently being explored at the Amsterdam Conservatory of Music, which is offering Bela classes to students in the Masters course "Live Electronics," and at the School of Music at the University of Auckland in the Bachelor of Music course "Musical Interface Design."[33]

Free Software Freedoms and Electronic Music Teaching

In this section, we discuss how the hacking approach that we described in the previous section cannot be fully supported with closed proprietary solutions.

When closed software is used in electronic music classes, students mostly learn specific and discrete software functionalities (e.g., adding reverb to a track) and processes (e.g., most Max objects cannot be accessed, and users, therefore, have no way of knowing their functioning). In this case, students cannot look under the hood and learn—and hack—the code. Their creative exploration is thus bound by these functionalities, through which the software de facto exercises control over what users are allowed or not allowed to do. By contrast, when electronic music teaching is structured around hacking and appropriation of open-source technology, students learn to see their musical practice as an explorative, open-ended activity. In this context, it is useful to recall the FSF's manifesto in which they identified the essential freedoms that software is required to meet in order to be considered free.[34] These freedoms can offer a starting point to support the continuation of the playful exploration that has character- ized music hacking movements since the 1950s:

> Freedom 1: *The freedom to run the program as you wish, for any purpose.* When teaching electronic music, practices of technol- ogy appropriation should be included. These practices are useful to develop an idiosyncratic relationship with technology, whose ontology and functionalities can be constantly reinvented by students. Notably, this process also favors the development of a critical approach to technology, which allows students to make informed decisions concerning the extent to which they might use computing solutions as they gain awareness of the role that tech- nology plays in their practice.
>
> Freedom 2. *The freedom to study how the program works and change it so it does your computing as you wish.* This freedom is composed of two parts—*studying* and *changing*—both relevant in the context of computer music pedagogy. With respect to the studying part, a thorough understanding of the code and the underlying algorithms that are used in music and sound comput- ing is central to the profile of contemporary electronic musicians, as it allows them to learn precisely how these algorithms work. This knowledge is not bound to any specific software but can be easily transferred when learning new platforms and programming languages. With respect to the changing part, once the code has been learned students can tweak it to their liking. The ability to modify open-source code thus becomes necessary to meet each

individual's artistic needs and to allow composers to use computers to the extent that is needed, rather than being limited and influenced by the constraints embedded in all closed software solutions.

Freedom 3. *The freedom to redistribute copies so you can help others* and Freedom 4: *The freedom to distribute copies of your modified versions to others*. The benefits of embedding these two freedoms in an electronic music classroom are related to the collaborative aspects of community building and peer-to-peer sharing. Both aspects are central to developing interdisciplinary skills. However, teachers should be mindful to educate students that the benefits of collaboration are not limited to a growth of the self; rather, they extend to the broader community. Nicholas Rowe has recently offered a note of warning, observing that tertiary educators' attitudes toward developing collaboration in their students are prompting them "towards an increasingly narrow, neoliberal mindset that simply seeks to exploit collaboration for private advantage."[35]

Practical Suggestions

To conclude this chapter, we propose some practical suggestions for electronic music teachers to consider when developing hacking-based courses.

1) Design coursework activities aimed at developing critical thinking concerning the complex relationship between technological and musical choices and developing the musically meaningful use of technology. Open-source technology is not a take-it-or-leave-it closed box; rather, it allows a modular approach and virtually infinite customization. Developing the ability to critically reflect on the implications and relationships between technology and music, students will form attitudes that will enable them to critically reflect on the implications of using technology in general.

2) Teach students how to appropriate existing tools and instruments or create completely new ones. In addition to the technical skills embedded in this objective, students should learn to use computers and technologies to the extent that is required by their compositional point of view rather than developing their practice on the basis of what is available, thus limiting it to what is offered by closed software that is inescapably constrained. Notably, the creation of new tools will, in turn, contribute to the development of new technologies.

3) Teach students to develop a compositional use of technology by learning to create composed instruments—that is, instruments that embed the aesthetic characteristics of a musical piece. By developing

their own instruments with their own aesthetics, students can join the ongoing debate over new musical instruments and be involved in shaping the future of music technology.

4) Support students in developing collaborative and sharing attitudes toward computer music practice. It is crucial that instructors stress the importance of the intrinsic motivations to collaborate, such as the development of social capital to foster common values through joint effort. Students will then learn to resist neoliberal ideologies that are infiltrating many forms of (music) technologies. By learning to work with free software and open hardware, they will be exposed to peer-to-peer communities that approach computing from an alternative perspective, defying economies of scale, refusing the necessity of mass production, and rejecting proprietary software and private property copyrights.

5) We also highlight some musicological implications of this proposed approach. The musicologist Magnusson has recently called for a *musicology of code*, one that looks "under the hood and read[s] the algorithmic composition of the piece in the form of code."[36] Magnusson continues:

> [We] would need to read the code and listen to variations of its output. Since reading scores is a common practice in musicology, this should be a natural extension of the musicologist's skill set in the modern age. However, this puts a pressure on composers to make the code accessible.[37]

Our suggested approach has a twofold beneficial effect on this perspective. From a technical point of view, it offers students the tools and skills they need to be familiar with programming and hacking hardware and software. From a socio-political side, it educates musicians on the importance of knowledge sharing, specifically to avoid the "pressure" mentioned by Magnusson.

6) From an organological perspective, code sharing offers a systematic and quantitative methodology to classify music. By analyzing code, organologists will be able to identify interconnections among digital instruments, algorithmic compositions, and—in general—technologies for music composition and performance.[38]

Notes

1. On the hacker movement, see Steven Levy, *Hackers: Heroes of the Computer Revolution* (Garden City, NY: Anchor Press/Doubleday, 1984) and Richard Stallman, "On Hacking," accessed February 24, 2020, https://stallman.org/articles/on-hacking.html.
2. Levy, *Hackers*, 12–26.
3. Levy, *Hackers*, 10.

4. Stallman, "On Hacking"; the "free" in "Free Software Foundation" stands for *freedon* rather than *free of charge.*
5. See the organization's website at https://fsf.org.
6. Silvia Lindtner, Shaowen Bardzell, and Jeffrey Bardzell, "Reconstituting the Utopian Vision of Making: HCI after Technosolutionism," *Proceedings of the 2016 CHI Conference on Human Factors in Computing Systems,* CHI '16, Association for Computing Machinery, San Jose, CA, 2016, 1390–402.
7. Stacey Kuznetsov and Eric Paulos, "Rise of the Expert Amateur: DIY Projects, Communities, and Cultures," *Proceedings of the 6th Nordic Conference on Human-Computer Interaction: Extending Boundaries,* NordiCHI '10, Association for Computing Machinery, Reykjavik, Iceland, 2010, 295–304.
8. Etienne Wenger, *Communities of Practice: Learning, Meaning, and Identity* (Cambridge: Cambridge University Press, 1999).
9. More information on people's motivation to collaborate can be found in Shin-Yuan Hung et al., "The Influence of Intrinsic and Extrinsic Motivation on Individuals' Knowledge Sharing Behavior," *International Journal of Human-Computer Studies* 69, no. 6 (2011): 415–27. A study of the motivations underlying participation in open source communities is found in Rishab A. Ghosh et al., *Free/Libre and Open Source Software: Survey and Study* (Deliverable report), International Institute of Infonomics, University of Maastricht, The Netherlands, 2002.
10. Helen Leigh, "Hackers & Makers Changing Music Technology," accessed August 10, 2020, https://media.ccc.de/v/36c3-10548-hackers_makers_chang ing_music_technology.
11. Steve Reich, *Writings on Music, 1965–2000* (Oxford and New York: Oxford University Press, 2002), 20–1.
12. Thom Holmes, *Electronic and Experimental Music: Technology, Music, and Culture,* 6th ed. (New York and London: Routledge, 2020), 247.
13. Alvin Lucier, *Music 109: Notes on Experimental Music* (Middletown, CT: Wesleyan University Press, 2012), 74–5.
14. Dan Newton and Mark T. Marshall, "Examining How Musicians Create Augmented Musical Instruments," *Proceedings of the International Conference on New Interfaces for Musical Expression,* Zenodo, 2011, 155–60.
15. Alvin Lucier, "Origins of a Form: Acoustical Exploration, Science and Incessancy," *Leonardo Music Journal* 8 (1998): 6.
16. Thor Magnusson, *Sonic Writing: Technologies of Material, Symbolic, and Signal Inscriptions* (New York and London: Bloomsbury Academic, 2019).
17. Nicolas Collins, *Handmade Electronic Music: The Art of Hardware Hacking,* 3rd ed. (New York: Routledge, 2020).
18. Perry Cook, "2001: Principles for Designing Computer Music Controllers," in *A NIME Reader: Fifteen Years of New Interfaces for Musical Expression,* ed. Alexander Refsum Jensenius and Michael J. Lyons (Cham, Switzerland: Springer, 2017), 1–13.
19. Cook, "2001: Principles for Designing Computer Music Controllers," 1–13.
20. Norbert Schnell and Marc Battier, "Introducing Composed Instruments, Technical and Musicological Implications," *Proceedings of the International Conference on New Interfaces for Musical Expression,* Zenodo, 2002, 156–60.
21. Till Bovermann et al., eds., *Musical Instruments in the 21st Century: Identities, Configurations, Practices* (Singapore: Springer Singapore, 2017) and Jensenius and Lyons, *A NIME Reader,* 127–36, 181–206, and 225–42.
22. Fabio Morreale, Andrew P. McPherson, and Marcelo Wanderley, "NIME Identity from the Performer's Perspective," *Proceedings of the International Conference on New Interfaces for Musical Expression,* Zenodo, 2018, 168–73.

23. Morreale, McPherson, and Wanderley, "NIME Identity from the Performer's Perspective," 171.
24. Morreale, McPherson, and Wanderley, "NIME Identity from the Performer's Perspective," 171.
25. Joe Cantrell, "Designing Intent: Defining Critical Meaning for NIME Practitioners," *Proceedings of the International Conference on New Interfaces for Musical Expression*, Zenodo, 2017, 169–73.
26. On autotelic experiences, see Mihaly Csikszentmihalyi, *Flow: The Psychology of Optimal Experience* (New York: Harper & Row, 1990).
27. Cantrell, "Designing Intent," 171.
28. Edgar Berdahl and Wendy Ju, "2011: Satellite CCRMA: A Musical Interaction and Sound Synthesis Platform," in Jensenius and Lyons, *A NIME Reader*, 373–89.
29. See the website https://bela.io; for more information on Bela, consult Giulio Moro et al., "Making High-Performance Embedded Instruments with Bela and Pure Data," *Proceedings of the International Conference on Live Interfaces*, 2016, https://www.eecs.qmul.ac.uk/~andrewm/moro_icli2016.pdf.
30. Victor Zappi and Andrew McPherson, "Design and Use of a Hackable Digital Instrument," *Proceedings of the International Conference on Live Interfaces*, 2014, https://www.eecs.qmul.ac.uk/~andrewm/zappi_icli14.pdf.
31. Andrew P. McPherson and Victor Zappi, "An Environment for Submillisecond-Latency Audio and Sensor Processing on BeagleBone Black," Audio Engineering Society Convention 138, Audio Engineering Society, 2015, https://www.eecs.qmul.ac.uk/~andrewm/mcpherson_aes2015.pdf.
32. Fabio Morreale et al., "Building a Maker Community around an Open Hardware Platform," *Proceedings of the 2017 CHI Conference on Human Factors in Computing Systems*, CHI '17, Association for Computing Machinery, Denver, CO, 2017, 6948–59.
33. "Live Electronics at the Conservatorium van Amsterdam with Bela Mini," accessed August 10, 2020, https://blog.bela.io/2018/11/18/bela-conservatorium-van-amsterdam/.
34. "What Is Free Software?," accessed August 10, 2020, www.gnu.org/philosophy/free-sw.en.html.
35. Nicholas Rowe, "The Great Neoliberal Hijack of Collaboration: A Critical History of Group-Based Learning in Tertiary Education," *Higher Education Research & Development* 39, no. 4 (2020): 10.
36. Magnusson, *Sonic Writing*, 115.
37. Magnusson, *Sonic Writing*, 123.
38. The first author wishes to thank Mauro Graziani, whose mentorship has played a fundamental role in his development of a critical view of music technology. Acknowledgment is also made to ARDITI—Agência Regional para o Desenvolvimento e Tecnologia under the scope of the Project M1420–09-5369-FSE-000002—PhD Studentship, and to the University of Auckland (Faculty of Creative Arts and Industries FRDF grant 3719326) for funding this research.

Selected Bibliography

Berdahl, Edgar, and Wendy Ju. "2011: Satellite CCRMA: A Musical Interaction and Sound Synthesis Platform." In Jensenius and Lyons, *A NIME Reader*, 373–89.
Bovermann, Till, Alberto de Campo, Hauke Egermann, Sarah-Indriyati Hardjowirogo, and Stefan Weinzierl, eds. *Musical Instruments in the 21st Century: Identities, Configurations, Practices*. Singapore: Springer Singapore, 2017.

Cantrell, Joe. "Designing Intent: Defining Critical Meaning for NIME Practitioners." In *Proceedings of the International Conference on New Interfaces for Musical Expression*, 169–73, Zenodo, 2017.

Collins, Nicolas. *Handmade Electronic Music: The Art of Hardware Hacking.* 3rd ed. New York: Routledge, 2020.

Cook, Perry. "2001: Principles for Designing Computer Music Controllers." In Jensenius and Lyons, *A NIME Reader*, 1–13.

Czikszentmihalyi, Mihaly. *Flow: The Psychology of Optimal Experience.* New York: Harper & Row, 1990.

Dix, Alan. "Designing for Appropriation." *Proceedings of the 21st British HCI Group Annual Conference on People and Computers: HCI . . . But Not as We Know It, vol. 2, 27–30*, BCS Learning & Development Ltd, Swindon, UK, 2007.

Ghosh, Rishab A., Ruediger Glott, Bernhard Krieger, and Gregorio Robles. *Free/Libre and Open Source Software: Survey and Study.* Deliverable report. International Institute of Infonomics, University of Maastricht, The Netherlands, 2002.

Groth, Sanne Krogh. "Provoking, Disturbing, Hacking: Media Archaeology as a Framework for the Understanding of Contemporary DIY Composers' Instruments and Ideas." *Organised Sound* 18, no. 3 (2013): 266–73.

Holmes, Thom. *Electronic and Experimental Music: Technology, Music, and Culture.* 6th ed. New York and London: Routledge, 2020.

Hughes, Alayna. "Maker Music: Incorporating the Maker and Hacker Community Into Music Technology Education." *Journal of Music, Technology and Education* 11, no. 3 (2018): 287–300.

Hung, Shin-Yuan, Alexandra Durcikova, Hui-Min Lai, and Wan-Mei Lin. "The Influence of Intrinsic and Extrinsic Motivation on Individuals' Knowledge Sharing Behavior." *International Journal of Human-Computer Studies* 69, no. 6 (2011): 415–27.

Jensenius, Alexander Refsum, and Michael J. Lyons, eds. *A NIME Reader: Fifteen Years of New Interfaces for Musical Expression.* Cham, Switzerland: Springer, 2017.

Kuznetsov, Stacey, and Eric Paulos. "Rise of the Expert Amateur: DIY Projects, Communities, and Cultures." *Proceedings of the 6th Nordic Conference on Human-Computer Interaction: Extending Boundaries*, NordiCHI '10, 295–304, Association for Computing Machinery, Reykjavik, 2010.

Levy, Steven. *Hackers: Heroes of the Computer Revolution.* Garden City, NY: Anchor Press/Doubleday, 1984.

Lindtner, Silvia, Shaowen Bardzell, and Jeffrey Bardzell. "Reconstituting the Utopian Vision of Making: HCI after Technosolutionism." *Proceedings of the 2016 CHI Conference on Human Factors in Computing Systems*, CHI '16, 1390–1402, Association for Computing Machinery, San Jose, CA, 2016.

Lucier, Alvin. *Music 109: Notes on Experimental Music.* Middletown, CT: Wesleyan University Press, 2012.

Lucier, Alvin. "Origins of a Form: Acoustical Exploration, Science and Incessancy." *Leonardo Music Journal* 8 (1998): 5–11.

Magnusson, Thor. *Sonic Writing: Technologies of Material, Symbolic, and Signal Inscriptions.* New York and London: Bloomsbury Academic, 2019.

McPherson, Andrew P., and Victor Zappi. "An Environment for Submillisecond-Latency Audio and Sensor Processing on BeagleBone Black." *Audio Engineering Society Convention*, 138 (Audio Engineering Society), 2015. https://www.eecs.qmul.ac.uk/~andrewm/mcpherson_aes2015.pdf.

Moro, Giulio, Astrid Bin, Robert H. Jack, Christian Heinrichs, and Andrew P. McPherson. "Making High-Performance Embedded Instruments with Bela and Pure Data." *Proceedings of the International Conference on Live Interfaces*, 2016. https://www.eecs.qmul.ac.uk/~andrewm/moro_icli2016.pdf.

Morreale, Fabio, Andrew P. McPherson, and Marcelo Wanderley. "NIME Identity from the Performer's Perspective." *Proceedings of the International Conference on New Interfaces for Musical Expression*, 168–73, Zenodo, 2018.

Morreale, Fabio, Giulio Moro, Alan Chamberlain, Steve Benford, and Andrew P. McPherson. "Building a Maker Community Around an Open Hardware Platform." *Proceedings of the 2017 CHI Conference on Human Factors in Computing Systems*, CHI '17, 6948–59, Association for Computing Machinery, Denver, CO, 2017.

Newton, Dan, and Mark T. Marshall. "Examining How Musicians Create Augmented Musical Instruments." *Proceedings of the International Conference on New Interfaces for Musical Expression*, 155–60, Zenodo, 2011.

Reich, Steve. *Writings on Music, 1965–2000*. Oxford and New York: Oxford University Press, 2002.

Rowe, Nicholas. "The Great Neoliberal Hijack of Collaboration: A Critical History of Group-Based Learning in Tertiary Education." *Higher Education Research & Development* 39, no. 4 (2020): 1–14.

Schnell, Norbert, and Marc Battier. "Introducing Composed Instruments, Technical and Musicological Implications." *Proceedings of the International Conference on New Interfaces for Musical Expression*, 156–60, Zenodo, 2002.

Tomás, Enrique, and Martin Kaltenbrunner. "Tangible Scores: Shaping the Inherent Instrument Score." *Proceedings of the International Conference on New Interfaces for Musical Expression*, 609–14, Zenodo, 2014.

Wenger, Etienne. *Communities of Practice: Learning, Meaning, and Identity*. Cambridge: Cambridge University Press, 1999.

Zappi, Victor, and Andrew McPherson. "Design and Use of a Hackable Digital Instrument." *Proceedings of the International Conference on Live Interfaces*, 2014. https://www.eecs.qmul.ac.uk/~andrewm/zappi_icli14.pdf.

10 Listening to and Sampling the Land

On the Decolonization of Electronic Music Pedagogy

Kate Galloway

There are inherent challenges and strategies involved in teaching extractive electronic music—including practices that sample the nonhuman soundscape such as soundscape composition, sound art, and video game sound—in an era of perpetual ecological violence and catastrophe, institutionalized climate change denial, and ongoing settler-colonial destruction and extraction of traditional Indigenous lands. By making analytical and descriptive strategies for electronic music more inclusive by embracing both settler-descendant and Indigenous approaches, we diversify accounts of who is working in electronic music and how they approach compositional resources that are connected to specific environments and nonhuman actors. In this essay, I sketch out the challenges and strategies involved in destabilizing narratives and soundscapes of colonialism in North American electronic music. I use these strategies as a mode of diversifying electronic music histories and pedagogy beyond categories such as gender to include Indigenous perspectives and how they inform our creative use and analysis of source materials that have their own agency and sonic lives prior to remediation. Informed by scholars theorizing Indigenous modernities—where tradition and contemporary practices are complexly interwoven to articulate a continuum between past and present in the expressive arts—I argue for the adoption of modes of electronic music analysis and pedagogy that listen to the timbres of sampled sonic fragments of place from settler-listener and Indigenous-listener perspectives. When we select case studies for inclusion in how we convey electronic music history, it is essential that we address issues of unacknowledged borrowing and the extraction of field recordings from culturally significant lands, particularly in genres that focus on the timbre and texture of sampled materials.

My pedagogical approach to teaching electronic music within the context of courses in the areas of musicology, ethnomusicology, and sound studies places the soundscape compositions of Hildegard Westerkamp, some of which use field recordings of unceded lands in Vancouver, in dialogue with the electronic music of Indigenous composer-performers, drawing primarily from the work of Raven Chacon, including his collaborations as a part of the Native American interdisciplinary arts collective "Postcommodity." German-Canadian settler-immigrant composer, radio artist, and sound ecologist Hildegard Westerkamp's approach to soundscape composition highlights processes of sonic witnessing and explores the political and musical potential of remediated field recordings. In her soundscape compositions and sonic practice for radio broadcast, Westerkamp has taken a very specific approach to the medium as a conveyor of environmental sounds by listening to, recording, playing back, and contextualizing local soundscapes. Through her work with the World Soundscape Project, Westerkamp developed a nuanced understanding of the soundscape, and through community radio, she organized and broadcast her field recordings in ways that "listened to" and would "speak back" to the community using "the sounds of its own making."[1]

Raven Chacon is a composer, performer of experimental noise music, and installation artist from Fort Defiance, Navajo Nation, and is based in Albuquerque, New Mexico, and Toronto, Ontario. From 2009 to 2018, he was a member of the Native American multidisciplinary artist collective Postcommodity, composed at different times of Chacon (Navajo), Cristóbal Martínez (mestizo), Kade L. Twist (Cherokee), Steven Yazzie (Laguna/Navajo), and Nathan Young (Delaware/Kiowa/Pawnee), who are based in different cities throughout New Mexico and Arizona. Founded in 2007, Postcommodity works to advance Indigenous cultural self-determination and decolonization within the global climate of instability, ethnocentric violence, and neo-liberalism. These politics resonate through Chacon's solo work as well. A student of James Tenney, Wadada Leo Smith, Morton Subotnick, and Michael Pisaro, among others, Chacon's work in electronic music explores the sonic potential of do-it-yourself (DIY) electronic instruments and handmade electronic sound.

To decolonize electronic music is to shift the listening perspective and center Indigenous voices and ways of being-in-the-world, while also subverting systems of power and creating spaces and opportunity for Indigenous communities to tell their stories, convey their expressive culture, and participate in self-determination. As Dylan Robinson, a xwélméxw (Stó:lō) scholar of Indigenous sound, public art, activism, and affect, explains,

> a sovereign listening may hear differently the soundscape of the territory we are from as a soundscape of subsistence (hunting) rather than one of leisure (with pleasant birdsong and quiet nature), while a sovereign sense of touch for Indigenous material culture (for instance a raven rattle) might be understood as intercorporeal (that is, between human and other-than-human relations) and interrelational rather than as a singular touch upon a nonacting object.[2]

In order to decolonize electronic music production, reception, and pedagogy, including how we listen to, compose with, and play with diverse kinds of electronic music, we must create the necessary physical, collaborative, and creative spaces for Indigenous voices and systems of representation. Electronic music that incorporates soundscape samples can do more than simply avoid extractive technological processes and stereotypical soundscape representations. To address this problem in electronic music, as scholars and pedagogues, it is necessary to engage students in dialogue that addresses the sources, politics, and identities that soundscape samples reference and amplify or erase and silence.

The inclusion of Indigenous knowledge systems in the ways we write and unravel the histories of electronic music is one entry point into the decolonization and diversification of electronic music histories and compositional lineages. In his solo work and pan-Indigenous cross-disciplinary collaborations, Chacon creates experiences rooted in human–nonhuman relationships, traditional storytelling, and transmissions of expressive culture that are similarly rooted in collaborative relationships that value stewardship, generosity, and reciprocity. Technology is not inherently in conflict with tradition and storytelling protocols. As ethnomusicologist Thomas Hilder has explained, diverse technologies such as platforms for digital communication, video games, electronic music, and sound art have been adopted by Indigenous makers "to assist in cultural revival, repatriation, and transmission—processes which have helped to 'decolonize' earlier media spaces and practices."[3] In *Indians in Unexpected Places*, Philip J. Deloria writes that the custom of imagining Indigenous peoples in terms of "primitivism, technological incompetence, physical distance, and cultural difference" has remained "familiar currency in contemporary dealings with Native people."[4] Redressing this conventional narrative, Deloria describes Indigenous peoples doing things—singing opera, driving cars, acting in Hollywood—that conflict with the expectations of non-Indigenous settlers.

When I present Indigenous electronic music in my teaching and research, I avoid framing the work and ideas of these artists as electronic music that pushes against new music norms, instead emphasizing that their approach to sound, technology, and music-making originates from a different cultural perspective and worldview. If we want to diversify the music history narratives constructed and conveyed in the classroom, this includes presenting a wide range of approaches to musicking in a global context.[5] Chacon explains,

> Everything I do I consider music. The way I define music would be, finding instances of beauty to align up with other instances of beauty. Sometimes those other instances are already happening in nature. It is just a matter of organizing or creating new beauty to superimpose on top of that.[6]

When Chacon speaks of the significance of sound in his work and everyday life, he is approaching sound with an Indigenous-specific perspective. He notes, "As we always say, sound is such a big part of everyday life, and yet it is often neglected. I think indigenous people are more conscious of how sound is used in everyday life."[7] Framed as a form of Indigenous Futurism, electronic music produced by Indigenous composer-performers focuses on issues of self-determination, subverting stereotypes, and approaching performance, technology, and music using a lens informed by Indigenous knowledge production and aesthetics.[8]

Grace Dillon (Bay Mills-Garden River Ojibwe) first established and explored the term "Indigenous Futurism" in her 2012 book *Walking the Clouds*, a collection of science fiction stories by Indigenous authors.[9] Indigenous peoples and their expressive culture are so often viewed as either vanishing or existing in the past. They are not positioned as an active and vibrant presence in and contributor to contemporary society and cultural life. Through Indigenous Futurism, as Suzanne Fricke observes, artists

> have addressed a range of difficult topics, including the long impact of colonization, institutional racism, destruction of the environment, and genocide. While many of these artists work in historic media such as painting, drawing, beadwork, and photography, the field encourages artists to explore new media including digital art, virtual reality, and websites.[10]

Adapting concepts from Afrofuturism to speak to the needs and experiences of global Indigenous peoples, often layering images, ideas, narratives, or sounds from popular culture and everyday life with specific Indigenous aesthetics, ideas, materials, and content, "Indigenous Futurisms offer new ways of reading our own ancient natures."[11] Indigenous Futurisms, as Dillon notes, "are not the product of a victimized people's wishful amelioration of their past, but instead a continuation of a spiritual and cultural path that remains unbroken by genocide and war."[12] This project involves Indigenous representation in futurist genres, seeing Indigenous peoples in science and science fiction, and hearing Indigenous voices and aesthetics in electronic music. Expressions of Indigenous modernity, manifested through activist play, design, code, art, and sound, indigenize cultural objects and experiences through creative acts of remaking. Indigenization is the process of making something, like sound art, video games, and electronic music, among other cultural forms, but altering it to make it fit into Indigenous culture and contribute to the needs of the Indigenous community. Often, these are objects, spaces, genres, and cultural experiences that are not typically regarded as spaces and media of Indigenous expression, aesthetics, participation, and worldviews.[13]

Westerkamp and Soundscape Composition: *Streetmusic* and *Lighthouse Park Soundwalk*

To introduce my students to soundscape composition, I play an excerpt of Westerkamp's *Streetmusic* (1982) and ask them to make an inventory of sounds as they listen and consider the position of the field recorder in relation to these sound sources. Some of the sound sources they list with great accuracy include the honking of car horns, the chatter of conversation, the squeal of vehicle wheels, and the music of buskers performing on the street corner, yet they always perceive Westerkamp's microphone as fixed and grounded on the street. They imagine her standing still, listening to the city move and buzz around her. They are surprised to hear that in *Streetmusic*, Westerkamp extends her recording equipment into the local community—literally dangling her microphone from the radio studio window down into the streets—listening to, exploring, collecting, celebrating, and (re)circulating the musical life and musicality of the city.[14] As a member of the World Soundscape Project, in her own creative practice and radiowork for Vancouver Co-op Radio,[15] and as the founder of the Vancouver Soundwalk Collective, Westerkamp ventured into the Greater Vancouver region with a tape recorder and stereo microphone in-hand, recording natural and urban community sounds: the snowfall in the mountains at the edge of North Vancouver, the shopping malls, parks, factories, and iconic street corners and communities, including the airport flight path.

Westerkamp first developed soundwalking as a research-creation methodology and community outreach through sound while she was engaged in research with the World Soundscape Project in the late 1960s to the early 1970s, and she further refined the practice throughout her career.[16] Westerkamp provides a purposefully broad definition of soundwalking, referring to the process as "any excursion whose main purpose is listening to the environment. It is exposing our ears to every sound around us no matter where we are."[17] Andra McCartney further defines soundwalking as a "creative and research practice that involves listening and sometimes recording while moving through a place at a walking pace. It is concerned with the relationship between sound-walkers and their surrounding sonic environment."[18] McCartney highlights in her own soundwalking practice an emphasis on "slowness, human movement and a focus on particular places [that] brings attention to the presence of the soundwalkers and their ways of interaction in that place."[19] Slowness is a measured, embodied listening pace that McCartney has observed in both Westerkamp's practice and her own.

Westerkamp's creative and community practice with sound is unified by her use of community sounds for members of those communities to listen back and sonically identify with place. Describing her weekly program *Soundwalking*, on Vancouver Co-op Radio in the late 1970s, for example, Westerkamp has remarked that she "brought community soundscapes into listeners' homes" and "simultaneously extended listeners' ears into the soundscape of the community."[20] The sonic content of Westerkamp's weekly programming is presented to listeners from her own point of audition via her microphone and the recording choices she makes as a recordist. "Radio that listens," Westerkamp explains,

> is about the recordist's position and perspective, the physical, psychological, political and cultural stance shaping the choices when recording. My choices are influenced by an understanding of the sonic environment as an intimate reflection of the social, technological and natural conditions of the area.[21]

The same is true for her soundscape compositions. In these works, Westerkamp manipulates and arranges recordings that she made while soundwalking and other forms of field recordings to compose a sonic narrative that conveys her embodied experience of a specific location. These are most often actual-world places—the places where she collected her recordings. Even when she is not composing, Westerkamp organizes and leads community soundwalks (or conducts soundwalks on her own) that are geared toward retuning residents' ears to the places where they live so that they may better understand their dynamic surroundings and come to know places through sound.

Her sonic practice is defined by her use of a variety of recording techniques to frame and re-present the sonic environment to listeners. These techniques include recorded soundwalks and mobile recording, stationary recording, the searching microphone, and close-miking. Westerkamp's "radio that listens" listens to different sounds and records them with a different sound politics in comparison to the choices and sounds that may be made by another recordist exploring similar places. Westerkamp foregrounds her environmental and pedagogical politics, articulating that she uses her compositions, installations, and modes of transmission (e.g., radio) to raise awareness of the present state of the soundscape and make listeners and soundmakers aware of their social and sonic responsibility as sounding bodies in the soundscape. Westerkamp is also conscious of her own social and sonic responsibility as a curator and composer of soundwalks and soundscape compositions, yet there are gaps in her perspective and land knowledge.[22]

Westerkamp composed *Lighthouse Park Soundwalk* using field recordings made while soundwalking through Lighthouse Park, which is located near a residential area in West Vancouver across the bay from downtown Vancouver. A popular tourist attraction and recognized in 1994 as a National Historic Site of Canada, Lighthouse Park was founded on ancestral Indigenous lands and occupies a significant place in the lives of

Vancouver residents and tourists, whether they visit and listen in real life or through Westerkamp's soundscape composition.

This work is one of many Westerkamp produced for her radio program *Soundwalking*. On these experimental radio programs, Westerkamp was concerned with listening to the city from multiple perspectives, yet her recordings were primarily made from sound-recording equipment that she held, moved with, and dangled into places while exploring the city by ear and the listening body. Like her more frequently taught *Kits Beach Soundwalk* of 1989, Westerkamp's voice figures prominently in the sound mix. Westerkamp recorded her spoken voice live, on location, as she did with her other soundwalking programs and compositions, while enveloped in the soundwalk rather than after the fact in the studio while listening back to her recordings—that is, in the moment rather than in response to sonic recall and recorded memories. There are often sounds we hear in the final mix that Westerkamp does not refer to in her live commentary and sounds that make it into her improvisational text because she responded to them in the live listening moment, given that the positioning of the microphone did not adequately record what was a heightened visceral sonic experience in that in situ moment.[23] What sets *Lighthouse Park Soundwalk* apart from other soundscape compositions where Westerkamp weaves her own voice through the mix is her inclusion of spoken word fragments and longer quotes from Emily Carr, a settler-descendant Canadian painter and writer whose work is inspired by the Indigenous nations of the Pacific Northwest Coast. Westerkamp uncritically selected and included specific passages from Carr's diary-like reflections on the sounds of the Northwest forests she lived in and painted, some of which are colored by her encounters with Indigenous communities, primarily the Haida, Gitxsan, and Tsimshian, and their expressive culture. Her selection of passages reflects a concern for presenting evocative textual images of place, despite instances of Indigenous exoticism and the legacies of salvage ethnographic practices embedded in these texts. Generally associated with the legacy of anthropologist Franz Boas and his students at the turn of the twentieth century, "salvage ethnography" involved the collection, extraction, and preservation of cultural objects and expressive culture, particularly those from Indigenous communities, who white North American and European scholars feared were vulnerable to extinction from aggressive settler colonialism and the forces of modernity and capitalism. Although Carr is considered a Canadian icon, she is also a contentious figure in Canadian art history. It was not until she shifted the subject matter of her paintings to Indigenous images and subject matter that she began to gain recognition in the art community, and she notoriously crafted replica artifacts in the name of cultural preservation and sold them for profit. After she left the Indigenous villages, she adopted the

"Indian" name "Klee Wyck" to symbolize the lasting impression these encounters had on her and her work.[24]

I have listened to *Lighthouse Park Soundwalk* multiple times and have used it frequently across my courses, yet only in the past few years have I engaged my students in discussions of the silences and erased voices in Lighthouse Park's soundscape. The field recordings in *Lighthouse Park Soundwalk* document Westerkamp's unique listening position while moving through and experiencing the location. Although Westerkamp's work is driven by an ethics of sound that strives to focus the ears of the public on the details of landscape formations and lived experiences of a place, there are sonic histories embedded in these places that remain unheard.

I ask my students: What is *Lighthouse Park Soundwalk* missing? What would a more inclusive *Lighthouse Park Soundwalk* sound like? What might it include? What do inclusive compositional approaches to soundscape composition sound like? What would a crowd-sourced *Lighthouse Park Soundwalk* sound like? The discussion that results from these open-ended exploratory questions reveals the frictions, voices, and silences in field-recording methodologies as we deconstruct the strong structures of geographic, cultural, and aesthetic privilege embedded in electronic music based in field-recording practices. In contrast to *Lighthouse Park Soundwalk*, Indigenous modes of listening and composing with field recordings support the urgent need to diversify existing modes of environmental monitoring and sensory perception. For instance, Chacon's sonic practice for the collaborative durational multimedia piece *Gauge* (2013–15) includes dramatic sonic imagery of climate change, including circumpolar field recordings, noise, and uncomfortable silences.

Westerkamp's soundscape compositions present field recordings of place as my students expect to hear them. The sound sources are identifiable, they can listen and name what they hear, and although they realize that editing processes have been applied to the field recordings, these recordings have been only nominally altered. Westerkamp presents them with a pristine and accurate recording of a specific location with little "interruption" by human-produced actions. However, even the earliest nature recordings and other forms of on-location recording are also only mere imitations and abstractions of the real thing. And while copyright does not extend to the sounds of nonhuman living things and the land, this does not mean we should not consider the ethics of sampling these voices and the politics of land rights connected to them.[25] If we teach soundscape compositions that include field recordings made on traditional Indigenous lands (whether or not they acknowledge Indigenous land rights) or focus on non-Indigenous electronic music with Indigenous content, we should also be including electronic music composed by Indigenous artists informed by their perspectives on sound and recording technology.

Raven Chacon and *Field Recordings*

In contrast to Westerkamp's approach and to shift the conversation toward voices that are obscured from narratives of electronic music, I turn to Raven Chacon's *Field Recordings* (1999), a work that decolonizes the practices of field recording and soundscape composition. Listeners may approach *Field Recordings* with the same expectations of pristine and accurate representations of nonhuman nature that Westerkamp provides. Chacon, however, surprises, discomforts, and displaces his listeners, confronting them with waves of noise. Field recording, referred to earlier to describe Westerkamp's method of collecting sounds, describes both an activity and a genre.[26] Instead of making recordings in a recording studio, field recordings are made in everyday environments using portable recording equipment; thus, they often record various environmental sounds in addition to the sound(s) that the field recordist targets with their microphone.

For *Field Recordings*, Chacon made recordings in three places on the Navajo Nation and New Mexico and set out on his field-recording excursions without strict sound-recording goals to hear and be open to the many possible sounds he could capture with his audio-recording equipment: Window Rock, 4:00 am; Sandia Mountains, 11:00 pm; Canyon De Chelly, 10:00 am. These locations and times of day were chosen for their quietness, and they are places that Chacon has a personal connection to and intimately knows. Like Westerkamp, Chacon is interested in drawing listeners' attention to specific sounds and magnifying them. Instead of framing specific sounds with his voice and using transparent editing techniques as Westerkamp does, in *Field Recordings*, Chacon amplifies the desert by turning up the recordings to full volume, creating a confrontational, constant wash of colorful noise. The pinks, browns, whites, and greens of the desert remain, obscuring the specific details of the sparse vegetation and textured landmasses. What connects Westerkamp and Chacon's sonic practice is that they are both concerned with looking and listening to things in new ways or sounds that they (and their listeners) had not noticed before.

Field Recordings and a number of Chacon's solo and collaborative projects question what gets amplified. As Chacon explained in conversation with the composer, vocal performer, and sound energy practitioner Wendalyn Bartley, describing one of his field recordings from Canyon de Chelly that he played back and manipulated during one of his noise performances,

> It was made in a quiet place at a quiet time of day. In the studio, I turned the volume up to the max. It's not about the pristine anthropological capturing or listening to this place. It's about letting *this* place scream. Speak and scream.[27]

In his electronic noise set for the festival, Chacon used a pair of hyper-directional speakers to direct sound onto audience members and place them in confrontation with field recordings he made at Standing Rock during the Dakota Access Oil Pipeline protests.

For Chacon, sound extends beyond what is heard by the ear. His noise performances and work in DIY handmade electronics are designed to be listened to using all of our senses and heard across the body, highlighting the tactile and bodily experience of sound through noise performance. In a performance organized by Vancouver New Music that I attended, Chacon's electronic manipulations and sculpting of sound explored percussive timbres and noisy punctuations, evoking the tactile and embodied understandings and experiences of sound. I heard and felt the percussive bursts and abstract and mimetic noises, some of which were reminiscent of the trotting and cantering of horses' hooves and the machinations of aircraft or automotive combustion engines. In other moments, I felt the wind and heard chirping birds emerge from the electronic beeps, squeals, and bloops of Chacon's electronics station. Many of these sounds were fashioned from static and overdriven microphones, played through lo-fi everyday directional speakers, like those used in retail stores. Chacon's focus on the entire body as a listening receptor recalls Dian Million's concept of Indigenous "felt theory," an Indigenous feminist approach to history and affect that foregrounds the multisensory palimpsestic nature of the past and future, lived experience, and emotional knowledge when approached using an Indigenous lens.[28] The dynamic interplay between quiet intensity and spiking loudness was felt as sound resonated through my body as I stood toward the back of the venue.

Decolonizing Electronic Sound Art: Postcommodity

Soundwalks and soundscape compositions compel their participants to listen to the layers of sound that define the places in which they live. Electronic sound art using site- and material-specific sound sources similarly reframes participants' listening, directing them to attend to both human- and nonhuman-produced voices in their sonic environment.[29] Postcommodity's mixed-media installation piece *P'oe iwe naví ûnp'oe dînmuu (My Blood is in the Water)*, from 2010, was a commissioned Indigenous response to Santa Fe's 400th anniversary memorializing the mule deer as a "spiritual mediator of the landscape," and it honors Indigenous food-ways and the community's sustainable resource practices in relation to the nonhuman world and the land.[30] The materials of *My Blood is in the Water* consist of mule deer taxidermy, wood poles, water, an amplifier, and electronics in the form of an amplified Pueblo drum, all of which collectively and relationally perform.[31] In the installation, the taxidermied buck mule deer carcass is hung upside down and drips blood/water to create sounds on an amplified drum beneath it, "'memorialising the mule deer as a spiritual mediator of the landscape and [paying] tribute to the traditional means by which indigenous people put food on the table' without destroying whole species," as Lucy R. Lippard observes, citing the artists; the striking image of the deer—simultaneously beautiful and tragic—is intended to turn around "'the dominant culture's process of commoditisation, demand/supply and convenience'."[32]

When I first introduced Postcommodity's installation into class discussion to address the resonance and sonic character of the materials used in electronic sound and installation art, my students focused immediately on the collisions among materials and sounds they sensed. I found it useful in this context to introduce actor-network theory as a way of addressing the varied ecologies of contemporary musical practices and their communities. The materials in *My Blood is in the Water*, for instance, constitute an "assemblage" in Jane Bennett's sense of an ad hoc grouping "of diverse elements, of vibrant materials of all sorts."[33] Building on Bruno Latour's notion of "actant," Bennett characterizes an actant as a "source of action that can be either human or nonhuman" and that can involve such assemblages.[34] In his examination of actor-network theory, Benjamin Piekut conceptualizes the interconnections among human and nonhuman actors and sounding bodies in contemporary experimental music as a form of ecology. He writes,

> An ecology is a web of relations, an amalgamation of organic and inorganic, or biological and technological, elements that are interconnecting and mutually affecting. In other words, like experimentalism or anything else, an ecology is an emergent, hybrid grouping that connects many different kinds of things. It has real boundaries that mark it off as distinct from its surrounding environment, but those boundaries are variable and open.[35]

The nonhuman actants who perform in *My Blood is in the Water* include four poles tied with rope at the top to create a tripod-like shape, and from that rope, the deer, which hangs by its back hooves, precariously suspended several feet above a suspended drum that is tied to the base of each of the four poles (Figure 10.1). The deer was hunted, prepared, and then taxidermied in preparation for the work. Red water (mimicking blood) drips from the deer carcass down onto the head of the drum. A microphone attached to the drum then amplifies the sound of these drops hitting the drumhead. The height, density, and materiality of each object and how they relate to each other shape the sounds produced by this assemblage of nonhuman co-actants. This use of nonhuman material as sound source illustrates how the artists of Postcommodity "use the forms of musical instruments as containers, or vehicles, to get ideas out there."[36]

I show a detail photo of the installation to my students, prompting a discussion of what sounds are produced as the red blood water (the

Figure 10.1 Detail from Postcommodity, *P'oe iwe naví ûnp'oe dînmuu* (*My Blood is in the Water*)

blood) drips down and strikes the animal-hide drumhead, pools on the surface of the hide, and accumulates as the taxidermy continues to spill blood. After four days of installation, the water/blood saturates the drumhead. We also discuss the role of electronics, focusing on how the contact microphone and amplifier affixed to the drum amplify the resonance, articulation, and decay of these sounds. As part of this prompt, I frame our discussion with Postcommodity's description of the artistic and political work this installation performs, to ensure that the voices of Indigenous artists and their perspectives are properly centered. In this description, the members of Postcommodity observe that "With blood dripping from the hanging deer carcass onto the amplified Pueblo drum, the piece becomes an ephemeral time-keeping instrument relaying the history and intonation of this land."[37] When we collectively view installation footage taken from the work's four-day durational installation in 2010, it is revealed to the students that from looking at the image they had focused on the sounds made by the immediate contact of the water droplets against the drumhead rather than the sounds produced by the slow durational pooling of water/blood on the drumhead as it spreads across and seeps into the hide over the four-day period of installation (Figure 10.2).[38] The water/blood vibrates, activated by the amplified drum sample that booms from inside the structure. Our conversations in the classroom frequently address issues of nonhuman agency and sound-making in this installation, how the work draws our attention to the land through the selection and assemblage of sounding bodies (e.g., the drum, the water/blood, the deer), and the ways that electronic systems

Figure 10.2 Detail of drumhead from Postcommodity, *P'oe iwe naví ûnp'oe dînmuu* (*My Blood is in the Water*)

of amplification highlight the rhythmic and musical properties of these unconventional sound objects. Technologies of amplification and electronic sound subtly insinuate themselves into this piece and its politics, simultaneously amplifying the message of the installation and actively contributing to the Indigenization of both sound and installation art.

On the Politics of Amplification

I would like to close by returning to the question: what and who gets amplified? While this question of amplification is often posed in reference to genres such as soundscape composition and field recording for acts that draw listeners' attention to specific sonic experiences and marginalized sounds, we must also consider whose voices and sonic practices are amplified in the narratives of electronic music we discuss with students. Promoting diversity across electronic music history includes using our pedagogical spaces as platforms for Indigenous-made electronic music and hidden Indigenous labor in music technology that is bound up with the racialized cultural history of early electronic manufacture, as well as new media and electronic music.[39] In her history of the communities of Navajo women in early electronic manufacture in the United States, Lisa Nakamura extends Donna Haraway's foundational feminist technocultural thought in arguing that

> the women of color workers who create the material circuits and other digital components that allow content to be created are all integrated within the 'circuit' of technoculture. Their bodies become

part of the digital platforms by providing the human labor needed to make them.[40]

Innovations in the history of electronic manufacture took place not only in Silicon Valley but also on Navajo land in Shiprock, New Mexico, owned and leased out by the Navajo Tribal Council to Fairchild Semiconductor. Fairchild, an influential and pioneering electronics company founded during Silicon Valley's formative years, opened a state-of-the-art semiconductor assembly plant on the Navajo reservation and exploited Navajo women who translated their traditional craftwork training into exquisite electronic assembly. If we turn our attention to developments in video game sound, specifically voice acting, the first voice-over actors for *The Sims* video game series were Navajo and spoke their language during character interactions, yet these voices were ultimately silenced during the game's development. *The Sims* is now known for its fictional generalizable language "Simlish" dominated by gibberish sounds, which does not require translation for different regional releases. These early contributions by Navajo voice actors were rejected by the series' creator Will Wright because they sounded too culturally specific.[41] By contrast, as educators, we should advocate for and center culturally specific perspectives on sound, technology, and the nonhuman environment. This responsibility is particularly pertinent when we are introducing compositions that are based on field recordings of places with contested histories and that are intimately known by human and nonhuman listeners of diverse positionalities and subjectivities.

Chacon and Westerkamp sound their relationships with the land that sustains them, and their work emphasizes how creating representational electronic music made from field recordings in relation to land-based ways of knowing and relationality is simultaneously subversive, experiential, and entertaining. These acts of listening and creating reconnect a variety of human bodies to the land and invite us to reconsider what constitutes environmental evidence, data, and knowledge to include fleshy, vibrational, and corporeal data that traces changes in how people perceive and relate to environments that they know intimately. By attending to diverse epistemologies of the land, including an ethics of kinship with the nonhuman as expressed by artists who work with sonic practices in public-facing ways—such as public radio and sound installations—we can develop a healthier understanding of human actions on the environment, perhaps cultivating more sustainable human–environment relations and ways of knowing.

Recommended Indigenous and Settler-Descendant Artists for Course Integration

Eliot Britton
Raven Chacon

Postcommodity
A Tribe Called Red
Cris Derksen
Tanya Tagaq
Casey Koyczan
Jeremy Dutcher
Andrew Balfour
Janet Rogers
Hildegard Westerkamp*
Andra McCartney*

*Settler-Descendant Artist

Notes

1. Hildegard Westerkamp, "The Soundscape on Radio," in *Radio Rethink: Art, Sound and Transmission*, ed. Daina Augaitis and Dan Lander (Banff, AB: Walter Phillips Gallery, Banff Centre for the Arts, 1994), 87.
2. Dylan Robinson, *Hungry Listening: Resonant Theory for Indigenous Sound Studies* (Minneapolis: University of Minnesota Press, 2020), 68.
3. Thomas R. Hilder, "Music, Indigeneity, Digital Media: An Introduction," in *Music, Indigeneity, Digital Media*, ed. Thomas R. Hilder, Henry Stobart, and Shzr Ee Tan (Rochester, NY: University of Rochester Press, 2017), 2.
4. Philip J. Deloria, *Indians in Unexpected Places* (Lawrence, KS: University Press of Kansas, 2004), 4.
5. Christopher Small, *Musicking: The Meanings of Performing and Listening* (Middletown, CT: Wesleyan University Press, 1998). Small famously coined the term "musicking" to highlight that music is not a static thing (e.g., the musical "work") but rather a broad and inclusive "activity, something that people do" (2). He wrote that "to pay attention in any way to a musical performance, including a recorded performance, even to Muzak in an elevator, is to music" (9).
6. The New School, "Raven Chacon – GIDEST Seminar Video," YouTube video, 9:02, November 27, 2017, www.youtube.com/watch?v=EJdaJuklZGA.
7. Bill Kelley, Jr., "Reimagining Ceremonies: A Conversation with Postcommodity," *Afterall: A Journal of Art, Context and Enquiry* 39 (2015): 28.
8. For an introduction to Indigenous Futurism, see Grace L. Dillon, "Introduction: Indigenous Futurisms, *Bimaashi Biidaas Mose, Flying* and *Walking towards You*," *Extrapolation* 57, nos. 1–2 (2016): 1–6; Joanna Hearne, "Native to the Device: Thoughts on Digital Indigenous Studies," *Studies in American Indian Literatures* 29, no. 1 (2017): 3–26; William Lempert, "Indigenous Media Futures: An Introduction," *Cultural Anthropology* 33, no. 2 (2018): 173–9.
9. Grace L. Dillon, ed., *Walking the Clouds: An Anthology of Indigenous Science Fiction* (Tucson: University of Arizona Press, 2012).
10. Suzanne Newman Fricke, "Introduction: Indigenous Futurisms in the Hyperpresent Now," *World Art* 9, no. 2 (2019): 107–21.
11. Dillon, "Introduction," 6. See also CBC Radio, "How Indigenous and Black Artists Are Using Science Fiction to Imagine a Better Future," *CBC Radio*, November 14, 2017, accessed June 1, 2020, www.cbc.ca/radio/thecurrent/the-current-for-november-14-2017-1.4400378/how-indigenous-and-black-artists-are-using-science-fiction-to-imagine-a-better-future-1.4400425.

12. Dillon, "Introduction," 2.
13. For further scholarship on Indigenous modernity, see Victoria Lindsay Levine and Dylan Robinson, eds., *Music and Modernity among First Peoples of North America* (Middletown, CT: Wesleyan University Press, 2019).
14. *Streetmusic* (1982) was first broadcast and commissioned by Vancouver Co-operative Radio and has also been broadcast on CBC Radio's "Hornby Collection" series, an anthology of plays, documentaries, interviews, and selected fiction for radio that were all written, prepared, and produced in British Columbia.
15. The medium of radio operated as an important source for soundscape programing and composition in the 1970s and 1980s: as a media tool, it engaged a local listenership in soundscape aesthetics while circulating the sonic life of the city over the radio.
16. For further scholarship addressing issues of access, embodied and emplaced histories, and intersectionality in the practice of soundwalking, see Amanda M. Black and Andrea F. Bohlman, "Resounding the Campus: Pedagogy, Race, and the Environment," *Journal of Music History Pedagogy* 8, no. 1 (2017): 6–27; Allie Martin, "Hearing Change in the Chocolate City: Soundwalking as Black Feminist Method," *SoundingOut!*, August 5, 2019, https://soundstudiesblog.com/2019/08/05/hearing-change-in-the-chocolate-city-soundwalking-as-black-feminist-method/; Andra McCartney, "Ethical Questions about Working with Soundscapes," *Soundscape: The Journal of Acoustic Ecology* 10, no. 1 (2010): 24–6.
17. Hildegard Westerkamp, "Soundwalking," in *Autumn Leaves: Sound and the Environment in Artistic Practice*, ed. A. Carlyle (Paris: Double Entendre and CRISAP, 2007), 49. See also R. Murray Schafer, *The Tuning of the World* (Toronto: McClelland and Stewart, 1977), 147, 212–13; and Westerkamp, "Soundwalking as Ecological Practice," *International Conference on Acoustic Ecology*, Hirosaki University, Hirosaki, Japan, November 2–4, 2006.
18. Andra McCartney, "Soundwalking: Creating Moving Environmental Sound Narratives," in *The Oxford Handbook of Mobile Media Studies*, vol. 2, ed. Sumanth Gopinath and Jason Stanyek (New York: Oxford University Press, 2014), 212.
19. McCartney, "Soundwalking," 213.
20. Westerkamp, "The Soundscape on Radio," 89–90.
21. Westerkamp, "The Soundscape on Radio," 89.
22. A reader might wonder why R. Murray Schafer is not prominently positioned in this narrative of soundscape compositions and the sonic environment. This is a deliberate reparative measure on my part in response to electronic music and sound studies historiography that has diminished the roles of Westerkamp and Barry Truax. Schafer is too often the only person who makes it into the classroom, yet the ideas presented in his widely cited and read book *The Tuning of the World* (1977) were developed by the entire collective of The World Soundscape Project. Westerkamp was a central member and the only woman in this research-creation group, and following the departure of Schafer from the group Westerkamp continued and productively extended the legacy of the World Soundscape Project alongside Truax at Simon Fraser University.
23. For more detail on Westerkamp's recording and compositional process, see Andra McCartney, "Circumscribed Journeys through Soundscape Composition," *Organised Sound* 7, no. 1 (2002): 1–3; Hildegard Westerkamp, "Linking Soundscape Composition and Acoustic Ecology," *Organised Sound* 7, no. 1 (2002): 51–6; Westerkamp, "Soundscape Composition: Linking Inner and Outer Worlds," *Soundscape Newsletter, Amsterdam, Holland*, 1999, http://ecoear.proscenia.net/wfaelibrary/library/articles/westerkamp_linking.

pdf. See also David Kolber, "Hildegard Westerkamp's *Kits Beach Sound-walk*: Shifting Perspectives in Real World Music," *Organised Sound* 7, no. 1 (2002): 41–3; Alexa Woloshyn, "Playing with the Voice and Blurring Boundaries in Hildegard Westerkamp's 'MotherVoiceTalk'," *eContact!* 14, no. 4 (2013), http://econtact.ca/14_4/ woloshyn_westerkamp.html.

24. Janice Stewart, "Cultural Appropriations and Identificatory Practices in Emily Carr's 'Indian Stories'," *Frontiers: A Journal of Women Studies* 26, no. 2 (2005): 59–72.

25. For an extended history of sound recording and nature imitation in relation to bird calls, see Craig Eley, "'A Birdlike Act': Sound Recording, Nature Imitation, and Performance Whistling," *The Velvet Light Trap* 74 (2014): 4–15.

26. For further scholarship on the practice of field recording, including the work of Leah Barclay, Francisco López, Christopher DeLaurenti, and Andra McCartney, among others, see Leah Barclay and Toby Gifford, "The Art and Science of Recording the Environment," *Leonardo* 51, no. 2 (2018): 184; Joanna Demers, "Field Recording, Sound Art and Objecthood," *Organised Sound* 14, no. 1 (2009): 39–45; Christopher DeLaurenti, "Making Activist Sound," *Leonardo Music Journal* 25 (2015): 93–4; Andra McCartney, "In and Out of the Sound Studio," *Organised Sound* 8, no. 1 (2003): 89–96.

27. Wendalyn Bartley, "The Music of Raven Chacon," *The WholeNote*, March 29, 2019, www.thewholenote.com/index.php/newsroom/beatcolumns-sp-2121861476/newmusic2/28910-the-music-of-raven-chacon.

28. Dian Million, "Felt Theory: An Indigenous Feminist Approach to Affect and History," *Wicazo Sa Review* 24, no. 2 (2009): 53–76.

29. For further scholarship on Indigenous sound art, see Sara Nicole England, "Lines, Waves, Contours: (Re)Mapping and Recording Space in Indigenous Sound Art," *Public Art Dialogue* 9, no. 1 (2019): 8–30; Kate Galloway, "Listening to Indigenous Knowledge of the Land in Two Contemporary Sound Art Installations," *Feminist Media Histories* 6, no. 2 (2020): 176–206; Robinson, *Hungry Listening*.

30. Postcommodity, "My Blood Is in the Water," accessed May 3, 2020, http://postcommodity.com/MyBloodIsInTheWater.html.

31. The dimensions of the installation structure are variable. In the version of the installation archived on Postcommodity's website, the dimensions of the structure were 15' in height with a 10' × 10' base, the taxidermy was 70" long, and the drum was 36" tall and 22" in diameter.

32. Lucy R. Lippard, "Postmodern Ambush," *Afterall: A Journal of Art, Context and Enquiry* 39 (2015): 19–20.

33. Jane Bennett, *Vibrant Matter: A Political Ecology of Things* (Durham, NC: Duke University Press, 2010), 23.

34. Bennett, *Vibrant Matter*, viii.

35. Benjamin Piekut, "Actor-Networks in Music History: Clarifications and Critiques," *Twentieth-Century Music* 11, no. 2 (2014): 191–215.

36. Kelley, "Reimagining Ceremonies," 27.

37. Postcommodity, "My Blood Is in the Water."

38. Footage of the 2010 installation can be accessed from Postcommodity's YouTube account: Postcommodity Collective, "Postcommodity: My Blood is in the Water – 2010," YouTube video, 2:00, October 19, 2010, www.youtube.com/watch?v=M86drs2pLOg&feature=emb_logo.

39. Lisa Nakamura, "Indigenous Circuits: Navajo Women and the Racialization of Early Electronic Manufacture," *American Quarterly* 66, no. 4 (2014): 919–41. For further scholarship on the intersectionality that can inform diverse pedagogies of music, sound, and technoculture in the histories of electronic music, see Ruha Benjamin, *Race after Technology: Abolitionist Tools*

for the *New Jim Code* (Medford, MA: Polity Press, 2019); André Brock, Jr., *Distributed Blackness: African American Cybercultures* (New York: New York University Press, 2020); Steven Loft and Kerry Swanson, eds., *Coded Territories: Tracing Indigenous Pathways in New Media Art* (Calgary, AB: University of Calgary Press, 2014); Lisa Nakamura, *Digitizing Race: Visual Cultures of the Internet* (Minneapolis: University of Minnesota Press, 2008); Tara Rodgers, "Tinkering with Cultural Memory: Gender and the Politics of Synthesizer Historiography," *Feminist Media Histories* 1, no. 4 (2015): 5–30; Lucie Vágnerová, "'Nimble Fingers' in Electronic Music: Rethinking Sound through Neo-Colonial Labour," *Organised Sound* 22, no. 2 (2017): 250–8.
40. Nakamura, "Indigenous Circuits," 920.
41. Megan Condis, "Building Languages, Building Worlds: An Interview with Jessica Sams," *Resilience: A Journal of the Environmental Humanities* 4, no. 1 (2016): 151; Brennan Kilbane, "A History of Simlish, the Language That Defined the Sims," *The Verge*, February 7, 2020, accessed March 21, 2020, www.theverge.com/2020/2/7/21126705/the-sims-simlish-language-history-20th-anniversary-game. See also "Facts about Simlish," *Sims Simlish: Your Comprehensive Simlish Guide*, 2010, accessed June 25, 2020, http://learnsimlish.blogspot.com /p/facts-about-simlish.html.

Selected Bibliography

Barclay, Leah, and Toby Gifford. "The Art and Science of Recording the Environment." *Leonardo* 51, no. 2 (2018): 184.
Bartley, Wendalyn. "The Music of Raven Chacon." *The WholeNote*, March 29, 2019. Accessed March 20, 2020. www.thewholenote.com/index.php/newsroom/beatcolumns-sp-2121861476/newmusic2/28910-the-music-of-raven-chacon.
Benjamin, Ruha. *Race after Technology: Abolitionist Tools for the New Jim Code*. Medford, MA: Polity Press, 2019.
Bennett, Jane. *Vibrant Matter: A Political Ecology of Things*. Durham, NC: Duke University Press, 2010.
Black, Amanda M., and Andrea F. Bohlman. "Resounding the Campus: Pedagogy, Race, and the Environment." *Journal of Music History Pedagogy* 8, no. 1 (2017): 6–27.
Brock Jr., André. *Distributed Blackness: African American Cybercultures*. New York: New York University Press, 2020.
CBC Radio. "How Indigenous and Black Artists Are Using Science Fiction to Imagine a Better Future." *CBC Radio*, November 14, 2017. Accessed June 1, 2020. www.cbc.ca/radio/thecurrent/the-current-for-november-14-2017-1.4400378/how-indigenous-and-black-artists-are-using-science-fiction-to-imagine-a-better-future-1.4400425.
Collins, Nicolas. *Handmade Electronic Music: The Art of Hardware Hacking*. 3rd ed. New York: Routledge, 2020.
Condis, Megan. "Building Languages, Building Worlds: An Interview with Jessica Sams." *Resilience: A Journal of the Environmental Humanities* 4, no. 1 (2016): 150–61.
DeLaurenti, Christopher. "Making Activist Sound." *Leonardo Music Journal* 25 (2015): 93–4.
Deloria, Philip J. *Indians in Unexpected Places*. Lawrence, KS: University Press of Kansas, 2004.

Demers, Joanna. "Field Recording, Sound Art and Objecthood." *Organised Sound* 14, no. 1 (2009): 39–45.

Dillon, Grace L. "Introduction: Indigenous Futurisms, *Bimaashi Biidaas Mose, Flying* and *Walking towards You.*" *Extrapolation* 57, nos. 1–2 (2016): 1–6.

Dillon, Grace L., ed. *Walking the Clouds: An Anthology of Indigenous Science Fiction.* Tucson: University of Arizona Press, 2012.

Eley, Craig. "'A Birdlike Act': Sound Recording, Nature Imitation, and Performance Whistling." *The Velvet Light Trap* 74 (2014): 4–15.

England, Sara Nicole. "Lines, Waves, Contours: (Re)Mapping and Recording Space in Indigenous Sound Art." *Public Art Dialogue* 9, no. 1 (2019): 8–30.

"Facts about Simlish." *Sims Simlish: Your Comprehensive Simlish Guide,* 2010. Accessed June 25, 2020. http://learnsimlish.blogspot.com/p/facts-about-simlish.html.

Fricke, Suzanne Newman. "Introduction: Indigenous Futurisms in the Hyperpresent Now." *World Art* 9, no. 2 (2019): 107–21.

Galloway, Kate. "Listening to Indigenous Knowledge of the Land in Two Contemporary Sound Art Installations." *Feminist Media Histories* 6, no. 2 (2020): 176–206.

Hearne, Joanna. "Native to the Device: Thoughts on Digital Indigenous Studies." *Studies in American Indian Literatures* 29, no. 1 (2017): 3–26.

Hilder, Thomas R. "Music, Indigeneity, Digital Media: An Introduction." In *Music, Indigeneity, Digital Media,* edited by Thomas R. Hilder, Henry Stobart, and Shzr Ee Tan, 1–27. Rochester, NY: University of Rochester Press, 2017.

Kelley, Bill, Jr. "Reimagining Ceremonies: A Conversation with Postcommodity." *Afterall: A Journal of Art, Context and Enquiry* 39 (2015): 26–35.

Kilbane, Brennan. "A History of Simlish, the Language That Defined the Sims." *The Verge,* February 7, 2020. Accessed March 21, 2020. www.theverge.com/2020/2/7/21126705/the-sims-simlish-language-history-20th-anniversary-game.

Kolber, David. "Hildegard Westerkamp's *Kits Beach Soundwalk*: Shifting Perspectives in Real World Music." *Organised Sound* 7, no. 1 (2002): 41–3.

Lempert, William. "Indigenous Media Futures: An Introduction." *Cultural Anthropology* 33, no. 2 (2018): 173–9.

Levine, Victoria Lindsay, and Dylan Robinson. *Music and Modernity among First Peoples of North America.* Middletown, CT: Wesleyan University Press, 2019.

Lippard, Lucy R. "Postmodern Ambush." *Afterall: A Journal of Art, Context and Enquiry* 39 (2015): 14–25.

Loft, Steven, and Kerry Swanson, eds. *Coded Territories: Tracing Indigenous Pathways in New Media Art.* Calgary, AB: University of Calgary Press, 2014.

Martin, Allie. "Hearing Change in the Chocolate City: Soundwalking as Black Feminist Method." *SoundingOut!,* August 5, 2019. Accessed March 25, 2020. https://soundstudiesblog.com/2019/08/05/hearing-change-in-the-chocolate-city-soundwalking-as-black-feminist-method/.

McCartney, Andra. "Circumscribed Journeys through Soundscape Composition." *Organised Sound* 7, no. 1 (2002): 1–3.

McCartney, Andra. "Ethical Questions about Working with Soundscapes." *Soundscape: The Journal of Acoustic Ecology* 10, no. 1 (2010): 24–6. Reprinted in *Organised Sound* 21, no. 2 (2016): 160–5.

McCartney, Andra. "In and Out of the Sound Studio." *Organised Sound* 8, no. 1 (2003): 89–96.

McCartney, Andra. "Soundwalking: Creating Moving Environmental Sound Narratives." In *The Oxford Handbook of Mobile Media Studies*. Vol. 2, edited by Sumanth Gopinath and Jason Stanyek, 212–37. New York: Oxford University Press, 2014.

Million, Dian. "Felt Theory: An Indigenous Feminist Approach to Affect and History." *Wicazo Sa Review* 24, no. 2 (2009): 53–76.

Nakamura, Lisa. *Digitizing Race: Visual Cultures of the Internet*. Minneapolis: University of Minnesota Press, 2008.

Nakamura, Lisa. "Indigenous Circuits: Navajo Women and the Racialization of Early Electronic Manufacture." *American Quarterly* 66, no. 4 (2014): 919–41.

The New School. "Raven Chacon – GIDEST Seminar Video." YouTube video, 9:02. November 27, 2017. www.youtube.com/watch?v=EJdaJuklZGA.

Perea, Jessica Bissett, and Gabriel Solis. "Asking the Indigeneity Question of American Music Studies." *Journal of the Society for American Music* 13, no. 4 (2019): 401–10.

Piekut, Benjamin. "Actor-Networks in Music History: Clarifications and Critiques." *Twentieth-Century Music* 11, no. 2 (2014): 191–215.

Postcommodity. "My Blood Is in the Water." Accessed May 3, 2020. http://postcommodity.com/MyBloodIsInTheWater.html.

Postcommodity Collective. "Postcommodity: My Blood is in the Water – 2010." YouTube video, 2:00. October 19, 2010. www.youtube.com/watch?v=M86drs 2pLOg&feature=emb_logo.

Robinson, Dylan. *Hungry Listening: Resonant Theory for Indigenous Sound Studies*. Minneapolis: University of Minnesota Press, 2020.

Rodgers, Tara. "Tinkering with Cultural Memory: Gender and the Politics of Synthesizer Historiography." *Feminist Media Histories* 1, no. 4 (2015): 5–30.

Schafer, R. Murray. *The Tuning of the World*. Toronto: McClelland and Stewart, 1977.

Small, Christopher. *Musicking: The Meanings of Performing and Listening*. Middletown, CT: Wesleyan University Press, 1998.

Stewart, Janice. "Cultural Appropriations and Identificatory Practices in Emily Carr's 'Indian Stories'." *Frontiers: A Journal of Women Studies* 26, no. 2 (2005): 59–72.

Vágnerová, Lucie. "'Nimble Fingers' in Electronic Music: Rethinking Sound through Neo-Colonial Labour." *Organised Sound* 22, no. 2 (2017): 250–8.

Westerkamp, Hildegard. "Linking Soundscape Composition and Acoustic Ecology." *Organised Sound* 7, no. 1 (2002): 51–6.

Westerkamp, Hildegard. "Soundscape Composition: Linking Inner and Outer Worlds." *Soundscape Newsletter, Amsterdam, Holland*, 1999. Accessed May 10, 2020. http://ecoear.proscenia.net/wfaelibrary/library/articles/westerkamp_linking.pdf.

Westerkamp, Hildegard. "The Soundscape on Radio." In *Radio Rethink: Art, Sound and Transmission*, edited by Daina Augaitis and Dan Lander, 87–94. Banff, AB: Walter Phillips Gallery, Banff Centre for the Arts, 1994.

Westerkamp, Hildegard. "Soundwalking." In *Autumn Leaves: Sound and the Environment in Artistic Practice*, edited by A. Carlyle, 49–54. Paris: Double Entendre and CRISAP, 2007.

Westerkamp, Hildegard. "Soundwalking as Ecological Practice." *International Conference on Acoustic Ecology*, Hirosaki University, Hirosaki, Japan, November 2–4, 2006. www.hildegardwesterkamp.ca/writings/writingsby/?post_id=14& title=%E2%80%8Bsoundwalking-as-ecological-practice-.

Woloshyn, Alexa. "Playing with the Voice and Blurring Boundaries in Hildegard Westerkamp's 'MotherVoiceTalk'." *eContact!* 14, no. 4 (2013). http://econtact. ca/14_4/woloshyn_westerkamp.html.

11 Technological Mediation and Traditional Culture in Chinese Electroacoustic Music

Annie Yen-Ling Liu and Yang Yinuo

Introductory courses in ethnomusicology often present a selected cluster of practices or geographical regions as case studies to analyze the complex relationships among sound, culture, and society. These materials and concepts ideally help students to cultivate broad and critical perspectives of musical experiences across different cultures, as well as establishing disciplinary concepts and methodological tools. Instructors of such classes must often strike a balance between selective introductions to specific practices, the study of how these practices may be transformed in the context of globalization and modernization, and establishing disciplinary knowledge. Because students are often unfamiliar with traditional practices, instructors may on occasion choose to introduce them through processes of appropriation and hybridization.

For instance, recent critical interest in virtual idols and Vocaloid software offers an opportunity for instructors to relate online musicking to aspects of traditional Asian cultures, adopting a "reverse narrative" approach that leads to historical study of these traditions. The popular songs that circulate through both Chinese and Japanese communities of online producers are often based on historical epics and characters. For instance, commenting on Japanese Vocaloid avatars, Louise H. Jackson and Mike Dines have argued that this practice should be understood through the lens of the continuing cultural significance of Bunraku, a form of puppet theatre developed during Japan's Imperial age. Vocaloid culture is marked by traces of the paradoxical relationship between "illusion" and "reality" that informs traditional aesthetics in Bunraku.[1] The implications of this study expand beyond Bunraku and Vocaloid avatars to consider larger questions of technological culture in modern Japan:

> If an understanding of vocaloids can be drawn from the cultural and aesthetic realm of the Bunraku, then the vocaloid can also furnish an aesthetic framework in which to unravel the relationship between Japan in the present and its relationship with technology.[2]

Depending on geographical location and student population, one can select examples of greater or lesser familiarity that draw upon students' shared cultural background. Examples from virtual idol culture may help students to understand how popular culture is shaped by "traditional" practices, and this pedagogical approach may also help motivate students to study unfamiliar cultures and ideas by taking advantage of relative immediacy and novelty.

By the same token, electroacoustic music produced in East Asia offers a platform for connecting contemporary practices to traditional art forms and aesthetics within a context defined by hybridity as well as interactions between the "East" and the "West," a dualism that comparative analysis may help to question and refine. Chinese composers have stressed the importance of retaining elements of traditional culture in dialogue with Western practices they commonly view as privileging abstract sonic experimentation. This agenda, which has formed an aesthetic core of Chinese electroacoustic music from its emergence in the 1980s to the present, derives from both a collective mission and the personal ambition of individual composers. The result is a body of musical works produced over the past several decades that is rich in allusions to Chinese visual art, philosophy, regional religions and folk customs, literature, and court dance.

Exploration of Chinese electroacoustic music may be incorporated into many different types of courses, whether ethnomusicological or musicological in focus, and it may help diversify courses on electronic music or twentieth- and twenty-first–century music more broadly. In this way, the pedagogical goals that are often more associated with introductory ethnomusicological courses that we sketched earlier can inform the teaching of electronic music. The development of electroacoustic music in China is a fascinating case study of the exchange and transformation of compositional techniques and aesthetic perspectives. While many of the most prominent figures in Chinese electroacoustic music were trained at least in part in Western studios and institutions, and while many of the techniques they use originated in Western experimental music, these composers have used traditional themes and topics as a way of developing a distinct compositional practice. As Leigh Landy has argued, "the proportion of [electroacoustic] music that consciously involves aspects from the musicians' own culture—China in general but also its diverse regions—is also higher than in most other nations in which there is an active electroacoustic music scene."[3] The "three paths" Landy identifies as being characteristic of Chinese musicians are "sampling," "the use of Chinese instruments and/or musical approaches," and "inspiration from Chinese culture (e.g., Buddhism, Taoism, poetry, philosophy)."[4] These techniques and tendencies, along with the greater use of "mixed music" combining tape and instruments, set Chinese electroacoustic music apart from that of other countries.

We can extend Landy's account by exploring the historical and cultural conditions that have led Chinese composers to follow these aesthetic paths. A principal reason is the desire of Chinese composers to create what the composer Zhang Xiaofu has called a "Chinese model" of electroacoustic music. As we consider in greater detail later, Chinese electroacoustic music emerged relatively late in comparison with other regions, and this late start likely contributed to the urgency with which Chinese composers sought to distinguish themselves from composers in Europe, the United States, and other East Asian countries. This first generation of composers, rising to prominence in the 1990s, not only had to master complex techniques of electronic sound production but also had to devise ways of using these techniques to create a distinctively Chinese practice. As a result, critical judgment of this body of work has often centered not on the creative manipulation of sound in an abstract and technical sense but on how insightfully and skillfully composers have communicated elements of traditional culture with audiences. Representation is accordingly an aesthetic norm. So too is what we might characterize in a Western context as a "nonalienated" relationship between experimental composers and their audiences, as communication is critically important for reasons that include the institutional and political frameworks that support musical production.

Because Chinese composers have reimagined their inherited traditions by repurposing Western techniques, their music offers an array of possibilities for instructors: it can introduce elements of traditional Chinese culture, particularly philosophical, religious, and cosmological ideas; it allows for exploring the dialectical relationship between local and global practices by examining the training and subsequent careers of Chinese composers who have continued to engage with "Western" practices; it offers a model of electroacoustic music that foregrounds representation and can, therefore, be contrasted with more abstract techniques. In the following sections, we first position Chinese electroacoustic music within an East Asian context by highlighting its particular historical background and compositional traits; we then introduce four works that belong to an emerging canon and that demonstrate how composers have reimagined traditional concepts through electroacoustic sound.

The Historical Background of Chinese Electroacoustic Music

The production of electroacoustic music in East Asia has developed rapidly since its beginnings in Japan in the early 1950s, and numerous exchanges between the West and East Asia have marked this growth. For instance, Toshirō Mayuzumi (1929–97) drew upon firsthand exposure to *musique concrète* in France in 1952 to compose *Myûjikku konkurêto no tame no sakuhin "X.Y.Z."* (*Work XYZ for musique concrète*, 1953), which was among the first and most significant tape compositions in East Asia. Also in the early 1950s, the NHK (Japan Broadcasting Corporation in Tokyo) established an electronic studio modeled after the Studio for

Electronic Music of the West German Radio (WDR) in Cologne. Early work at the NHK Studio, therefore, reflected the techniques of serialism, sound synthesis, and audio processing that characterized *elektronische Musik*. As Marc Battier and Liao Lin-Ni have shown, the flourishing of electronic music in Japan in the 1950s and 1960s eventually came to involve diverse stylistic exploration, which remains a prominent feature of Japanese electroacoustic music.[5]

Electronic music in South Korea developed later than in Japan yet also closely followed the model of *elektronische Musik* in its beginnings. South Korea has now become one of the most important global centers for electronic music in terms of composition, performance, education, and research.[6] Taiwanese composers have also participated in the development of the field, dating back to Lin Erh's study and composition of computer music in the United States and Germany from the late 1950s to the early 1970s. Lin Erh's experiments during this period became a model for later musicians.[7]

By comparison, electroacoustic music emerged only recently in China. Zhang Xiaofu (b. 1954), a member of the first generation of Chinese composers of electronic music and a director of the CEMC (Center for Electronic Music of China), has attributed its delayed inception to political and social factors: at the same time that Pierre Schaeffer and Pierre Henry were developing *musique concrète* in post-war Paris in the late 1940s and early 1950s, China was still engaged in war and political conflict; as tape music and other forms of electronic music gained increasing prominence in Europe and the United States, China was undergoing the Cultural Revolution (between 1966 and 1976); as computer music advanced in complexity and sophistication abroad, China was experiencing sweeping social reforms (the "Reform and Opening-Up" beginning in 1978).[8] The result, according to Zhang, was a "gap in core conceptions and fundamental techniques" due to the absence of the traditions of "concrete music" and "tape music" in China.[9]

The social reforms and the easing of political turmoil at the end of the 1970s led to an environment more open to electronic music. Among the events that are most often invoked as foundational for this development is a synthesizer concert featuring music by Tan Dun, Chen Yi, Chen Yuanlin, and Zhang at the Central Conservatory of Music in Beijing in 1984. For Wu Lin-Li, this concert signaled the introduction of electronic music to the young generation in China.[10] Landy, however, has argued that the story of Chinese electronic music really begins with Jean-Michel Jarre's performances in Beijing and Shanghai in 1981.[11] This view is shared by Xu Xibao, who cites both Jarre's 1981 Beijing concert and the 1984 Shanghai concert by the Japanese musician Kitarō as the two events that introduced electronic music into China.[12]

During the 1980s and 1990s, Chinese composers were able to travel to gain knowledge of electronic music in Europe and the United States. These composers include Zhang, Xu Shuya, and Chen Yuanlin, among others. Zhang, for example, traveled to Paris to study in 1989, and after returning to the Central Conservatory of Music in 1993, he introduced many electronic techniques and concepts into China. Since its founding in 2004 as an outgrowth of the Electronic Music Week, the Musicacoustica-Beijing has become a satellite connecting many well-known international institutions. The festival's host, the Central Conservatory of Music, typically defines a specific theme for each year that highlights the most cutting-edge issues in the field.[13]

As a pioneer in this new field of musical activity, Zhang has expressed the hope that Chinese electroacoustic music may "form a unique school that will occupy a unique position in the world in the near future."[14] At the basis of this "unique school" is the integration of Western technologies and Chinese national characteristics to express national identity; he argues that "the core motivation seems to be the conception of securing our inheritance and the inspiration for artistic innovation from Chinese cultural heritage."[15]

Before moving on to consider more detailed case studies, several brief examples will speak to the range of these cultural influences. In the series of works *Visages peints dans les Opéras de Pekin*, Zhang draws inspiration from Peking (Beijing) opera by sampling and transforming its instrumental and vocal styles. Chen Yuanlin's *Flying Swan* (1995) draws upon ancient poetry from the Han Dynasty and adopts the formal structure of ancient Chinese music. Liu Jian's *Black Pearl* (2000) is based on the folk music of the Wa, a tribe located in Yunnan Province that possesses distinctive linguistic features and whose striking eyes have inspired the expression "black pearls" to describe members of the tribe. Liu drew upon religious practices of the Yao tribe for his *Daughter of King Pan* (1998). Another important source of themes for these composers has been Chinese religion and philosophy. Zhang's *Nuo Ri Lang* (1996), for instance, is inspired by Tibetan Buddhism, and Taoist philosophical doctrines are invoked in Leng Censong's *Wu Xing* (1996) and Xu Shuya's *Taiyi* (for tape, 1990) and *Taiyi II* (for flute and tape, 1991).

Four Case Studies

We select four works that illustrate a wide range of styles and techniques, both in terms of electronic sound production and references to traditional culture. Among these works, we offer the most detailed introduction to Zhang's *Nuo Ri Lang*.

Liu Jian, Daughter of King Pan

Liu Jian (1954–2012) composed *Daughter of King Pan* in 1998. It is a nine-movement musical epic based on the culture of the Yao people, an ethnic minority in China and Vietnam. The materials used by Liu are diverse: he samples folk songs he collected from the Yao and juxtaposes these expressions with electronically generated sounds, pop music, and orchestral music. According to Liu, the purpose of the work was "to find the intersection between traditional folk music and modern music in order to allow the audience to experience the perennial charm of Chinese folk music."[16]

The first movement ("Daughter of King Pan") samples solo women's songs, drumming, and a male chorus. The drumming and male chorus are combined with electronic sounds to create an ethereal atmosphere that evokes the remote past. In the second movement ("Mountain Song"), the foreground sound is a Yao recitation that describes the history of the Yao culture and is supported by electronic sounds, cello, Chinese wood flute, sporadic drumming, and a choir. For Liu, the Yao people's singing style was distinguished by its elegance and melancholy character; the role of electronic sounds and the cello in this context seems to lend the movement a mysterious, remote atmosphere as well as a modern and global character that connects the Yao tribe's past to the present and future.

The work may serve as the basis for a meaningful discussion concerning the relationship between directly cited source material (folk songs) and electronic sound production and modulation. While Liu retains the original Yao songs, preserving their distinct vocal quality and thus seeming to foreground this work as a vocal genre, the instrumental parts and electronic sounds are not treated merely as "accompaniment" for the voice. Feng Jian has suggested that Liu has created a new vehicle for mediating music rooted in a tribal context for contemporary audiences and that *Daughter of King Pan* may be understood as a "source of new folk music."[17]

Xu Shuya, Taiyi II

Xu Shuya (b. 1961) composed *Taiyi II* for flute and tape in 1991 during his studies in Paris.[18] Working at the INA-GRM, Xu used the GRM Tools software to realize the tape part. At the time, Xu was studying orchestration with Gérard Grisey, and Bai Zhao has argued that this early landmark of Chinese electroacoustic music handles "sound color" and "time and space concepts" in ways reminiscent of Grisey's music.[19] Instructors might capitalize on this link to draw out the multiple influences of Spectralism in late twentieth- and early twenty-first–century music, here adapted to an aesthetic shaped by Taoist philosophy.

Xu drew upon Taoist ideas for both the work's title and certain of its compositional strategies. The concept of "Taiyi" (the Great One) originates in the *Lüshi Chunqiu* (*c.* 239 BCE), which equates it with the *tao* (or *dao*) and describes it as the source of music:

> Music . . . finds its root in the Great One. The Great One produced the two principles; the two principles produced *yin* and *yang*. *Yin*

and *yang* metamorphosed, one ascending and one descending. Joining, they form a pattern. Mixed and murky, they separate and then come together again. They come together and then separate. This is what is called celestial constancy.[20]

According to the Taoist conception of "Taiyi," music reflects the essence of the cosmos, whose energy is manifested through diverse and constant movements such as repulsion, attraction, ascendance, and descendance.

In the work, Xu places samples of a *xiao* (bamboo flute) and transverse flute in dialogue with a live flute. The tape part also includes electronically generated sounds and samples of other acoustic instruments, and the musical language is atonal and microtonal. The interplay of the sampled *xiao* and the transverse flute, placing a Chinese instrument alongside a Western instrument, symbolizes the principles of *yin* and *yang* as articulated in Taoist philosophy: the soft sounds of the wooden *xiao* are veiled and breathy, suggestive of clouds, wind, and water, and therefore *yin*; the flute, by contrast, is metallic and bright, symbolizing the *yang* principle.[21] The tape part creates a sense of formal and timbral continuity between the *xiao* and flute, expressing both the unity and constant movement between the *yin* and *yang* principles.

The Taoist cosmological model of music has affinities with classical Greek and medieval thought, as well as with *Naturphilosophie* in German culture in the first half of the nineteenth century. Both Taoism and *Naturphilosophie* place importance on the harmony of the cosmos and conceive the universe as a holistic, coherent organism. For Eduard Hanslick, the founder of musical formalism in aesthetics, music offered a sounding image of "the motions of the cosmos."[22] Instructors may place Taoist ideas in parallel with *Naturphilosophie* to guide students in exploring how abstract cosmological ideas have shaped both aesthetic theory and compositions like *Taiyi II*.[23] In addition to exploring these resonances, students may consider how the work explores the issue of representation in electroacoustic music, a key aspect of the "Chinese model" posited by Zhang—in this case, attempting to represent or invoke the most abstract idea in Taoism through electroacoustic means.

Leng Censong, Wu Xing

Composed by Leng Censong (b. 1966) in 1996, *Wu Xing* features sampled sounds, tape processing, and computer-generated sounds. The concept of "Wuxing" originates in the *Daodejing* (*Tao Te Ching*). According to Taoist belief, the universe is composed of five elements that are derived from or repel each other, reflecting traditional belief systems in which everything in the world consists of five elements: metal, wood, water, fire, and earth. "Wuxing" involves the cyclical movement of these elements within a holistic cosmological paradigm, whereas the principles of *ying* and *yang* focus more on a dialectical relationship, as we explored in our discussion of *Taiyi II*. Both concepts are essential to Taoism and have exerted a powerful influence on traditional Chinese medicine, geomancy (*feng shui*), numerology, physiognomy, and divination.

The key concept for Leng's *Wu Xing* is the idea that the relationship among these elements may be mutually derivative or mutually exclusive. For the sampled sounds, Leng chose traditional Chinese instruments and everyday sounds to symbolize the five elements: bell, wooden drum, samples of water, firecrackers, and the *xun* (a vessel flute). The work is organized into two parts and ends with a brief coda. The first part depicts how the five elements are derived from each other: the order in which the sounds appear follows the laws according to which the elements are derived from each other—that is, water is derived from wood, wood from fire, fire from earth, and earth from metal. The second part depicts the conflict among these elements. Whereas Leng uses looping techniques to represent the cycle of the derivation of the elements, he uses tape reversal (creating a mirroring effect) to show the phenomenon of repulsion among the elements in the work's second part.

Zhang Xiaofu, Nuo Ri Lang

Zhang's *Nuo Ri Lang*, which combines percussion, digital images, and electronic sound, was commissioned by the INA-GRM and produced using GRM Tools.[24] The work premiered at the 1996 Paris International Contemporary Music Festival, and it has since been featured in numerous international music festivals. Zhang has accordingly adapted the work into numerous versions or "variants," a tendency that Landy has identified as a distinctive feature of Zhang's compositional practice.[25] In this discussion of the work, we consider the version of the 1996 premiere (for Chinese percussion instruments and electroacoustic media, a "mixed" work combining a live musician and a fixed recording).

"Nuo Ri Lang," meaning "male god," is the Tibetan transliteration of the name of a waterfall located in Jiuzhaigou, Sichuan Province, in the Aba Tibetan Autonomous prefecture. The waterfall's name symbolizes qualities of height, majesty, justice, and masculinity, as well as the people of the area who are reputedly endowed with unusually good health. Tibetan Buddhism and its folk legends constitute a strong, distinct local tradition in this region. In this form of Buddhism, *zhuanjing* (转经) is a religious activity in which one walks along a particular path and prays with a prayer wheel moving around and around in one's hand.[26] The practice of *zhuanjing* can be seen widely in Tibet; it is understood to be equivalent to chanting as an effective means of repenting of the past, avoiding future disaster, and accumulating merit (see Figure 11.1). Most practitioners pray for future happiness and even their own reincarnation, expressing the cycle of life and death through the prayer wheel. *Zhuanjing* is

Figure 11.1 An elderly Tibetan woman holding a prayer wheel in Lhasa, Barkhor

also understood to create a form of communication between the Buddha and practitioners.

Zhang intended *Nuo Ri Lang* to reflect this aspect of Tibetan culture so that listeners would have the impression of crowds of people practicing *zhuanjing* on the street. He hoped that the work would evoke the physical characteristics of the landscape, such as its sunlight and mountains, as well as its sacred quality and the communication between the Buddha and practitioners.[27] The sonic material in the work comes from sampled sounds, percussion instruments, and electronically generated sounds. The sampled sounds are primarily derived from a Lama chanting and a female Tibetan singer. Zhang uses cortex, bronze, wooden, and stone percussion instruments for their ancient (even "primitive") symbolic evocations, combining these with modern performance techniques and multichannel electronics. The distribution of percussion instruments is meant to create a virtual space in which the dialogue between the Buddha and human beings takes place, and the interaction of instruments and electronic sounds evokes not only *zhuanjing* but also the principle of reincarnation in Tibetan Buddhism. This strategy reflects Zhang's broader aesthetic agenda: he has characterized "mixed-media" composition, which presents live performers interacting with sampled sounds, as "an efficient way to form sound combinations to invoke national characteristics."[28]

The sample of the Lama chanting is based on the six-syllable mantra "Ong, Ma, Ni, Bei, Mei, Hong" (*Om mani padme hum*). A core tenet of Tibetan Buddhist practice is the belief that the more one chants, the more pious one becomes, allowing one to escape the suffering of reincarnation. In addition to chanting, therefore, Tibetan Buddhists also place scriptures in the prayer wheel, with each rotation being equivalent to chanting. In this way, they repeat the six-syllable mantra hundreds to thousands of times. Zhang loops the sampled sounds to depict the repetition of chanting and the action of the constantly rotating prayer wheel. The first and fourth parts of the work are made up of repetitions, variations, and sonic deformations of the same sample. In the looping process, the elements of the Lama chant constantly change in pitch, strength, length, and density. By altering sound volume and density, Zhang produces sound levels from the far to the near listening field. At 2'29", for instance, he places the sampled sound in a different channel, creating the effect that as one chanting sample falls, another rises. Zhang uses micropolyphony and "intensive" counterpoint as well as looping to develop a 2-second sample into a large cycle of 3 minutes and 30 seconds, a compositional approach that avoids the static repetition of an unaltered loop. The technique symbolizes the circular, repetitive action of *zhuanjing* and the process of reincarnation, reinforcing the semantic value of the Lama chant through technical means.

Looping is not only used at the local level in processing sampled sound; it also informs the work's large-scale structure. In the transition between the third part and the fourth part (beginning at 11'17"), the Lama chant reappears and continues in various states of deformation. The work ends with the Lama sample, so that the final section completes a large circle of the whole work that mirrors the opening.

Because the sampled sounds and the looping techniques are easily recognized, *Nuo Ri Lang* may serve as a highly effective example to introduce the practices of Tibetan chanting and *zhuanjing* and its associated spiritual significance for practitioners. Zhang's handing of sampled sounds, acoustic instruments, and electronic sounds is also of aesthetic and technical interest. The abstract and mysterious electronic sounds in the work can also be related to Tibetan mysticism as well as to the concept of the "unrepresentable" in Taoism. As with Xu Shuya's *Taiyi II* and its engagement with Taoist cosmology, Zhang's *Nuo Ri Lang* may offer a listening experience that invites students to contemplate core ideas in Tibetan Buddhism.

Referentiality and Poetic Interpretation

Referentiality is a central aspect not only of Zhang's compositions but of Chinese electroacoustic music as a whole. In the works we have discussed, most of the sampled sounds retain some degree of recognizable links to their origins, and in some cases, these samples comprise entire folk songs. For the "Chinese model" that Zhang and his contemporaries have elaborated in many works over the past several decades, electroacoustic music must maintain a social and cultural function linked to the listening attitudes and abilities of audiences. Zhang has stressed the importance of passing down the "legacy" of tradition through electroacoustic music.[29] In this way, he hopes to balance the elite status of institutionally supported electroacoustic music with the experience and interests of the general public.

Given these objectives, Chinese electroacoustic music invites exploration of the intersections between techniques of sound production and poetic meaning, the tensions between representation and abstraction, and the role of cultural and historical knowledge in the acousmatic experience. The works introduced here illustrate a range of these topics, including folk narratives, Taoist philosophy, the experience of landscape, and daily religious practice in Tibetan Buddhism. Perhaps a particular attraction in studying these and related works is how they bring sonic immediacy to seemingly remote aspects of Chinese traditional culture. They also demonstrate forms of exchange and influence between the traditional and the modern as well as between the "East" and the "West," presenting opportunities to analyze the effects of globalization and questions of national identity as they have shaped modern Chinese (and world) history.

Notes

1. Louise H. Jackson and Mike Dines, "Vocaloids and Japanese Virtual Vocal Performance: The Cultural Heritage and Technological Futures of Vocal Puppetry," in *The Oxford Handbook of Music and Virtuality*, ed. Sheila Whiteley and Shara Rambarran (New York: Oxford University Press, 2016), 101–10.
2. Jackson and Dines, "Vocaloids and Japanese Virtual Vocal Performance," 103.
3. Leigh Landy, "The Three Paths: Cultural Retention in Contemporary Chinese Electroacoustic Music," in *The Routledge Research Companion to Electronic Music: Reaching Out with Technology*, ed. Simon Emmerson (New York: Routledge, 2018), 80.
4. Landy, "The Three Paths," 81–2.
5. Marc Battier and Liao Lin-Ni, "Electronic Music in East Asia," in *The Routledge Research Companion to Electronic Music*, 49, 58–61. More detailed and specialized studies appear in Marc Battier and Kenneth Fields, eds., *Electroacoustic Music in East Asia* (London and New York: Routledge, 2020). Also recommended is the survey of the region in Thom Holmes, *Electronic and Experimental Music: Technology, Music, and Culture*, 6th ed. (New York and London: Routledge, 2020), 373–84, which focuses principally on Japanese electronic music but includes sections on China and Indonesia.
6. For more on developments in Korea, consult Hee Seng Kye and Jongwoo Yim, "Excavating the History of Electroacoustic Music in Korea, 1966–2016," *Contemporary Music Review* 37, nos. 1–2 (2018): 174–87.
7. See Battier and Liao, "Electronic Music in East Asia," 56.

8. Zhang Xiaofu, "The Development of Chinese Electroacoustic Music: Historical Discussion and Evaluation," *Journal of Art Criticism* 4 (2012): 29
   [Chinese language].
9. Zhang Xiaofu, "The Power of Arterial Language in Constructing a Musical
   Vocabulary of One's Own: Inheriting the Inspiration and Gene of Innovation in Electroacoustic Music from Chinese Culture," *Contemporary Music
   Review* 37, nos. 1–2 (2018): 129. Marc Battier surveys early developments
   in Chinese electroacoustic music and their political context in his essay "*Nuo
   Ri Lang* by Zhang Xiaofu," in *Between the Tracks: Musicians on Selected
   Electronic Music*, ed. Miller Puckette and Kerry L. Hagan (Cambridge, MA
   and London: The MIT Press, 2020), 176–80.
10. Wu Lin-Li, *Research on Chinese Electroacoustic Music: The Integration of
    Modernity and Nationality in Five Compositions* (Beijing: Culture and Art
    Publishing House, 2011), 1 [Chinese language].
11. Landy, "The Three Paths," 78.
12. Xu Xibao, "The Expectation for the Prosperous Development of Modern
    Chinese Electroacoustic Music," *Journal of Music Research* 2 (2007): 113
    [Chinese language].
13. The festival's history is surveyed in Hefei Wang, "Exploration and Innova-
    tion, the Chinese Model of the Musicacoustica-Beijing Festival," *Contempo-
    rary Music Review* 37, nos. 1–2 (2018): 147–60.
14. Zhang, "The Development of Chinese Electroacoustic Music," 40.
15. Zhang, "The Power of Arterial Language," 129. The composer Xu Shuya
    has expressed a similar outlook; see Li Qiuxiao, "Characteristics of Early
    Electronic Music Composition in China's Mainland," *Contemporary Music
    Review* 37, nos. 1–2 (2018): 136–7.
16. See Qian Renping, "From 'Ornamentation' to 'Daughter of King Pan': The
    Markov Process in Liu Jian's Compositions," *Journal of the Music Lover* 3
    (2001): 23 [Chinese language].
17. See Feng Jian, "Composition, Research, and Education of Electronic Music
    in the Wuhan Conservatory of Music," in *The Collection of Electro-Acoustic
    Music Composition and Study*, ed. Liu Jian, Qian Renping, and Feng Jian
    (Shanghai: Shanghai Conservatory of Music Press, 2007), 3 [Chinese language].
18. Xu Shuya, *Taiyi II: pour flûte et bande* (Paris: Editions Jobert, 2017); the
    score includes a CD recording of the tape part.
19. Bai Zhao, "Heritage of Gérard Grisey in China," *Proceedings of the Electro-
    acoustic Music Studies Network Conference: Electroacoustic Music beyond
    Performance*, Berlin, June 2014, 4 (web address listed in the selected bibli-
    ography). Analytical observations and discussion of the work as it relates
    to "national" musical characteristics appear in Li, "Characteristics of Early
    Electronic Music Composition in China's Mainland," 136–8 and 144–5.
20. Cited in Sarah Allan, "The Great One, Water, and the *Laozi*: New Light from
    Guodian," *T'oung Pao* (Second Series) 89, Fasc. 4/5 (2003): 268. This article
    is a useful resource on Laozi and Taoist cosmology, focusing on the 1993
    discovery of bamboo slips transmitting early Chinese philosophical texts,
    including a version of the *Daodejing* (*Tao Te Ching*), an essential source for
    philosophical Taoism that can traced back to the late 4th century BCE.
21. See Wu Lin-Li, *Research on Chinese Electroacoustic Music*, 10–30.
22. Mark Evan Bonds, "Aesthetic Amputations: Absolute Music and the Deleted
    Endings of Hanslick's *Vom Musikalisch-Schönen*," *19th-Century Music* 36,
    no. 1 (2012): 12–13.
23. Useful in this light is the comparative study of Chinese and Western philoso-
    phy centered on the *dao* and *logos* in Ming Dong Gu, "The Universal 'One':

Toward a Common Conceptual Basis for Chinese and Western Studies," *Diacritics* 32, no. 2 (2002): 86–105.
24. Zhang briefly describes his intentions with the work in "The Power of Arterial Language," 130–1. Detailed discussion of the work and its various versions appears in Battier, "*Nuo Ri Lang* by Zhang Xiaofu," 173–6 and 181–91.
25. Landy, "The Three Paths," 83–5.
26. For an account of the significance of the practice, consult Lorne Ladner, ed., *The Wheel of Great Compassion: The Practice of the Prayer Wheel in Tibetan Buddhism* (Boston: Wisdom Publications, 2000).
27. Wu Lin-Li, "To Pursue a Syncretism of Chinese and Western Cultures: Analysis of Xiaofu Zhang's *Nuo Ri Lang*," *Chinese Musicology* 2 (2010): 130 [Chinese language].
28. Zhang, "The Power of Arterial Language," 131.
29. Zhang Xiaofu, interviewed by Yang Yinuo, Beijing, March 2016.

Selected Bibliography

English-Language Sources

Allan, Sarah. "The Great One, Water, and the *Laozi*: New Light from Guodian." *T'oung Pao* (Second Series) 89, Fasc. 4/5 (2003): 237–85.

Battier, Marc. "*Nuo Ri Lang* by Zhang Xiaofu." In *Between the Tracks: Musicians on Selected Electronic Music*, edited by Miller Puckette and Kerry L. Hagan, 173–93. Cambridge, MA and London: The MIT Press, 2020.

Battier, Marc, and Kenneth Fields, eds. *Electroacoustic Music in East Asia*. London and New York: Routledge, 2020.

Battier, Marc, and Liao Lin-Ni. "Electronic Music in East Asia." In *The Routledge Research Companion to Electronic Music*, edited by Simon Emmerson, 49–76.

Bell, Sarah A. "The dB in the .db: Vocaloid Software as Posthuman Instrument." *Popular Music and Society* 39, no. 2 (2016): 222–40.

Bonds, Mark Evan. "Aesthetic Amputations: Absolute Music and the Deleted Endings of Hanslick's *Vom Musikalisch-Schönen*." *19th-Century Music* 36, no. 1 (2012): 3–23.

Emmerson, Simon, ed. *The Routledge Research Companion to Electronic Music: Reaching Out with Technology*. New York: Routledge, 2018.

Gu, Ming Dong. "The Universal 'One': Toward a Common Conceptual Basis for Chinese and Western Studies." *Diacritics* 32, no. 2 (2002): 86–105.

Holmes, Thom. *Electronic and Experimental Music: Technology, Music, and Culture*. 6th ed. New York and London: Routledge, 2020.

Jackson, Louise H., and Mike Dines. "Vocaloids and Japanese Virtual Vocal Performance: The Cultural Heritage and Technological Futures of Vocal Puppetry." In *The Oxford Handbook of Music and Virtuality*, edited by Sheila Whiteley and Shara Rambarran, 101–10. New York: Oxford University Press, 2016.

Kye, Hee Seng, and Jongwoo Yim. "Excavating the History of Electroacoustic Music in Korea, 1966–2016." *Contemporary Music Review* 37, nos. 1–2 (2018): 174–87. (Reprinted in Battier and Fields, *Electroacoustic Music in East Asia*).

Ladner, Lorne, ed. *The Wheel of Great Compassion: The Practice of the Prayer Wheel in Tibetan Buddhism*. Boston: Wisdom Publications, 2000.

Landy, Leigh. "The Three Paths: Cultural Retention in Contemporary Chinese Electroacoustic Music." In *The Routledge Research Companion to Electronic Music,* edited by Simon Emmerson, 77–95.

Lau, Frederick. *Music in China: Experiencing Music, Expressing Culture.* New York and Oxford: Oxford University Press, 2008.

Li, Qiuxiao. "Characteristics of Early Electronic Music Composition in China's Mainland." *Contemporary Music Review* 37, nos. 1–2 (2018): 135–46. (Reprinted in Battier and Fields, *Electroacoustic Music in East Asia*).

Wang, Hefei. "Exploration and Innovation, the Chinese Model of the Musicacoustica-Beijing Festival." *Contemporary Music Review* 37, nos. 1–2 (2018): 147–60. (Reprinted in Battier and Fields, *Electroacoustic Music in East Asia*).

Xu, Shuya. *Taiyi II: pour flûte et bande.* Paris: Editions Jobert, 2017.

Zhang, Xiaofu. "The Power of Arterial Language in Constructing a Musical Vocabulary of One's Own: Inheriting the Inspiration and Gene of Innovation in Electroacoustic Music from Chinese Culture." *Contemporary Music Review* 37, nos. 1–2 (2018): 126–34. (Reprinted in Battier and Fields, *Electroacoustic Music in East Asia*).

Zhao, Bai. "Heritage of Gérard Grisey in China." *Proceedings of the Electroacoustic Music Studies Network Conference: Electroacoustic Music Beyond Performance,* 1–6, Berlin, June 2014. Accessed September 19, 2020. www.ems-network.org/IMG/pdf_EMS14_zhao.pdf.

Chinese-Language Sources

Huang Zhipeng. "The Origin and the Future of Chinese Electroacoustic Music and Its Related Disciplines." *Music Research* 2 (2008): 123–7.

Li Pengyun. "Musical Portrait of the Wa Ethnicity: An Analysis of the Sound Organization of Hei Zhenzhu." *Journal of Guizhou University* (Art edition) 2 (2007): 68–73.

Li Pengyun. "A Study of Liu Jian's Musical Thoughts in His Electroacoustic Music." *Journal of Xinghai Conservatory of Music* 4 (2007): 53–9.

Li Qiuxiao. "An Investigation Into the Compositional Characteristics of Early Chinese Electroacoustic Music." *Music Communication* 2 (2013): 98–104.

Liu, Jian, Qian Renping, and Feng Jian, eds. *The Collection of Electroacoustic Music Composition and Study.* Shanghai: Shanghai Conservatory of Music Press, 2007.

Lü Zhenbin. "The Exploration and Development of Chinese Electroacoustic Music." *Hundred Schools in Art* 6 (2006): 81–3.

Peng Zhimin. "Kudi, Mission, Fusion, and More: Liu Jian's Newly-Created *Panwang zhi nü.*" *People's Music* 2 (1999): 10–11.

Pian Yundi. "The Development of Tone Color in Chinese Electroacoustic Music in Zhang Xiaofu's *Nuo Ri Lang.*" *Journal of Fuyang Teachers College* 4 (2013): 151–6.

Qian Renping. "From 'Ornamentation' to 'Daughter of King Pan': The Markov Process in Liu Jian's Compositions." *Journal of the Music Lover* 3 (2001): 22–4.

Wang Cizhao. "The Beginning of Chinese Electroacoustic Music." *Journal of the Central Conservatory of Music* 4 (1984): 79.

Wang Xuan. "Innovation in Concept and Technique: Analysis of the Compositional Features of the Electronic Piece *Nuo Ri Lang.*" *People's Music* 9 (2010): 34–7.

Wang Xuan. "Pedagogy and Practice of Electroacoustic Music 1: Looping as a Technique and Its Application." *Instruments* 1 (2006): 53–5.

Wu Lin-Li. "An Ingenious Integration of Contemporary Electronic Technique and Ancient Eastern Philosophy: A Musical Analysis of Xu Shuya's *Taiyi II.*" *Art of Music (Journal of the Shanghai Conservatory of Music)* 2 (2010): 107–21.

Wu Lin-Li. "To Pursue a Syncretism of Chinese and Western Cultures: Analysis of Zhang Xiaofu's *Nuo Ri Lang.*" *Chinese Musicology* 2 (2010): 129–38.

Wu Lin-Li. *Research on Chinese Electroacoustic Music: The Integration of Modernity and Nationality in Five Compositions.* Beijing: Culture and Art Publishing House, 2011.

Xu Xibao. "The Expectation for the Prosperous Development of Modern Chinese Electroacoustic Music." *Journal of Music Research* 2 (2007): 113–18.

Xu Xibao. "Shaping Characters with Sound: Critical Analysis of Zhang Xiaofu's Electronic Music Piece *Lianpu II.*" *People's Music* 9 (2010): 38–40.

Zhang Xiaofu. "The Development of Chinese Electroacoustic Music: Historical Discussion and Evaluation." *Journal of Art Criticism* 4 (2012): 27–40.

12 Sound and Image in New Media Art

Marian Mazzone

This essay introduces musicians, composers, musicologists, and scholars working in related disciplines to the use of sound in new media art of the twenty-first century. My goal is to familiarize this audience with the ways that artists use sound in works intended and exhibited as visual art and that are accepted and understood by audiences as such. Musicians and scholars are likely aware of works called "sound art," a type that includes a wide variety of works using sound as the medium of expression. A growing literature on sound art already exists, and some of what I discuss tracks close to that broad category.[1] However, I intend to focus on examples in the recent art world that are recognized first and foremost as visual art but that also cohesively integrate sonic elements through electronics. This discussion furnishes diverse applications of sound for musicologists to consider and explains the value of the sonic to expression in the visual arts. For practitioners in the field of electronic music, studying visual artists' uses of sound may provide new models of sonic expression and experience. It can expand the repertoire of artists, works, and techniques that instructors choose to include in courses on electronic music, particularly given the connections between composers such as Éliane Radigue and John Cage and artists working with sound such as Yves Klein and Haroon Mirza. Of these new models of expression, it is the digitization of both sonic and visual elements in the course of the twentieth century that has profoundly changed artistic form in both fields, giving us a shared language of communication in the 0s and 1s of binary code.

Early Alliances Between Visual and Sonic Art

Art is, first, visual, but this does not preclude the involvement of other senses. In the history of the visual arts, the addition of new elements far beyond paint or marble characterized modern art. Responding to the experience of modern life, artists began incorporating a wide range of materials into their work, including sound. Earlier artists, Wassily Kandinsky being the best known, attempted to establish a synesthesia-based connection between sight and sound. Kandinsky, however, limited his medium to painting, developing theories about the perceptual effects of the visual elements of line, color, shape, and their parallel sounds. In the 1920s, Dada and the Constructivist artists experimented with the combination of visuals and sound. They primarily focused on music (not just sound) and the undoing of the compositional structure of fine art, poetry, and symphonic music. In this instance, we can think of Tristan Tzara and Kurt Schwitters' Dadaist "poetry" that disassembled poetic word structure and was meant to be sonified by being read aloud. On the Constructivist side, the new compositions of Hans Richter, Viking Eggeling, and László Moholy-Nagy paired the ordering visual language of geometry with rhythmic abstract sound in black-and-white film works.

By mid-century, technology had advanced such that electronic sound and music-making was fully viable. In most instances, visuals were still provided by the older technology of film. Such works are largely combinatory: bringing together experts from the various arts who create a collaborative work drawing on their different strengths. A prime example is *Poème électronique*, created for the 1958 Brussels World's Fair by Edgard Varèse, with architectural and visual components provided by Le Corbusier and Iannis Xenakis. Le Corbusier and Xenakis designed a pavilion structure to house and shape an experience for the audience. Varèse created one of the first electronic compositions of sounds to fill that space, and Le Corbusier accompanied the work with a film showing black-and-white photographs that he selected. Xenakis also provided one of his own compositions, *Concrèt PH*, for the pavilion entryway as the interlude between performances of the *Poème électronique*. Such collaborative works continue today; people trained in either music or visual art join their expertise in a complementary fashion. Sometimes the joint composition is done by two or more artists simultaneously, or it can be accomplished by having one discipline respond to an already completed creation of the other. In either case, two disparate tracks are paired: one sonic, one visual. I now narrow our focus to artists who create the two tracks together as solo practitioners.

One element making such fusion possible was the growing acceptance of multimedia practice and the loosening of boundaries between both the arts disciplines and within the individual arts themselves. By mid-century, the visual arts had already incorporated a wide range of materials into 2D work via the collage of the Cubists and Dadaists and the third dimension with the assemblages of Jean Dubuffet. The prime mover in the field of music was John Cage, who as part of his work with sound/noise quickly understood that the experience of the world was also a visual one. Perhaps his straying far from the bounds of traditional concert music allowed him the freedom to experiment in ways that no other music practitioner would. His "compositions" typically integrate substantial and necessary visual components. For example, *Water Walk* from 1952 "composes" any

number of real-world sounds and noises but does so by the active manipulation of an array of household objects, including a duck call, a bathtub,
several radios, and a kitchen full of home appliances. The experience of
Water Walk is inherently visual as well as aural: Cage performs the work
by showing us the making of the sounds while he moves about the stage
manipulating the objects.

Cage's influence to date has arguably been as much on visual artists as
on musicians. Cage taught at the New School where artists instrumental
in Fluxus and Happenings (including George Brecht, Dick Higgins, and
Alan Kaprow) took his classes, and at Black Mountain College where
Robert Rauschenberg became his mentee. Cage also inspired a number of
artists working in New York to create works that defied media and genre
boundaries. One key example that gives equal weight to sound and visuals is Robert Morris's *Box with the Sound of Its Own Making* (1961).
A plain six-sided wood box (9 inches) emits a 3½-hour recording of the
noises made during its construction. The sound is a constituent element
of the work, recording the process of the box's coming into being. When
Morris invited Cage to "see" it, Cage reportedly sat and listened intently
for the 3½ hours until it was completed.[2]

No discussion of Cage's relationship to visual artists would be complete
without mentioning Nam June Paik. Paik studied graduate-level music in
Germany, but there came under the influence of Karlheinz Stockhausen
and Cage, leading him away from the study of classical music into electronics and experimentation. Paik and Cage collaborated on numerous
works fusing sound and visuals, and all of Paik's works both within the
context of Fluxus and out of it demonstrate his mastery of both music/
sound and the visual arts. *Random Access* from 1963 is an early but
indicative example of Paik's ability to create works that conjoin sound
and visuals. Paik affixed a variety of cut pieces of recorded audio tape
onto a wall looking like an abstract linear drawing. Viewers/participants
were able to select any of the linear tapes in any order and play them with
a small audio head in their hand, thereby composing their own sound
work. *Random Access* allows the audience to literally play the lines of an
abstract composition that is both visual and aural.

In Paris, the birthplace of electronic music, the visual artist Yves Klein
made a significant contribution to the body of works that coinvent in
sound and visuals. Klein had a number of connections to the experiments in electronic music occurring in France, including a close friend-
ship with electronic music composer Éliane Radigue, who among other
things was a student of Pierre Schaeffer and an assistant to Pierre Henry.
Klein's 1960 *Monotone-Silence Symphony* originally paired a ten-piece
orchestra playing a 40-minute symphony (20 minutes of one chord, D
major, followed by 20 minutes of silence), while nude women pressed
their blue-painted bodies against a surface to make paintings.[3] For Klein,
the symphony created audible presence and suspended time; there was no

definitive beginning or end to the work, extending as it did the meditative and experiential mode of the creators and audience within a sonorous event. The monotone color of blue visually mirrored the monotone of sound and silence. Klein's death at an early age truncated this line of experimentation, but the *Monotone-Silence Symphony* remains a landmark work.

Noise: Non-Musical Sound and Audible Art

Most readers are likely familiar with the avant-garde use of noise by the Italian Futurists and the pioneering work of Cage that shifted our attention from composed music to all of the acoustical phenomena of our environment, otherwise known as *noise*. As a constituent part of the everyday world, this kind of un-composed sound became a key component in making art *real*. Artists have continued to use sound to maximize audience address and perceptual engagement and to extend the time and space in the work of art beyond the limits of the frame and the single moment. "Sound artists" use sound as their primary medium but do not compose music. Currently, the border between sound art and visual art that incorporates sound is distressingly porous. Clarifying the differences proves useful because as technology changes, conjoined creation in visuals and sound seems more likely. Therefore, an artist working primarily in sound or visuals makes a purposeful choice. Alan Licht contributes key ideas for scholars in the visual arts by attempting to define and explain what is and is not sound art.[4] The 2007 edition of his book identifies three types of sound art. First and most familiar is sound art as installation. In this paradigm, an artist uses sound to penetrate space and establish presence. We feel the sound in our bodies, perceive it with our ears, but do not have much to look at other than the equipment transmitting the sounds. Some sound artists include lights or other sensory elements to make the sound more palpable, but they are not required. Most sound artists of this type have a formal education in music and are using sound in an experimental manner to explore space and the emotional perception of sounds in space. Alvin Lucier and Maryanne Amacher are two examples of sound artists who are likely familiar to critics and scholars of contemporary music. Licht's second type is sound sculpture: a visual object that can produce sound. Licht might place Morris's *Box with the Sound of its own Making* in this category. But as we shall see, given Morris's professional position as a visual artist, lack of training in music, and preponderance of visual works in his oeuvre, I am not sure "sound art" accurately describes this work. Each sound object should be judged separately.

Before coming to Licht's third category, we may briefly consider how the art world determines whether something is "art," a discussion that may also aid us in separating sound art from other things. Ever since the practices of Marcel Duchamp in the early twentieth century, the art world has needed to continually refine its borders and its means of recognizing what is and is not art. Duchamp's provocative act of submitting *Fountain* (a signed urinal) for serious consideration in an art exhibition in 1917 began this process of reckoning, and contemporary art has continued to regularly challenge accepted conceptions of art. In my own teaching, I present three criteria for students to guide them through the process of deciding whether something is visual art: 1) it is made by an artist, 2) it appears in an art context (usually provided by an institution, e.g., a gallery or other art space), and 3) it is accepted as art by a preponderance of the art world (meaning by persons who are art professionals, practitioners, or collectors).[5] Of course, there can be exceptions to each of these three, but the criteria usually hold. This set of criteria can help us solve the problem of whether Morris' sound box is "sound art." Morris is an artist because his professional training was in visual art, he made and exhibited many works of visual art that were routinely shown in galleries and museums, and the scholarship on Morris is in the visual art literature written by critics and art historians.

Confusingly, there are a number of artists who currently occupy an in-between status: sound artists who are recognized in the visual art world and visual artists who use a preponderance of sound in their creations. Licht's third category is meant to encapsulate such in-betweens: "sound by visual artists that serves as an extension of the artist's particular aesthetic, generally expressed in other media."[6] In the 2019 edition of his text, however, Licht shifts this third category slightly, describing the type as "not nominally sound art"[7] and placing a number of examples in a separate chapter entitled "Sound and the Art World."[8] This chapter and the one that follows on recent sound art are useful resources for those interested in visual artists who have used sound in a variety of capacities. Some of his text rehearses the history covered earlier, but his selection of diverse contemporary examples is likely familiar to people both in music and the visual arts. Even if we cannot resolve the ambiguity and assign to each one the title "sound" or "visual" artist, we can learn more by testing where boundaries might be and how we might discern them. It can be a useful exercise to select recent examples of works from his text or other sources and write a formal description and analysis in a compare/contrast format. Applying ideas and terms to the specifics of what we see and hear focuses our tools of discernment. Where are the vocabulary and theory of visual art or music most pertinent? Which aspects of the works force a breakdown of the disciplinary tools and language? Are there other ways of describing what we see and hear that unite the work's elements with shared language? What, if anything, must we retain to distinguish visual and aural elements? And do the creators describe themselves as composers or visual artists, or as something else?

One such perplexing in-between case is Susan Philipsz. She was trained as a visual artist and, as we might expect in that instance, has no musical background beyond singing in a church choir, nor does she compose the music she uses in her installations. Philipsz uses already existing music, including folk songs and madrigals that she sings. She intends for the music she selects to have a psychological impact on the audience as her voice permeates space. Philipsz seems most interested in the bodily and emotional effects that voiced music has on people and how space influences the perceptual experience. The art world has accepted her as an installation artist, even though there is little to "see" beyond the already existing landscapes or galleries into which the songs are broadcast. Philipsz has noted, however, that since winning the Turner Prize in 2010 for *Lowlands*, she has found herself being classified as a "sound artist" and, much to her dismay, being separated out into sound art exhibitions. She notes that these "are very limiting criteria and you usually get a very mixed bag of artists. In time I think people will stop using the term sound art and I can go back to being a normal artist again."[9] I agree that "sound art" as a term is likely to disappear in the future, although I do not know if we share the same reasons for thinking it will. I believe that computation is likely to make the present category "sound art" obsolete, because electronic signals carry sound and visual information equally as numerical data, generated through various devices or machines by one artist. Media artists can work with either (sound, image) or both, simultaneously.

Considering the work of Christian Marclay enables us to focus on this shift. Marclay was trained in visual art but has a considerable history in composing and performing music, albeit largely self-taught. His visual work is not in painting or drawing but in video and film. Marclay collects sound equipment, modifies vintage vinyl records and other recordings, and experiments with making new sounds using turntables and modified technology (work he began in the early 1980s). We should consider this kind of work the manipulation of objects in space to make sounds while we watch. His fusion of sound and image has culminated in a series of installations featuring composite videos created by stringing together hundreds of image/sound clips from film and TV into new compositions. *The Clock* (2010) is the most famous of these. In the installation, viewers experience an entire 24-hour work of art featuring clips from movies, keyed throughout to the specific time of the day/night of the clock. Examining the process of creating this work makes the role of computation clear. Numerous assistants scanned thousands of films (already digitized) looking for references to time within their narratives. Using editing software, they spliced out the relevant portions of the films, taking both the visuals and then the sounds that were keyed to that time window. These were downloaded and stored as data—in other words, as numerical code. All of these hundreds of clips were then placed in chronological order according to their time references and stitched together with editing software. When using such editing software, the interface makes it appear that the user is visually manipulating video and audio segments or clips on the computer screen, but in actuality, the user is cutting and copying strings of code. In the original process of digitizing the films, all of the visuals and the sound were transferred entirely into numerical code, becoming data. For the computer doing the actual combining work, everything is numbers: both the video and the audio are rendered equally in lengthy numerical strings.

For our purposes, two things are critical: first, this work could not have been accomplished with the older technology of actually splicing film stock, cutting audio tape, matching them back up and then reassembling both tracks into a new order. It would take a team of people years to finish, would be too expensive and incredibly tedious to do, and mistakes would thus be legion. Second, and more importantly, computation asks a conceptual shift of artists: it forces the creator to rethink the material composition of their media, both sound and visuals. Rendering all media into numbers through digitization makes sound and visuals equal in a radical way. No matter the preference or tendencies of the maker, both "tracks" are the same at their roots, as they are numerical. Whether an artist goes into the creative process as a musician or as an artist, their biases and disciplinary tendencies are mitigated at the start by numerical transmutation into code. Clearly, how any creator works with the numerical strings, how they choose to make the sound and visuals instantiated in time and space, and how and why they "compose" the works are no less crucial questions. However, the starting situation establishes terms that cannot be evaded. Artists know that they are working with code, and to create original, high-quality work, they must consider how they will interact with that code.

A telltale sign of this change registers in the use of the word "compose," which among creators of electronic-based art and music stretches beyond the traditional meaning of writing music. One composes works that combine sound and visuals, with the word "composer" taking on the connotation of a compiler, arranger, and organizer of already existing material (coded sound/visuals) rather than a writer of music. By contrast, "writer" suggests creating something *ex nihilo*. We will encounter several artists who call themselves "composers" by way of saying that they create with both visuals and sound bound together equally, as a result of electronic processing. We find them in the visual arts under the category of "new media" artists.

New Media: Sound and Visuals Together

Given that this book is focused on electronic music, our primary examples consist of new media art that is electronic-based. "New media art" refers specifically to art composed computationally and stored and exhibited electronically. Therefore, we will not discuss many of the familiar 2D media such as drawing, print, painting, or 3D objects and sculpture. Instead, we explore the newly productive relationship that is developing between sound and art in the electronic environment. For the visual artist working on the digital screen, visual and sonic elements entwine as electronic data, and the manipulation and range of data outputs is what primarily engages the artist. By contrast, in the analog state in the visual arts, the materials remain stubbornly separate and singular: a unique painting, a discrete sculptural mass. Historically, the music world experienced the conversion to data earlier and more completely; conversion in the visual arts has been hesitant and far less comprehensive. This reluctance is not surprising, given the defining role that tangible material plays in visual art. For many, a "painting" must contain actual paint, and a "sculpture" must be carved or built from wood, stone, metal, or other materials. Making the conceptual shift to consider data-derived forms of line, shape, color, and composition clearly abstracts the notion of concrete materials and is not a choice all artists are willing to make. But for those who are, the transmutation of visual elements into data has fostered a new kind of thinking about artistic materials more abstractly, leading them to use the sonic as another data form in their toolkit. Digital technology has changed how such artists perceive materials and has expanded the options for connections between image and sound.

Haroon Mirza

New pathways of creation are forged when artists bind sound and visuals in ideation and manufacture at the beginning of the work. We can best understand the possibilities by looking closely at a few examples. Haroon Mirza is an artist whose primary format is kinetic sculpture and installation, but generating and shaping sound unites all of his practice. He has training in the visual arts, including a BA in painting and an MFA in Fine Art and Design, yet his website foregrounds sound: "All music is organized sound or organized noise. . . . So as long as you're organizing acoustic material, it's just the perception and the context that defines it as music or noise or sound or just a nuisance."[10] Mirza works with sound as "acoustic material": he structures devices to emit sound, creates sound/light experiences in anechoic chambers, and alters found objects that make noises. Mirza insists that he is not a sound artist because he includes "visual entities" that are responsible for making the sounds.[11] Licht describes the connection between sound and visuals in Mirza as a "codependence . . . as neither would function as completely as an artwork on their own."[12] I would argue that they are more profoundly co-generated than Licht's language suggests. Codependence connotes a relationship forged at a point in time only when the other is needed. But neither the sound nor the visuals could exist separately from each other in Mirza's compositions. Mirza's visual objects are chosen or created specifically to emit the sounds that they do. The objects must be reassembled and reconfigured to make the sounds and reflect the action of the sounds. The sound's work is perceptual and visual, such that we can "see" the sounds throughout his compositions because lights or shapes change as sound happens.

Such blended creation only happens by thinking electronically: linking the pulse (the electrical current) with the activation of both sound and visual data so that the audience can perceive the work as whole. Mirza calls himself a composer, but not in the strict musical sense. When denying that he is a sound artist, Mirza allows that composer might be more accurate. Crucially, though, he uses the term "composer" in the new media sense: "I'm not trying to transform space with sound. I'm composing acoustic space and also visual objects in that space, the way a painter would compose a painting. I think a composer is very different from a sound artist."[13] Mirza cites Cage, Max Neuhaus, and Karlheinz Stockhausen as inspiration, recognizing that they were musicians

> who pushed music to its peripheries and entered visual art space. I'm the opposite—a visual artist pushing visual language to the edge of music, and entering acoustic space. It doesn't have a beginning or end, and every time you enter the space it's a different experience. That's not designed. It's the nature of it.[14]

To my mind, the relevant comparison is Cage's *Water Walk*, in which the composer manipulates a variety of objects to make sounds, arranged together on a stage like an assemblage, while we watch what happens. A key part of our participation and perceptual experience depends on us seeing the manipulation of the objects orchestrated among a variety of compositional parts and watching while the objects are physically manipulated to make their sounds. Maximizing audience engagement is one result, as is enabling a wide range of perceptual or sensory responses.

A format Mirza has used to great effect is the anechoic chamber, such as in *The National Apavilion of Then and Now*, first installed at the 2011 Venice Biennale. The triangular chamber blocked all light and sound, except a ring of white light overhead, which became brighter as a drone sound increased in intensity, finally ceasing with a sensory pop.

Another favorite of Mirza's is the Technics turntable. Turntables are a kinetic object but also a means to emit and transform sounds. They are visible, familiar objects, and we are used to seeing DJs and hip-hop artists utilize them to create new sound experiences from already existing sonic material. Many works by Mirza contain turntables, whether visible or embedded in complex configurations of noise-making arrangements. For example, in *An_infinato* (2009), a video monitor plays a borrowed loop image of bats leaving a cave mouth, a film (with its celluloid hole-punched) flashes white circles on a big screen, and a garbage can filled with water rotates on a white disc of light.[15] As water fills the garbage can, a Casio keyboard (disassembled) hangs above. When viewers first step into the gallery room, they may be overwhelmed by the intensity and disjointed nature of the experience: flashing lights, a variety of objects moving and making sounds, and a lack of clear guidance as to how to find "the work." *An_infinato* exemplifies the ability of new media to extend time and space. People in music are used to thinking about time in an expansive way; however, for those of us in the visual arts, the time signature of a work of art is usually unitary: it is all present, all at once, all the time. True, a viewer takes time to scan and build up an experience of looking, but that is the bodily practice of the viewer as a human being. The work of art emits only one thing forever. Indeed, the questions of how to extend time beyond the single moment and how to extend the experience of the work beyond the limitations of the frame have bedeviled modern and contemporary art for a while. Sound art's primary concern seems to be spatial in that sound is broadcast into spaces and is tasked with inhabiting and holding architectural or landscape spaces the way visual art holds space. The audience enters a space and experiences the sound as connected with that spatial experience. The sound is also felt in the body. In Mirza's work, we get all of these sensations, strung together and activated by a computational network translating data between film, video, audio equipment, and a rotating disc under a garbage can in a timed sequence. The light flashes of the punched film set off the audio portion of the bat cave video and generate an LED light and movement reaction from the disc under the garbage can. Its flashing white light echoes the white flashing of the film reel. The movement of the mechanical disc makes the water inside the garbage can agitate, which we hear. Above the sloshing water we also detect random noise: as the water splashes, it hits the exposed note sensors disemboweled from the Casio, generating random plinking notes from the keyboard. To hear and see this, a viewer has to witness the work firsthand, exactly as one would expect to do with a work by John Cage, for example. What is happening has to be seen, heard, and experienced across time, all together.[16] The digital underpinning of film, video, audio, and mechanics makes the combination all the more seamless. Mirza is actually shaping the way the information, an electronic pulse at its base, is shared among and within all of the entities in that space. It will take time for the viewer entering that space to experience all that it contains and slowly begin to note the synchronization and communication patterns among the elements in the room as they shift and change.

Recently, Mirza has taken the dynamics of time, space, sound, and visuals outside the gallery space, evoking comparisons to earth and land art. *Stone Circle* (2018–) is an installation of nine huge stones in the desert near Marfa, Texas. Marfa was the home base of minimalist artist Donald Judd and has since become the site of the Judd collection and other artists' works sprawling throughout the landscape of desert flats. In Mirza's composition, one of the stones is equipped with a solar panel that collects energy and stores it in a bank of batteries underground. At the full moon, that energy disperses to the other eight stones, causing them to emit sound and their quartz veins to illuminate with LED lights. Each stone emits its own three distinct tones.[17] When speaking about the work, Mirza underscores the simultaneous switching on of both the sound and the lights, which allows us to perceive the electrical current. The current/ electronic pulse generates the work, and the artist understands that the energy current itself is what is being structured.[18] Furthermore, *Stone Circle* fully exists only when the electronic pulse is activated at the full moon, transferring a timed command to the stones to light up and emit their sounds. The *ring format* refers to Neolithic stone circles, but Mirza's is an electronic-dependent henge activated by data transfer from the lead stone at the full moon, its effects composed by the artist himself.[19] *Stone Circle* will remain in the desert for several years as a short-term work that only fires up to its full visual and sonic presence on a timed schedule with the moon. No matter how visible they are, the inert stones standing in the desert the other days of the month are not the work. To see the rocks is not enough, because we cannot hear them. In contrast, when one goes to see landmark earth art works such as Robert Smithson's *Spiral Jetty* (1970), it is important to see the spiral shape of the rocks and to note the visible changes that time, weather, and salty water have wrought on its form. The large stone spiral of Smithson's work remains in the Great Salt Lake, endlessly photographed and eternally present for those who pilgrimage to its site, whether it is visible above the water or lurking below the surface. Visuality is key, but not sound. Mirza's rocks are just rocks until they are activated by electronic pulses that render visible and audible the work of art, revealing the data that is the actual material of this art. The stones are a vehicle, a "screen" perhaps, that displays and sounds the data.

Ryoji Ikeda

Ryoji Ikeda is internationally known for the high quality of his integrated work in both visuals and sound. Ikeda also has a substantial practice as a musician and DJ. Ikeda, with fellow new media artist Carsten Nicolai, has been collaborating on a long-term audio/visual project called *Cyclo. id*, which I will discuss further. Ikeda, like Mirza, thinks of his practice as composing a variety of elements together with any number of possible outputs: as an art object, as installation, and as a concert. "I compose visual elements, sounds, colours, intensities, and data. . . . I love to orchestrate all these things into one single art form—sometimes as a concert, sometimes as an installation, sometimes as public art, sometimes as film."[20] Ikeda's work is technically complex and is based on his interest in mathematics and science. For example, he has had an artist residency at the particle physics laboratory at CERN (European Organization for Nuclear Research) in Switzerland. As should be familiar to us now, Ikeda probes the means and limits of human perception of sound and visuals, and he uses technology both to immerse his audience in a sensory experience and to test the transfer of information between computational units and the human senses.

Ikeda's forte is taking a concept and working it out in a variety of instantiations, somewhat like the practice of parameterization in computer science. *Test Pattern*, first launched in 2008, is a typical case. In *Test Pattern*, Ikeda converts data (of any kind) into binary code, that is, into a pattern of 0s and 1s. He makes the conceptual point of using all kinds of artifacts—including text, audio, photo, and film—to convert into data, demonstrating that all are translatable into binary code. It is the lingua franca of the computational world in which he works. The physical outputs of the coded patterns are as various as computation allows. *Test Patterns* (which are numbered) are printed onto aluminum-mounted paper and hung on gallery walls. Test patterns have been installed in art spaces with huge screens on the floors and walls so that people can literally walk in and on the data patterns. Installed test patterns include audio keyed to the bitstreams pumped into the space from a multitude of speakers. Test patterns have been printed on strips of film and framed in the gallery, and they have also been broadcast in Times Square, establishing their presence amid the neon advertising signs of that site. The striking quality of Ikeda's installations is the speed and complexity of the data patterns coursing through the visuals, and the intense experience of the sound as it pushes against the limits of what humans can hear. The installations are almost overwhelming in terms of their sensory information load and effect on the body. Ikeda's audience finds itself fully immersed in a data stream that is both palpably and physically present to them in image and sound.

As a mathematical thinker, Ikeda analyzes the elements, both visual and sonic, from which he builds his compositions. The *Cyclo.id* project demonstrates the modular thinking and abstracting approach that both Ikeda and Nicolai practice with their sound and visual data elements. They are compiling a "database of sound fragments" using the technology of the oscilloscope. Oscilloscopes (among other things) render an image of the relationship of time to voltage of sound waves on the (x, y) graph and are used particularly in calibrating stereo sound. Ikeda and Nicolai are interested in three aspects of sound that are plotted on the planar quadrant of the (x, y) graph: amplitude, frequency, and phase correlation.[21] Stereoscopic sounds create a pattern across the quadrant, with every sound possessing its own unique image. The challenge the artists have set themselves is to amass a vast array of sonic bits with accompanying image(s) in an ever-expanding archive.[22] The images are not merely the outputs of the sounds; instead, Nicolai and Ikeda have developed an interest in designing images that will create new sounds.[23] The patterns are charted mathematically and visually from oscilloscope data and in linear shapes. They propose that what is being discovered and generated is a substrate of structural patterning that could be useful in the future for designers and engineers. In essence, they are trying to find through data analysis inherent perceptual patterns for absorbing/perceiving visual and auditory information as human beings.

I hope this survey of selected artists working in image and sound is useful to people in musical disciplines. Seeing what visual artists are creating in the context of new media art reveals the ways in which electronic technology is impacting how artists conceptualize and create art forms that fuse sound and image. The transformation of sound and visuals into digital code has allowed artists to conceptualize vision and auditory perception differently. To be a composer is to orchestrate the relationship between these electronic elements and to render their manifestation in physical, spatial, and perceptual terms. Space and time are established in these works as the site of expanded audience perception and experience.

Notes

1. See the following sources listed in the bibliography: Cox (2018), Kahn (1999), Licht (2007, revised ed. 2019), Kelly (2011 and 2017), Kim-Cohen (2009), LaBelle (2015), Pardo (2017) and Weibel (2019). These sources provide critical and historical discussion of the relationship between sound and the visual arts, define and debate the terminology of sound art and sound in installation art, and provide examples of artists, works, and primary texts. For those interested in a greater range of digital media, the volume of collected essays edited by Carol Vernallis, Amy Herzog, and John Richardson (2013) may be useful. The visual focus in this volume is primarily on "screens" in cinema, video, and gaming.
2. This example is also cited in Alan Licht, *Sound Art Revisited* (London: Bloomsbury Academic, 2019), 62–3.
3. Details of the first performance in 1960 and Klein's connection with Radigue are available at www.yvesklein.com/en/articles/view/3/monotone-silence-symphony/.
4. Alan Licht, *Sound Art: Beyond Music, between Categories* (New York: Rizzoli Publications, 2007) and *Sound Art Revisited* (2019).
5. For a good introduction to the complicated philosophical questions about what art is and how it is defined, see the primer by Cynthia Freeland, *But Is It Art? An Introduction to Art Theory* (Oxford: Oxford University Press, 2002).
6. Licht, *Sound Art: Beyond Music, between Categories*, 17.
7. Licht, *Sound Art Revisited*, 6.
8. Licht, *Sound Art Revisited*, 83 and following.
9. As quoted in Licht, *Sound Art Revisited*, 127, note 5, quoted from Anna Savitskaya, "'Sound Has Always Been My Primary Tool': Interview with

Susan Philipsz About Her Sound Installations and More," artdependence. com, January 9, 2015, www.artdependence.com/articles/sound-has-always-been-my-primary-tool-interview-with-susan-philipsz-about-her-sound-installations-and-more/.

10. "Haroon Mirza," Lisson Gallery, accessed February 26, 2020, www.lisson gallery.com/artists/haroon-mirza.

11. Mirza in interview with Linda Yablonsky (September 14, 2015), *Flash Art*, accessed February 26, 2020, www.flashartonline.com/article/haroon-mirza/.

12. Licht, *Sound Art Revisited*, 131.

13. Quoted in Licht, *Sound Art Revisited*, 131, drawn from the Yablonsky interview at www.flashartonline.com/article/haroon-mirza/.

14. Quoted in Licht, *Sound Art Revisited*, 131, drawn from the Yablonsky interview at www.flashartonline.com/article/haroon-mirza/. Direct quotation of Mirza.

15. The video clip is by Jeremy Diller, and the film by Greg Sherwin.

16. In lieu of this firsthand experience one can get a sense of the work by a video in exhibition at Ikon Gallery available here: www.youtube.com/watch?v=AI CnKHznRI8&list=PLFD882B86A29610F0&index=52&t=491s.

17. Jennifer Boomer, "Marfa, Texas, Is Getting Its Own Solar-Powered Stonehenge," *The Wired*, May, 16, 2018, www.wired.com/story/marfa-solar-stone-circle/.

18. Ballroom Marfa interview with Haroon Mirza, available on Vimeo at https://vimeo.com/233549773.

19. Mirza cites The Nine Ladies in Yorkshire, England, as his local inspiration.

20. As quoted in Licht, *Sound Art Revisited*, 133. The quotation is drawn from Nicholas Forrest, "Ryoji Ikeda: Artistic Genuis or Maths Magician?," in *BlouinArtInfo Australia*, June 28, 2013.

21. From the artists' statement in the catalogue *Cyclo.id*, edited and with a preface by Ryoji Ikeda and Carsten Nicolai (Berlin and London: Die Gestalten Verlag, 2011). The book also includes a CD of additional cyclo.id forms.

22. The *Cyclo.id* databank has been published in book form (as noted earlier) and can be seen on Vimeo (https://vimeo.com/73860675) and on Ikeda's website.

23. Ikeda and Nicolai, *Cyclo.id*, preface.

Selected Bibliography

Cox, Christoph. *Sonic Flux: Sound, Art, and Metaphysics*. Chicago and London: University of Chicago Press, 2018.

Freeland, Cynthia. *But Is It Art? An Introduction to Art Theory*. Oxford: Oxford University Press, 2002.

Huttenlauch, Eva. "Art as an Explanatory Model of Universal Complexity: On Carsten Nicolai's Unidisplay." In *Carsten Nicolai: Unidisplay*, 9–13. Berlin: Die Gestalten Verlag, 2013.

Ikeda, Ryoji, and Carsten Nicolai. *Cyclo.id*. Edited and Preface by Ryoji Ikeda and Carsten Nicolai. Berlin and London: Die Gestalten Verlag, 2011.

Kahn, Douglas. *Noise, Water, Meat: A History of Sound in the Arts*. Cambridge, MA: The MIT Press, 1999.

Kelly, Caleb. *Gallery Sound*. New York: Bloomsbury Academic, 2017.

Kelly, Caleb, ed. *Sound: Documents of Contemporary Art*. London and Cambridge, MA: Whitechapel Gallery and The MIT Press, 2011.

Kim-Cohen, Seth. *In the Blink of an Ear: Toward a Non-Cochlear Sonic Art*. New York and London: Continuum, 2009.

LaBelle, Brandon. *Background Noise: Perspectives on Sound Art*. 2nd ed. New York: Bloomsbury Academic, 2015.

Licht, Alan. *Sound Art: Beyond Music, between Categories*. New York: Rizzoli Publications, 2007.

Licht, Alan. *Sound Art Revisited*. London: Bloomsbury Academic, 2019.

London, Barbara, curator and ed., and Anne Hilde Neset. *Soundings: A Contemporary Score*. New York: Museum of Modern Art, 2013.

Pardo, Carmen. "The Emergence of Sound Art: Opening the Cages of Sound." *The Journal of Aesthetics and Art Criticism* 75, no. 1 (Winter 2017): 35–48.

Vernallis, Carol, Amy Herzog, and John Richardson, eds. *The Oxford Handbook of Sound and Image in Digital Media*. New York: Oxford University Press, 2013.

Weibel, Peter, ed. *Sound Art: Sound as a Medium of Art*. Cambridge, MA: The MIT Press, 2019.

Contributors

Marc Battier is a composer of instrumental and electroacoustic music. After twenty years at IRCAM, Paris, he became full professor of musicology at Sorbonne University. Now emeritus, he joined Shenzhen University in China as a distinguished professor. He also taught at the University of California at San Diego, New York University, the University of Montreal, and the University of Music and Arts of Aichi, Japan. He funded a research network devoted to electronic music from Asia (EMSAN) and is co-founder of the Electroacoustic Music Studies Network. He has published many articles and several books on the history of electronic music. He is a board member of *Organised Sound* and the *Malaysian Journal of Music*, has served on the board of *Computer Music Journal* and *Leonardo Music Journal*, and was a founding member of the International Computer Music Association. His music is widely played in Asia, Europe, and North America. He is published by BabelScores.

Kate Galloway is on faculty at Rensselaer Polytechnic Institute. Her research and teaching addresses sonic responses to environmentalism, radio and broadcast sound media, Indigenous musical modernities and traditional ecological knowledge, sound studies, science and technology studies, new media, and digital humanities. Her monograph *Remix, Reuse, Recycle: Music, Media Technologies, and Remediating the Environment*, under contract with Oxford University Press, examines how and why contemporary artists remix and recycle sounds, musics, and texts encoded with environmental knowledge. Galloway's work is published in *American Music, Ethnomusicology, MUSICultures, Tourist Studies, Sound Studies, The Oxford Handbook of Hip Hop Music, Playing for Keeps: Improvisation in the Aftermath*, and *Music in the Role-Playing Game: Heroes & Harmonies*.

Lucy Ann Harrison is a composer and sound designer specializing in interactive sound. Recent work has included sound and music for an immersive art event in partnership with the National Trust, a motion sensitive sound installation for Girlguiding at Alexandra Palace, an

Interactive blanket fort in East London, and an interactive virtual library on SineSpace. She has a PhD in composition from Royal Holloway, University of London, where she investigated control, collaboration, and audience engagement in interactive sound installations. Lucy is a Senior lecturer in the Production and Games Academy courses at ACM (Academy for Contemporary Music) in London and Guildford where she teaches sound design, interactive audio, games audio, and research skills.

Patti Kilroy, violinist, pedagogue, and recording artist, has been praised for her "intensely focused" playing by *The New York Times*. A modern-minded musician, she is most known for giving the world premiere of over 100 works, with a particular focus on works incorporating looping, live processing electronics, and prepared violin. As a researcher, she documents new performance practices created as performers use electronics across contexts. Based in Los Angeles, she is an assistant professor of music at California State University, Los Angeles, and is a recipient of the PhD in Music Performance from New York University. To learn more, visit pattikilroy.com.

Leigh Landy (www.llandy.dmu.ac.uk) directs the Music, Technology and Innovation—Institute for Sonic Creativity (MTI^2) at De Montfort University (UK). His scholarship is divided between creative and musicological work. His compositions, many of which are sample based, include several for video, dance, and theatre and have been performed around the globe, including commissions from international festivals, radio stations, ensembles, and venues. His publications focus primarily on the studies of electroacoustic music. He is editor of *Organised Sound* (CUP) and author of eight books including *What's the Matter with Today's Experimental Music?* (Harwood), *Understanding the Art of Sound Organization* (MIT), *The Music of Sounds* (Routledge) and is currently completing the book *On the Music of Sounds and the Music of Things* with John Richards. He directs the ElectroAcoustic Resource Site (EARS) projects (www.ears.dmu.ac.uk, www.ears2.dmu.ac.uk) and is a founding director of the Electroacoustic Music Studies Network (EMS, www.ems-network.org).

Annie Yen-Ling Liu is professor of music history in the School of Music at Soochow University (Suzhou, China). Her research embraces both European and Chinese traditions, centering principally on German symphonic music from the eighteenth century to the late nineteenth century and contemporary Chinese electroacoustic music. She has lectured on traditional and modern Chinese music as a visiting professor at the Université Grenoble Alpes (Grenoble, France) and published articles on Liszt and Wagner in English and Chinese journals. Her book *"New Athens" in the Mid-Nineteenth Century: Franz Liszt and* *the New German School* was published by Southwest China Normal University Press in 2020.

V. J. Manzo, PhD, is associate professor of Music Technology and Cognition at Worcester Polytechnic Institute (WPI). He is a composer and guitarist with research interests in theory and composition, artificial intelligence, interactive music systems, and music cognition. V. J. is author of several books published by Oxford University Press, including *Max/MSP/Jitter for Music, Foundations of Music Technology*, and co-author of *Interactive Composition* and *Environmental Sound Artists*. He has created numerous software projects including the Modal Object Library, a collection of programming objects to control harmony in algorithmic and electroacoustic compositions, and EAMIR, an open-source project and nonprofit charity organization that supports composition, performance, education, and research through accessible technology-based musical instruments. At WPI, he is the founding director and principal investigator of the Interactive Music Systems Lab (IMSLab) and the Electric Guitar Innovation Lab (EGIL) and a co-director of the Media Arts Group Innovation Center (MAGIC).

Raul Masu is a PhD student in digital media at the Nova University of Lisbon and ITI/LARSyS (Portugal). He graduated in electronic music (BA) and composition (10-years diploma, master-level equivalent) from the Conservatory of Music of Trento (Italy). After his graduation, he worked as a research assistant at the interAction Lab—Department of Computer Science (University of Trento). He has presented and published papers in several international conferences and journals in the field of music computing and HCI. His music has been performed in several countries, including Germany, the United Kingdom, Italy, Switzerland, and Japan.

Marian Mazzone is an associate professor in the Art & Architectural History Department at the College of Charleston, teaching courses on contemporary art and new media art. She is an affiliate of the Art & Artificial Intelligence Lab at Rutgers University and one of the co-founders of the Computing in the Arts major at the College of Charleston. Mazzone has published on art, technology, and related issues in *Leonardo, Arts*, and *Technoetic Arts*.

Robert McClure's music attempts to discover beauty in unconventional places using nontraditional means. His work has been featured at festivals including NYCEMF, Beijing Modern Music Festival, ISCM, TIES, SEAMUS, and ICMC. His works may be found through ADJ·ective New Music, Bachovich Music Publications, Resolute Music Publications, and Tapspace Publications as well as on ABLAZE, Albany, and New Focus Record labels. Robert received his doctorate from Rice

University's Shepherd School of Music. Robert has previously held positions at the Shanghai Conservatory of Music and Soochow University in Suzhou, China. He serves as assistant professor of composition/theory at Ohio University.

Fabio Morreale is a lecturer of music technology and director of research at the School of Music of the University of Auckland (New Zealand). He teaches computer music, sound design, and musical interface design at the undergraduate and postgraduate levels. He holds a PhD in human–computer interaction (University of Trento) and an MSc and BSc in computer science (University of Verona). He also worked as a postdoctoral researcher at the Augmented Instruments Laboratory at Queen Mary University of London and at the interAction Lab of the University of Trento. His research is focused on understanding how computer technologies are shaping the way we perform, compose, learn, and listen to music, and on the analysis of the hackers and makers communities. He has also developed numerous musical instruments, interfaces, and installations that have been exhibited worldwide.

Rishabh Rajan is a music educator with over 10 years of experience in education, having taught in India, Malaysia, and now the United States. He is currently on the faculty at Berklee College of Music with the Electronic Production & Design Department. Rishabh has also been developing online courses for Ask.Video and macProVideo for the past eight years and, more recently, developed a course for Berklee Online, which won him a Silver Telly Award in April 2020. Rishabh has published ebooks on sound design techniques, which are available on the Apple iBookStore. Aside from teaching, Rishabh works as a writer for Ask.Audio reviewing hardware/software synthesizers and as a sample library developer for Crypto Cipher.

Andrew Selle is a continuing lecturer and the coordinator of music theory/composition at Purdue University Fort Wayne. He received his bachelor's and master's degrees in music composition from Bowling Green State University and his PhD in music theory from Florida State University. An active composer and scholar, Andrew has presented papers and compositions at many national and international events, including the International Computer Music Conference, the national conference of the Society for Electroacoustic Music in the United States (SEAMUS), the New York City Electroacoustic Music Festival, and the South-Central Society for Music Theory, as well as conferences at the University of North Texas, Louisiana State University, the University of Arizona, and the CUNY Graduate Center, among others. His research interests include electronic music, music cognition, and music theory pedagogy.

Blake Stevens is associate professor of music history at the College of Charleston. He has published on the pedagogy of electronic and computer music in the *Journal of Music, Technology & Education* and *Performing Arts As High-Impact Practice*. Research on the history of the *tragédie en musique* and music aesthetics in France, including studies of operatic monologues, the entr'acte, and spatial representation, has appeared in the *Journal of Musicology*, *Music and Letters*, *Word and Music Studies*, and *Eighteenth-Century Music*.

Yang Yinuo is a research assistant in educational management at the Graduate School of the Nanjing University of Art. She earned her master's degree in musicology from the School of Music at Soochow University (Suzhou, China) with a thesis on Chinese electroacoustic music, investigating its first generation of composers, transcultural phenomena, and the relationship between semiotics and listening behaviors in selected works. She has given papers on these and related topics at international conferences organized by the International Musicological Society (IMS), Analytical Approaches to World Music (AAWM), and the Electroacoustic Music Studies Network (EMS), and she has published research articles in the Chinese-language journals *Center for Drama* and *Modern Music*.

Index

Page numbers in *italics* indicate figures.

236   *Index*

Lightning Source UK Ltd.
Milton Keynes UK
UKHW021551091222
413458UK00025B/181